# EIGHT MILLION EXILES

# EIGHT MILLION EXILES

## Missional Action Research and the Crisis of Forced Migration

CHRISTOPHER M. HAYS

WILLIAM B. EERDMANS PUBLISHING COMPANY

*Grand Rapids, Michigan*

Wm. B. Eerdmans Publishing Co.
4035 Park East Court SE, Grand Rapids, Michigan 49546
www.eerdmans.com

Book design by Jamie McKee

Printed in the United States of America

30  29  28  27  26  25  24      1  2  3  4  5  6  7

ISBN 978-0-8028-8239-4

**Library of Congress Cataloging-in-Publication Data**

A catalog record for this book is available from the Library of Congress.

Scripture quotations, unless otherwise indicated, are from the New Revised Standard Version (NRSV).

For Milton, Guillermo, and Jhohan
*Compañeros del camino*

# Contents

# Foreword

The church is "browning." As the global pendulum of Christianity swings in the direction of Latin America, Africa, and Asia, it is estimated that the majority of Christians in the world will live in the Global South by 2050. The church of North America faces an interrelated future where, fueled by immigration, white representation is in decline, all other ethnic groups are together increasing, and one in three American evangelicals is already a person of color. Christianity is returning to its historical origins as a faith of the marginalized born in the Near East.

Christian immigrants from the Majority World bring with them a vibrant personal faith driven by radical dependence on Jesus made necessary by suffering and the struggle to survive. Flowing from the lens of their distinct God-given community cultural wealth (Rev 21:26), global theologians also bring fresh perspectives that have the potential to address many of the burning spiritual and social questions facing both the North American and universal church. *Eight Million Exiles* is a reflection of such transformative perspectives and a signpost of the ecclesial change that is to come.

In this book, Christopher M. Hays tells the story of "how a handful of theologians in a little seminary on the wrong side of Medellín responded when they came to comprehend that the lives of eight million of their countrymen had been destroyed by the violence of Colombia's armed conflict." Their response began with a small conference but led to the unexpected development of an innovative method of applied theological investigation called Missional Action Research (MAR) and a national ministry project called Faith and Displacement. Missional Action Research uniquely fuses the theological framework of integral missiology with insights from the social sciences and Participatory Action Research methods. In his discussion of MAR, Hays is careful to properly credit René Padilla, Samuel Escobar, and the Fraternidad Teológica Latinoamericana (Latin American Theological Fellowship) as the founders of integral missiology as well as to recognize his positionality as cultural outsider. Indeed, Hays was initially reluctant to play any leadership role in the project until pressed by Biblical Seminary of Colombia president Elizabeth Sendek: "Christopher, we asked you here because we want your opinion. And if you are wrong, we will tell you." Building upon the general framework of *misión integral*, the specific theological and pastoral contours of the MAR methodology were shaped by Colombian theologians Milton Acosta, Saskia Donner, Guillermo Mejía Castillo, Fernando Abilio Mosquera Brand, and Jhohan Centeno. The social science components of the methodology were developed by a dozen Colombian and Colombian American academics from the fields of psychology, sociology, education, politics, and economics, including Lina Marcela Cardona Sosa, Lisseth Rojas-Flores, Duberney Rojas Seguro, and Laura Cadavid. In keeping with the philosophical commitment of community-engaged scholarship, the research and project also incorporated the leadership and insights of many local Colombian pastors, leaders, professionals, and members of displaced communities. Hays served as coordinator of the massive interdisciplinary endeavor, which was ultimately composed of twenty-five scholars from four continents and six teams focused on economics, sociology, psychology, pedagogy, public sector interaction, and missiology.

The MAR and larger Faith and Displacement project are compelling to me because of their academic rigor and ecclesial rootedness—two features that do not usually accompany each other. Just as importantly, or perhaps even more so, I value *Eight Million Exiles* and the underlying Faith and Displacement project it describes because it represents an approach and methodology that center the scholarship, perspectives, and God-given community cultural wealth of the Colombian people and church themselves. Stated simply, such cultural stakeholders, guided by the Holy Spirit, are in the best position to understand and craft solutions to the problems that they face. The rest of us can come along for the ride if invited, but theirs is the most important perspective. *Eight Million Exiles* is essential reading for anyone interested in new missional research models that prioritize the perspectives and distinct God-given community cultural wealth of the Majority Church.

*Robert Chao Romero*

# Preface

This book is at once a theological methodological treatise and a story. In the former sense, it describes the creation of the Missional Action Research (MAR) method, an approach developed to transform theological and social-scientific scholarship into a mechanism for mobilizing churches to respond to a heinous humanitarian crisis. If you picked up this volume with an interest in the bare method, you might start with chapter 8, which provides a tight summation of the approach, just the brass tacks of MAR.

But this book is also the story of how a handful of theologians in a little seminary on the wrong side of Medellín responded when they came to comprehend that the lives of eight million of their countrymen had been destroyed by the violence of Colombia's armed conflict. We called that response Faith and Displacement. It's that story that has me convinced the MAR method is worth this book's pages, and your time.

Faith and Displacement was the work of dozens of theologians, social scientists, professionals, pastors, and survivors of displacement, people from four continents drawn together in a shared sense of calling to serve victims of the violent conflict. While the scope of this preface does not permit me to name all that deserve to be celebrated, I would be remiss not to highlight Faith and Displacement's deputy directors Milton Acosta and Saskia Donner, as well as the Fundación Universitaria Seminario Bíblico de Colombia (FUSBC) colleagues who first helped launch what felt like an impossibly audacious endeavor: Guillermo Mejía Castillo, Fernando Abilio Mosquera Brand, and Jhohan Centeno. I owe special thanks to Luz Jacqueline Mestra, the project administrator who deserves as much credit as anyone for the impact of this outlandish undertaking. Finally, I'm indebted to David Baer, my erstwhile missionary supervisor and next-door neighbor, whose detailed editing of this manuscript was a gift to all readers. I hope he never asks me to return the favor.

Words are clumsy tools for attempting to express how deeply grateful I am to my wife, Michelle, and our children Judah, Asher, and Zoe for all that they sacrificed in the name of this work with the churches and displaced communities of Colombia. My travels, absences, and risks cost them more than anyone else.

This publication represents research undertaken as part of a research project of the FUSBC, formally denominated "Integral missiology and the human flourishing of internally displaced persons in Colombia." The project was made possible through the support of generous grants from the Templeton World Charity Foundation, Inc. The opinions expressed in this publication are those of the author and do not necessarily reflect the views of the Templeton World Charity Foundation, Inc. (TWCF) or the FUSBC. But none of this would have been possible without the trust and support of both TWCF and FUSBC.

A few notes on method are required at the outset of this book on, well, method. In the first place, all of this work was originally conducted in Spanish. All translations from Spanish are mine and in the ensuing pages, I translate interview transcriptions and secondary citations without commenting each time I do so. Unless otherwise indicated, Scripture citations are from the NRSV.

Our field research engaged marginalized communities in order to coax forth voices hitherto unheard. Their testimonies underlie the conclusions to which we came and the interventions we created. Still, I wanted to ensure that at least some of them could speak in their own voices. Therefore, I braided this book's chapters together with seven biographical vignettes derived from interviews with project participants.[1] While I have at times filled in blanks for the reader, I have endeavored to translate and summarize in such a way as to facilitate their voices being heard directly, even if doing so means that rough edges persist in the accounts.

The protocols for the field research behind this volume were approved by the FUSBC Ethics Committee, as were the data protection practices. The most sensitive research protocols were also approved by the Fuller Theological Seminary Institutional Review Board. All interviews and focus groups were recorded, transcribed, analyzed, and archived, but are not available to the public, for security reasons. Names, geographic identifications, and dates are sometimes elided or altered for the protection of survivors and those who still risk their safety to work among them.

---

1. This approach was inspired by Michael Jackson, *The Wherewithal of Life: Ethics, Migration, and the Question of Well-Being* (Berkley: University of California Press, 2013).

# CHAPTER 1

# Opening Our Eyes

*Desplazamiento . . . desplazamiento.*

When you are new to a sociolinguistic context, you tend to follow conversations in an impressionistic rather than precise fashion. Unknown words whiz past your head while you furrow your brow and nod, feigning understanding and hoping your brain will catch up soon. You do your level best to piece together the gist of a discourse using the lexemes you have already memorized, all the while assuring yourself that the bits you missed were probably unimportant. Still, when a strange term knocks against your ear for the fourth or fifth time, you may begrudgingly tap it (or your best phonetic approximation of it) into your phone in search of a definition, just as I did in August 2013, sitting in a meeting with leaders from the Biblical Seminary of Colombia (FUSBC,[1] the seminary I was about to join) and a couple visiting academics from Fuller Theological Seminary. *Des-pla-za-mi-en-to. . .*

The meeting was a brainstorming session between the Californian and Colombian seminaries in an effort to identify a research topic of mutual interest. The scholars from Fuller had mentioned that many Latin Americans arriving in California were fleeing violence in Central America. My soon-to-be colleague, Milton Acosta (an Old Testament professor at FUSBC), pointed out that Colombia was likewise afflicted by massive forced *desplazamiento* due to decades of savage violence.

The sluggish internet finally produced a translation: *desplazamiento*, noun, meaning "displacement." Embarrassingly, the English term did not ring any bells for me. In 2013, the global migratory crisis had not yet become the topic of woke conversation at hipster bars. But since my senior Latin colleagues grew increasingly enthusiastic about the possibility of jointly researching this phenomenon called "forced displacement,"

---

1. Fundación Universitaria Seminario Bíblico de Colombia; the acronym FUSBC is pronounced *Foosbaysay*, which hardly rolls off the tongue.

I concluded that I would have to slink away and figure out what they were talking about.

What I discovered horrified me.

At that point, in 2013, 6.5 million Colombians had been driven from their homes and land by the savage violence that rampaged throughout the countryside. That number is equivalent to the population of a small nation: Uruguay has 3.5 million inhabitants; Costa Rica has 5 million; Nicaragua and El Salvador, 6.5 million each. And the Colombian displacement crisis was not dying down. Even after the Colombian government signed the Habana Peace Accords with the dreaded FARC[2] guerrilla group in 2016, numbers of displaced people continued to climb. As I draft this introduction, the Colombian government's official database for victims of the armed conflict, the Registro Único de Víctimas, puts the total number of internally displaced persons (IDPs) at over 8,150,000,[3] giving this already-notorious Latin American nation the dubious distinction of having the largest population of IDPs in the world. Colombian-forced internal displacement[4] is the biggest contemporary humanitarian crisis you have never heard of. Its resolution or perpetuation will define the future of the country for at least the next two generations.

This chapter tells the story of how the Biblical Seminary of Colombia, a little evangelical school nestled in the mountainside on the wrong end of Medellín, decided to make forced displacement the defining topic of its research and social action for nearly a decade. We begin with an

2. More accurately, FARC-EP, the Fuerzas Armadas Revolucionarias de Colombia-Ejército del Pueblo.

3. Red Nacional de Información, "Registro único de víctimas," https://www.unidadvictimas.gov.co/es/registro-unico-de-victimas-ruv/37394. The total number of displacement events is actually 9,150,000, since many IDPs are displaced multiple times.

4. Let me clarify a few terms up front. The two basic types of migration are "voluntary" and "involuntary," being differentiated by whether the migrant chooses or is forced to migrate. In practice, migration often falls somewhere on the spectrum between the extremes of voluntary and involuntary. One can also migrate internationally or domestically, the latter of which is referred to as internal migration. The term "refugee" refers to *international* forced migrants, who are subject to a myriad of international protections. By contrast, this book focuses on people who are *internally* displaced due to violence. They are, as it were, refugees within their own national borders. For a succinct Christian overview of the global migratory crisis, see Elizabeth W. Collier and Charles R. Strain, *Global Migration: What's Happening, Why, and a Just Response* (Winona, MN: Anselm Academic, 2017).

all-too-brief overview of the causes and consequences of involuntary migration due to violence in Colombia. I then describe how the seminary's initial collaboration with Fuller morphed into something much bigger. Thereafter, I lay out the epistemic and theological commitments that shaped the project's evolution. In the ensuing chapters, I will unpack how, from 2014 through 2022, we generated and implemented an innovative method of applied theological investigation, called Missional Action Research (MAR), and created a project called Faith and Displacement that now works with Christian communities and IDPs across the country to reconstruct the lives of victims of the armed conflict.

## The Crisis of Forced Displacement Due to Violence in Colombia

Since the history of the armed conflict is both complex and hotly contested,[5] the present chapter will confine itself to a broadly synchronic description (focusing mostly on the past twenty years) of the major causes and ramifications of the displacement crisis.

### The Causes of Displacement

In order to provide an overview of the causes of displacement, I will summarize the actors who generate displacement, the reasons they displace people, and the tools those actors use.

#### The Actors of Displacement

While it would be unfair to impute all the guilt of the Colombian conflict to them, guerrilla militias stand at the nexus of the crisis. In the last twenty years, two guerrilla groups[6] have been most influential: the

---

5. During the FARC peace talks, ten historians were asked to write a brief history of the war. After a few months, there were ten histories, rather than a single one. This illustrates how intractable of a problem it is to tell Colombia's story in a way that satisfies different sides. For serious attempts to write an even-handed representation of the recent history of Colombia, see Ricardo Arias Trujillo, *Historia de Colombia contemporánea (1920–2010)* (Bogotá: Universidad de los Andes, 2011); and Grupo de Memoria Histórica, *¡Basta Ya! Colombia: Memorias de guerra y dignidad* (Bogotá: Centro Nacional de Memoria Histórica, 2013), 110–94.

6. All known by acronyms; one of the few things that Latin Americans have in common with Germans is their love of a good acronym.

FARC-EP[7] and the ELN-UC (Ejército de Liberación Nacional).[8] Both of these groups have Marxist roots, and they conceive of themselves as defenders of the campesino. (Campesino refers to a lower-class rural Latin American farmer with a modest amount of land at their disposal. The suggested translation of campesino tends to be "peasant," an infelicitous rendering, given both its European, feudal evocations and the fact that it is pretty gauche for a White academic to refer to anyone as a peasant. This book will stick with the transliterated term *campesino*.) Still, the guerrilla's ideological proclamations ring hollow in the ears of anyone who knows the myriad forms of violence they have committed against people of all social stripes, including poor campesinos.

Guerrilla groups like the FARC and ELN began formally to constitute themselves in the mid-1960s. Over the subsequent decades, they clashed with national police and military forces and with local nongovernmental self-defense groups (*grupos de autodefensa*) that banded together to protect their own interests, often fighting in alignment with the national armed forces. In the 1980s and '90s, those informal citizen militias grew in power, becoming small private armies and, in due course, broadly right-wing terrorist groups.

These *autodefensas* are typically referred to as *paramilitares*, "paramilitary groups." Paramilitary forces have perpetrated some of the more heinous atrocities of the armed conflict, at times with the aid or complicity of the national army. An infamous case was *Operation Genesis*, a cooperative strike between the 17th Brigade of the Colombian army and the paramilitary group Bloque Elmer Cárdenas. *Operation Genesis* was launched against an Afro-Colombian community in the Chocó, in an effort to strike a blow against the FARC. In the course of this massacre, Marino Lopez Mena, an Afro-Colombian citizen, was brutally murdered, dismembered, and beheaded, after which his killers played soccer with his skull.[9]

---

7. Demobilized in 2016–2017, although a significant minority of the group, the so-called Disidencias de las FARC, remain active.

8. Formed 1964 and active until today, the ELN is the oldest guerrilla group in the world.

9. Comisión Intereclesial de Justicia y Paz, "Operación 'Génesis,' tortura y ejecución extrajudicial de Marino Lopez Mena," https://www.justiciaypazcolombia.com/operacion -genesis-tortura-y-ejecucion-extrajudicial-de-marino-lopez-mena/.

Paramilitary groups—such as the Clan de Golfo, the Caparrapos, and the Rastrojos—continue to savage the countryside of Colombia, the national military all too often turning a blind eye to their atrocities. At one point in Colombian history, it was possible to view the *autodefensas* as part of a solution to the guerrilla problem. Today, however, their odious actions make clear that the putative cure ended up being worse than the disease.

The precipitous ascendency of paramilitary forces in Colombia is owed in large measure to a massive capital inflow from drug cartels, especially the notorious Cartel de Medellín, led by Pablo Escobar. Paramilitary groups frequently allied themselves with the cartels, providing muscle to protect the cultivation and transport of narcotics. After Escobar was toppled in the late 1990s, the major cartels were somewhat broken up. Rather than disappear, though, they reorganized into large mafia organizations (called *bacrim*, short for *bandas criminales*) that traffic in drugs and murder for hire. Alliances between the diverse urban mafia and rural paramilitary groups (often called *narcoparamilitares*) may shift from one year to the next. But it is the proliferation and fluidity of criminal groups that make the Colombian conflict so intractable. Disarming guerrillas and paramilitary forces is like a sadistic game of whack-a-mole, in which the losers, time and again, are the people of Colombia.

Last, the Colombian armed forces and police contribute (in a lesser but not insignificant degree) to the ongoing violence in Colombia, and not just insofar as they are fighting on the "side of the angels." This is a sensitive topic, as many instances of alleged crimes against humanity perpetrated by Colombian military forces are under investigation and as the Colombian government has a vested interest in minimizing them. Nonetheless, the Habana Peace Accords recognized that crimes against humanity had been committed by members of the Colombian Armed Forces, and individual cases are being tried.

The most widespread human rights violations perpetrated by the Colombian army are known by the innocuous term "false positives." Under right-wing President Álvaro Uribe (2002–2010), the armed forces were pressured and incentivized to reach quotas of guerrilla fighters killed. In response, thousands of soldiers (often with the knowledge and complicity of their superiors) kidnapped campesinos, dressed them as guerrillas, and murdered them in order to fill their quotas. In 2021, a special tribunal established that at least 6,400 people were executed as "false positives" between 2002 and 2008.[10] Actions such as these not only feed continued resistance by guerrilla forces, but also generate, in some displaced persons, a deep-seated suspicion of the Colombian national government.[11]

## The Reasons People Are Forcibly Displaced

Armed groups' primary reason for invading new territories is to secure control of key spaces. Sometimes, the land itself holds significant economic potential and can be exploited for mining or for cultivating coca. Other territories provide geographic or topographic advantages in military skirmishes or guerrilla warfare. In some instances, armed groups seek to control strategic transportation corridors to facilitate the movement of drugs or people. Colombians are well accustomed to being stopped at highway roadblocks, typically operated by the national military or by protestors, but sometimes by guerrilla militia or *autodefensas*. The worry, when approaching a roadblock manned by people in camouflage and holding rifles, is that they will do more than simply examine your identity papers and baggage.

Sometimes, armed groups target specific individuals or groups, even after securing control of a given territory. If, for example, the Clan de Golfo suspects that a particular townsperson sympathizes with or supports the Caparrapos, or if the *guerrilla* think that someone is passing information to the military, that person might be singled out for execution.

In other instances, local leaders draw the attention of armed groups, who recognize that the elimination of a mayor, a community organizer, or a pastor will expedite the submission of the rest of the town. As a thirty-seven-year-old man from the department[12] of César narrated:

10. Jurisdicción especial para la paz, "Comunicado 019 de 2021," Bogotá, 2021; and BBC, "Peace Court: Colombia Army 'Behind 6,400 Extrajudicial Killings,'" BBC News, https://www.bbc.com/news/world-latin-america-56112386.

11. The corruption and collusion between paramilitaries and the national government is not limited to the armed forces. One displaced man I spoke to, who had informed on a paramilitary group, had to displace three times because the paramilitaries kept hunting him down, aided by corrupt government officials. It was only when he stopped registering with the Unidad de Víctimas (and forewent victims' support), stopped sending his daughter to school, and ceased to be formally employed that the paramilitaries could no longer find him.

12. Rather than being structured into different states, like the United States or Mexico, Colombia comprises thirty-two different "departments."

When I was a candidate for mayor, the guerrilla kidnapped me for three days and told me that if I wanted, I could support someone else [as a candidate], but that I could not run. So we supported someone else in the group and I was named the secretary of the [local] government. During that term, the guerrilla took the pueblo and attacked it terribly, and we tried to talk [with them]. So then the paramilitaries arrived and they fingered us as collaborators of the guerrilla. . . . The paramilitaries did not threaten me; they were [just] going to kill me. But someone I knew found out and called me and warned me that they were coming the next day to kill me. So my whole family had to leave.[13]

As the result of dynamics like these, community leaders in Colombia live in grave peril. According to statistics from February 2021, in the four years and three months following the signing of the Habana Peace Accords, over nine hundred social leaders and community organizers had been murdered.[14] When their leaders die, people typically flee.

### The Tools of Displacement

By definition, forced displacement results from the use or credible threat of violence; that is what distinguishes it from economic or environmental migration. The Registro Único de Victimas recognizes sixteen different categories of victimizing events. To date, it has catalogued a total of 12,140,000 victimizing events within the theatre of the armed conflict, 9,500,000 of which are forcible displacements.[15] Nonetheless, involuntary displacement is itself the result of other forms of victimization. That is to say, involuntary displacement is "forced" by something else.

Displacement frequently transpires in response to the explicitly stated threat of future violence. A given group will enter a settlement and give the inhabitants notice that they have a week, a day, or even an hour to vacate their homes, lest reprisals ensue. If the townspeople do not heed

13. Interview conducted by Laura Cadavid, cited in Laura Milena Cadavid Valencia, "Elementos para comprender el desplazamiento forzado en Colombia: un recorrido por normas, conceptos y experiencias," in *Conversaciones teológicas del sur global americano: violencia, desplazamiento y fe*, ed. Oscar Garcia-Johnson and Milton Acosta (Eugene, OR: Wipf & Stock, 2016), 21.

14. Deutsche Welle, "Más de 900 líderes sociales asesinados en Colombia desde 2016," Deutsche Welle, April 19, 2021, https://www.dw.com/es/m%C3%A1s-de-900-l%C3%ADderes-sociales-asesinados-en-colombia-desde-2016/a-57257906.

15. Red Nacional de Información, "Registro único de víctimas."

these verbal warnings, matters escalate precipitously. Members of one community with whom we work had their homes and farms burned after initially refusing to leave their land.

Other times, violence itself serves as the eviction notice, whether taking the form of physical battery, sexual assault,[16] torture, or murder. Additionally, people often displace after a family member has been kidnapped or disappeared, after being injured by the antipersonnel mines that litter certain contested territories, or after a child has been "recruited" by an armed group.[17]

The aforementioned violence may take the form of targeted assassinations of persons perceived to be a particular threat or obstacle, or of false positives by the military that have little to do with the specific identity of the victim. Often, however, there are large-scale massacres of whole villages, notionally for the purpose of rooting out members of or collaborators with an opposing armed group. When I say "often" I mean to say that, just in 2020, there were ninety-one massacres in Colombia, twenty-one of which were in Antioquia (the department in which FUSBC is located). As I draft this chapter in August 2021, the year's tally of massacres has already reached sixty-eight.[18]

[*The content of the following paragraphs is disturbing and could be triggering to some readers. Feel free to skip to the next section.*] Perhaps the best-documented massacre in the armed conflict occurred in the settlement of El Salado, in the Montes de María of the Caribbean coastal region of Colombia. I summarize this brutal event at this juncture in the

---

16. As of 2017, the Centro Nacional de Memoria Histórica had documented over fifteen thousand cases of sexual violence within the scope of the armed conflict (Centro Nacional de Memoria Histórica, *La guerra inscrita en el cuerpo: informe nacional de violencia sexual en el conflicto armado* [Bogotá: Centro Nacional de Memoria Histórica, 2017], 17), although the shame associated with such crimes ensures that the real figures are far higher than what is formally reported.

17. As of 2017, the Centro Nacional de Memoria Histórica had documented 16,879 cases of the recruitment of children and adolescents by guerrilla and paramilitary groups; Centro Nacional de Memoria Histórica, *Una guerra sin edad: informe nacional de reclutamiento y utilización de niños, niñas y adolescentes en el conflicto armado colombiano* (Bogotá: Centro Nacional de Memoria Histórica, 2017), 17.

18. Instituto de estudios para el desarrollo y la paz Indepaz, "Informe de masacres en Colombia durantes el 2020 y 2021," Indepaz, http://www.indepaz.org.co/informe-de -masacres-en-colombia-durante-el-2020-2021/.

volume, because it illustrates how diverse forms of violence are inter-connected in massacres and other displacement-precipitating events.[19]

In February 2000, a force of 450 paramilitary fighters took control of El Salado as part of their conflict with the FARC. Some residents attempted to flee to the mountains and were shot by paramilitaries surrounding the village. When the village had been taken, the fighters forced the inhab-itants at gunpoint to the football pitch (soccer field) at the center of the town, lining the men up along the edge of the field and locking the women and children in an adjacent house. They then interrogated the men of the town one by one, accusing them of collaborating with the guerrilla. The interrogation consisted of a macabre and twisted succession of beatings, mutilations, suffocations, and murders. Men had ropes tied around their necks and chests and were stretched to the point of strangulation; they were bayoneted in the throat, stabbed, and shot one after the other.

Throughout this process, the paramilitaries cranked up music on the stereos in the shops bordering the football pitch to create the atmosphere of a depraved *festivo* (festival). They even held raffles to decide whom to kill next, contributing to the psychological abuse of their victims.

Before long, women were dragged from the house where they had been imprisoned to be beaten, bayoneted, shot, raped, and tortured. In one gruesome instance, the invaders seized a twenty-one-year-old pregnant woman named Neivis Arrieta, raped her, broke her neck, and impaled her with a stick through the vagina. The youngest person to die in the massacre (aside from Neivis's unborn baby), however, was Neivis's seven-year-old sister, Helen Arrieta. Helen succumbed to dehydration as she hid in a mountain, refusing to drink the urine of the woman who concealed her there.

All told, sixty people were killed in the massacre. After the paramil-itaries withdrew, the surviving inhabitants of El Salado fled their homes and fields, leaving behind them a ghost town.

The heinous events of the massacre at El Salado illustrate how pro-foundly destructive the events that cause displacement can be. Without apprehending the precipitating events of forced migration, it would be all too easy to interpret it as an inconvenient relocation, as opposed to

---

19. The following paragraphs depend on the details chronicled in Gonzalo Sánchez G., Andrés Fernando Suárez, and Tatiana Rincón, *La masacre de El Salado: esa guerra no era nuestra* (Bogotá: Ediciones Semana, 2009), 31–69.

what it often is: scrambling flight in the wake or the pathway of appalling evil. Furthermore, the sick combination of torture, sexual assault, psychological abuse, and murder provides some glimpse into the profound multidimensional suffering that afflicts many displaced people who must somehow cobble together a new "life" after experiencing such atrocious death.

## The Consequences of Displacement

After the violence, people flee, perhaps with what they can fit into a vehicle, if they are lucky. At times they run for their lives with what they can carry, or with just the clothes on their backs and their remaining children in their arms. The violence may be a mere matter of minutes. The flight, a matter of days. But what happens thereafter defines the course of the rest of their lives.

Like a diabolical, trauma-inducing arachnid, displacement catches victims in a web of multidimensional suffering that festers for decades. The displaced are wounded psychologically, debilitated financially, crippled socially, disenfranchised politically, and crushed spiritually. Although a more detailed account of the consequences of violence-induced migration is available in appendix 1,[20] for the sake of concision let me pull in the following facts from that treatment, to articulate some of the key dynamics:

- The eight million people who have fled violence leave behind the graves of one million homicide victims: spouses, children, and friends.
- As a consequence, 39 percent of displaced families have only one parent, almost always a woman, and 39 percent of those women personally witnessed the murder of a husband or a male child.
- Sixty-seven percent of displaced households report psychosocial suffering; 24 percent report having sought help; staggeringly, only 2 percent report receiving any professional support for emotional or mental health.
- Campesinos displaced to cities experience an *extreme* poverty rate of 85 percent.

---

20. Refer to the appendix for citations substantiating the statistics below.

- On average, an adult Colombian IDP has only five years of formal education, and 11 percent have not even completed a year of schooling.
- The IDPs are marginalized in their arrival sites as a consequence of regional prejudices and the suspicion of their neighbors, who assume that the displaced must have done something sinister to deserve their misfortune. (*Por algo será* is the speculation: "It must have been for something.")

Much like a spider's web, if you tug on one strand of that suffering in hopes of providing relief in one aspect of the victim's life, you end up pulling at the entire sticky, constricting matrix. To give just one example: psychological trauma contributes to victims' chronic poverty because trauma undermines the sorts of economic behaviors congenial to financial recovery. Those afflicted by psychological disturbances manifest a striking preference for low-risk/low-reward economic behavior, such that they gravitate toward the saturated informal sector of the economy (selling candy on buses, washing windshields in intersections) and avoid the sorts of entrepreneurial activities that development economists often commend for nonmigrant, non-traumatized, low-income populations. The inability to put food on the table intensifies people's desperation, leading parents to withdraw children from school in order to supplement the family's income. This in turn heightens the likelihood of intergenerational poverty as well as affiliation with criminal groups, which perpetuates the cycle of violence.

In brief, the victimization of Colombian IDPs may begin with the violence they suffer, but it hardly ends there. They struggle on through decades, afflicted by poverty, psychological trauma, family dismemberment, government neglect, and social stigmatization and marginalization. While they have not crossed their nation's legal border, they live as refugees, as exiles in their own country. Yet, for all of that marginality, these domestic refugees account for 16 percent of the national population, one in six persons: eight million exiles.

## Initial Explorations into the Displacement Crisis

Of course, I did not grasp all of this back in 2013. My earliest attempts to wrap my head around the displacement crisis remained clumsy. After all, my starting point was attempting to sound out the spelling of the word *desplazamiento* so as to seek out a definition for the term. Notwithstanding the crudity of my initial understanding, however, the sheer scale of the tragedy more than convinced FUSBC and Fuller Theological Seminary that forced migration due to violence warranted attention (especially since a social topic of this sort would be evidence of that ever-elusive desideratum of academic research: "relevance"). We jointly agreed to spend the first half of 2014 researching forced migration in our respective geographic contexts, after which we planned to hold a conference at FUSBC and publish a wee edited volume. We surmised that the whole endeavor would amount to about a year's worth of work.

The intervening autumnal months of 2013 afforded me enough time to shuffle my family across the pond from Oxford to the United States (where I dragged myself through several weeks of the cross-cultural missions training mandated by my mission agency), and then down to Colombia. After my jarring first encounter with Advent celebrations in a *barrio popular* of Medellín (where the yuletide festivities are less characterized by soft hymns and the occasional troupe of carolers than by six successive weeks of raucous parties lasting through the night and punctuated by the unending racket of firecrackers), I arrived—keenly aware of my cultural alterity—at the first meeting Milton Acosta had convened to organize our faculty's research.

We were not exactly an elite cadre of thinkers. As we gulped acidic black coffee and kicked ideas around, onlookers (had they existed) would not have conjured up images of Sartre, Beauvoir, Hemingway, Picasso, and Camus sipping espresso together in Paris. Even setting aside the fact that our ensemble boasted fewer doctorates than one could count on a single hand (sans thumb), we were all theologians (mostly professors of the Bible), hardly accustomed to examining contemporary social phenomena. We agreed rapidly that we would need help wrapping our heads around the crisis.

Accordingly, Milton did something odd: he contracted a sociologist to consult with us. Laura Cadavid (from whom I skimmed some of the quotations above) did not have a PhD and was only twenty-eight years old. But she was a Christian sociologist (a combination hard to come by in Colombia) and had legit experience performing field work with displaced people. Her remit was to help us understand the social and political dynamics affecting the experiences of the displaced, lest we be left to our own speculative devices.

At the same time, Milton invited local Christian leaders with ministries to IDPs to meet with us monthly in order to share their experiences and help us identify the most pressing obstacles to IDP recovery. As they shared, not only did the plight of the displaced lose some of its abstraction, but we also glimpsed how complicated it would be to do anything about it. The intractability of the crisis, owing to the interconnections among poverty, psychological trauma, political ineptitude and corruption, educational disadvantages, and overly spiritualizing theology, began to come into focus.

Meanwhile, our team members started conducting research on whatever aspects of displacement struck our interest, each person sharing their perspectives on successive weeks. But I was wrestling with an additional problem: I felt unsure as to whether I had the right to say anything.

After all, I had lived on Colombian soil for only a few months, most of them within the same four square miles of Medellín. A middle-class White millennial from California who had spent the previous seven years studying in Europe, I continued to screw up my subjunctive verbs in Spanish. Moreover, my time in the United Kingdom had been accompanied by a steady drip of postcolonial awareness (and guilt). That in turn was complemented (strangely) by my few months of cross-cultural missions training in the United States, which drilled into me that I, as a foreign missionary, should defer to the superior cultural understanding of my national partners. As will be clear to anyone who has read *The Poisonwood Bible*, such sensitivities are vital for a White male missionary from the United States. The history of modern missions, laudable in many respects, has been blighted by cultural imperialism. All this left me in a bind. How could I work as a professor and a researcher, without succumbing to the temptation to foist my paradigms upon my students and colleagues?

My initial strategy consisted of deflecting questions and querying others for their thoughts on the topics at hand. Being a facilitator, rather than a constructive thinker, seemed a safe route. Eventually, however, the seminary's Colombian president Elizabeth Sendek pressed me to give my own opinions. I wrung my hands and voiced postcolonial truisms about my own cultural situatedness and my concern that I would inappropriately prejudice the group with my imperialist theological and social sensitivities. Elizabeth listened patiently, blinking slowly in a way that (I would eventually realize) reflected that she had heard my schtick before and was waiting for me to conclude. When I had finally run out of words, she responded simply, "Christopher, we asked you here because we want your opinion. And if you are wrong, we will tell you."

"If you are wrong, we will tell you." Elizabeth's tone was kind, but her words bore a gentle reproach. My efforts at postcolonial circumspection and cultural caution—motivated, I later understood, by a mixture of earnest good intentions and a bit of intellectual hubris—effectively revealed the paternalistic assumption that I would bowl over my colleagues (almost all of whom were my seniors) with my impressive academic qualifications. Elizabeth helped me see that the national faculty were no strangers to working alongside foreign professors. They were perfectly capable of identifying our cultural bias and politely backing us down. My fear of imposing my worldview on my colleagues betrayed a fair measure of patronizing condescension. But nobody on faculty was at risk of blithely accepting my views; nobody saw me as a missionary nerd messiah. Only I thought I had that much power.[21]

Therefore, Elizabeth and the rest of my colleagues invited me to be involved: self-aware, yes, but not self-quarantining as a consequence. I realized I needed to pitch into a larger dialogue and collaborative endeavor, adding my culturally situated perspective to the insights of non-theologians like Laura and nonacademics like the church ministers who shared with us each month. I learned that listening did not mean that I never talked, and that respecting national partners meant trusting that they were capable of correcting me.

## Three Streams of Insight That Shaped Our Project

Looking back at those early months, I can identify the emerging epistemic considerations that eventually formed Faith and Displacement. To be clear, we did not articulate robust epistemology at our project's outset. But given the unconventional style of this book, it would be best to begin with an outline of the epistemic intuitions that shaped our project.

---

21. I should clarify that this observation applies only to my faculty colleagues. It would not typically be true of seminary students, local pastors, or Colombian laity, who often accord excessive authority to foreign missionaries.

Three major streams of insight or, indeed, revelation, fed into Faith and Displacement: the social sciences, Christian Scripture, and experience.[22] The structure and generic oscillation of the ensuing chapters (from personal narratives to social-scientific research to biblical studies) keep each of these streams in view.

## Social Sciences

The hiring of a sociologist like Laura Cadavid set into motion the project's long-term and sustained engagement with social-scientific literature and methodologies. She was the first of a dozen social scientists—researchers in psychology, sociology, education, politics, and economics—to contribute to our work. Faith and Displacement ultimately organized itself into six different teams, five of which were explicitly social-scientific in their remit. Each team synthesized social-scientific and theological theory in their constructive educational interventions and utilized empirical investigative methods from the social sciences to build their proposals. Correspondingly, every chapter in this volume will include contributions from social-scientific research. Although in 2014, our work remained more theologically abstract, we ultimately wanted to ensure that we achieved concrete, practical impact. And for that, we needed the social sciences.

## Christian Scripture

Perhaps it will appear obvious that the second stream of revelation that fed our project was Christian Scripture. After all, I'm a New Testament scholar; Faith and Displacement is a project of the *Biblical* Seminary of Colombia, an evangelical institution that prides itself on the Bible occupying a more central place in its curriculum than other protestant seminaries in Colombia;[23] and evangelicals in the Americas assert that

---

22. Being a fan of the Wesleyan Quadrilateral, I wish I could say that self-aware engagement with Christian tradition also played a significant role. Sadly, it did not. Colombian Protestantism is typically evangelical in its wariness of church tradition and its attendant notional reliance only upon the Bible for the elaboration of doctrine and ethics. Although we did call on bits and bobs of historical Christian tradition at various junctures in the project, such appeals were matters of convenience, not the consequence of disciplined historical-theological engagement.

23. Christopher M. Hays, "The State of Protestant Academic Theology in Colombia," in *Glaube und Theologie: Reformatorische Grundeinsichten in der ökumenischen Diskussion / Faith and Theology: Basic Insights of the Reformation in Ecumenical Debate,*

the Bible is the primary font of their faith and morals. In fact, Colombian evangelicals often are suspicious of systematic theology unless it is presented in terms that they understand to be biblical, preferring what they understand to be "the Word of God" rather than "human doctrines" (cf. Eph. 4:14). So it is probably unsurprising that Scripture was a major source of insight for this undertaking. Still, a few more points that might not be self-evident require clarification.

First of all, the Bible played an important role in our social-scientific research. A number of our academic publications fused theology and the social sciences (in relation to, e.g., trauma theory, politics, and acculturation), and yet the theological contributions in those publications came from Scripture studies, rather than from dogmatics.[24]

Second, the Bible figured pervasively in our response to the displacement crisis. As will be described in chapter 5, each project team elaborated an educational intervention through which to confront aspects of displacement pertinent to their team. Even when discussing, say, formal employment or trauma-informed care, Scriptural texts and reflections mediated the message, precisely because the Bible is the way in which many Colombian IDPs understand the world.[25]

Given the role of Scripture in both our field research and our interventions with IDPs, it seemed incongruous to write the present book without incorporating Scriptural study as well. Consequently, each of the following chapters will incorporate insights from the Gospel of Luke and the Acts of the Apostles, in order to showcase how aspects of the biblical witness reinforce and complement the lessons learned from social-scientific research and local experiences.

ed. Wolfram Kinzig and Julia Winnebeck, Veröffentlichungen der Wissenschaftlichen Gesellschaft für Theologie (Leipzig: Evangelische Verlagsanstalt, 2019), 103.

24. So Christopher M. Hays and Milton Acosta, "A Concubine's Rape, an Apostle's Flight, and a Nation's Reconciliation: Biblical Interpretation, Collective Trauma Narratives, and the Armed Conflict in Colombia," *Biblical Interpretation* 28 (2020): 56–83; Robert W. Heimburger, Christopher M. Hays, and Guillermo Mejía Castillo, "Forgiveness and Politics: Reading Matthew 18:21–35 with Survivors of the Armed Conflict in Colombia," *HTS Teologiese Studies / Theological Studies* 75, no. 4 (2019): 1–9; and Christopher M. Hays, "What Is the Place of My Rest? Being Migrant People(s) of the God of All the Earth," *Open Theology* 7, no. 2 (2021): 150–68.

25. The vast majority of our eighteen project curricula use Scriptural reflections or studies in every lesson.

The works of Luke are congenial for this purpose given their deep attention to matters of both migration and missions. Naturally, Acts provides the only extended canonical narrative on the missional expansion of the early church,[26] which makes it especially pertinent for a book that expounds a new approach to missiological research. But beyond that, geographic migration runs throughout both Lukan books, making them topically relevant to the present work on displacement. Luke's Jesus travels constantly as an itinerant preacher, a messianic figure who nonetheless has "nowhere to lay his head" (Luke 9:58). This aligns with the way that Mark and especially Matthew characterize Jesus's ministry,[27] but Luke extends this motif in his second volume, as the book of Acts represents the expansion of the gospel through repeated tales of migration (often forced migration),[28] taking the gospel from Jerusalem, to Judea and Samaria, and to the ends of the earth (Acts 1:8).[29] Additionally, according to the traditional construal of the works' authorship,[30] Luke himself was the "beloved physician" mentioned in the Pauline Epistles (Col. 4:14; Philem. 24; 2 Tim. 4:11) and traveled with Paul (Acts 16:10–17; 20:5–15; 21:1–18; 27:1–28:16; see further, chapter 4), meaning that he himself was a migrant minister. For these reasons, insights from the academic study of Luke and Acts run through this volume like a red thread, exemplifying the pervasive role of the Bible in shaping the research and interventions of Faith and Displacement.

26. On mission in Acts, see, e.g., Beverly Roberts Gaventa, "'You Will Be My Witnesses': Aspects of Mission in the Acts of the Apostles," *Missiology* 10, no. 4 (1982): 413–25; and Peter G. Bolt, "Mission and Witness," in *Witness to the Gospel: The Theology of Acts*, ed. I. Howard Marshall and David Peterson (Grand Rapids: Eerdmans, 1998), 169–90.

27. On Jesus's migrant identity in Matthew, and its relationship to contemporary migratory crises, see Christopher M. Hays and Milton Acosta, "Jesus as Missional Migrant: Latin American Christologies, the New Testament Witness, and Twenty-first Century Migration," in *Who Do You Say I Am? On the Humanity of Jesus*, ed. George Kalantzis, David B. Capes, and Ty Kieser (Eugene, OR: Cascade, 2020), 158–77.

28. Acts 8:1–4; 9:23–30; 13:50–51; 14:19–20; 16:39–40; 17:5–15; 18:2; 19:20; 23:16–33; and 27:1–28:15.

29. See, e.g., Christoph W. Stenschke, "Migration and Mission: According to the Book of Acts," *Missionalia* 44, no. 2 (2016): 129–51; and Hays, "What Is the Place?," 150–68.

30. On the case for the traditional identity of Luke, see Craig S. Keener, *Acts: An Exegetical Commentary*, 4 vols. (Grand Rapids: Baker, 2012), 1:402–16.

## Experience

This brings us to the third stream of insight that fed Faith and Displacement: the experiences of the project participants, including the academic researchers, local Christian leaders, and members of displaced communities.

Admittedly, for Christian theologians, Experience, the avenue of revelation most beset by the vulnerabilities of interpretive subjectivity, remains the most problematic side of the Wesleyan Quadrilateral.[31] Scripture, Tradition, and Reason can be analyzed within the methodological frameworks developed by biblical scholarship, historical theology, and philosophy. But Experience in good measure resists critical evaluation by third parties and risks throwing a free-spirited wrench into the carefully calibrated theological reflections of exegetes, historians, and philosophers. Accordingly, however much I would privately have credited my subjective perceptions of what "I felt the Lord was teaching me" within the sphere of my own spirituality, such experientially based intuitions remained relegated to homiletical anecdotes, without playing any explicit role in academic publication. (In a published work, the citation and the syllogism reign supreme.)

But here's the problem: Faith and Displacement did not unfold in a spiritual vacuum. Notwithstanding the extensive methodological reflection that shaped the project, our decisions were also significantly influenced by a sense of how God was leading us (whether through prayer, or pleas from local leaders, or a sense of inner conviction, or the extraordinary confluence of circumstances). To omit the role of personal and corporate spiritual discernment from this account, all the while attempting to commend our research method to other scholars, would effectively amount to tearing a key chapter out of the instruction manual. Indeed, however methodologically slippery it might be to pay attention to personal experiences, to ignore such experience would be to operate as if God did not exist.

Several years into the Faith and Displacement project, I stumbled across the work of Clare Watkins. Watkins argues that scholars of applied theology ought to adopt a spiritual practice marked by three traits: "An attentiveness in *humility before multiple voices* in conversation; an

---

31. The Wesleyan Quadrilateral refers to the four sources of revelation celebrated in the Methodist tradition: Scripture, Reason, Tradition, and Experience.

*eschatologically formed expectation regarding outcome*; and, above all, a *pneumatological understanding* of the reading *of incarnational realities* of faith."[32] This framework eloquently describes the intuitions and spirituality that governed the project's attention to Experience.

In relation to the first trait, Watkins explains that curating a conversation between diverse voices requires "a *kenotic* quality, which names the position of the researcher so as to de-power it in an act of self-emptying before what is other."[33] This point was impressed upon us by the Participatory Action Research method (chapter 3). A diversity of voices needed to come together in our project, and an understandable desire to hear them in harmony should not allow the distortion or silencing of any one singer.

Nonetheless, hearing the voice of the other requires that I drop the guise of impartial detachment. A mere caveat admission of my own subjectivity falls short of the candor required from a practical theological or missional action researcher. However much we researchers try to keep our biases at bay, we are too heavily implicated in the research to hide ourselves behind the narrative curtain. The truth of the researcher's identity needs to be disclosed so that subsequent readers can see how that researcher's identity shaped their approach—perhaps in prejudicial fashion, but perhaps as a graced serendipity, as God uses the cultural particularity of the researcher for good.

This brings us to the second component of the spirituality of practical theological research that Watkins commends: "An *eschatological* attitude, an openness to an unknown but promised 'outcome.'"[34] Here, Watkins fuses the belief that God is acting in the theological research with humility to allow that work to deviate dramatically from the route originally planned. Such research requires an attitude of both faith and following. In later chapters, I will continue to share how our team followed divine twists and turns that led us into fields that were as unexpected as they were fruitful.

Third, Watkins's spirituality of theological research calls for a "personally appropriated *pneumatology*—a lived sense of the presence and

---

32. Clare Watkins, "Reflections on Particularity and Unity," in *Ecclesiology in the Trenches: Theory and Method under Construction*, ed. Sune Fahlgren and Jonas Ideström (Cambridge: James Clarke, 2015), 152, emphasis mine.

33. Watkins, "Particularity and Unity," 152.

34. Watkins, "Particularity and Unity," 152.

activity of the Holy Spirit not only in the ecclesial practices being studied, but also in the very practice of practical ecclesiological research itself."[35] If one believes that the Spirit works in contemporary situations, then the specifics of those situations become windows into the divine character and will. Let's not forget: revelation only ever occurs as enculturated and contextualized; God never encounters historically and culturally abstracted people. Since revelation only transpires in and as particularity, then the scrutiny of contemporary experience should be a fundamental aspect of theological research,[36] unless we simply deny the continued activity of the Spirit of God.

Watkins proposes that this sort of spirituality would "return us to the longer theological tradition of our faith—a tradition of faith seeking understanding, of discernment of divine presence, and of a refusal to allow our lived realities of ecclesial faith to be boxed into any one discipline or theory."[37] In our most graced moments of MAR, our team did bear a strong sense of God's presence drawing us beyond our disciplinary bounds and into the movement of the Spirit in Colombia.

Since experiences are loci of ongoing revelation, and since practical theological research requires an openness to the Spirit, the present volume does not bracket out our experiences. Rather, in an effort to shine a light on where we believe God to have acted, this book is shot through with narrative and testimony. To do so might be methodologically heterodox, but it is also methodologically honest, revealing what we have actually done.

The attempt to combine three streams of revelation—social sciences, Christian Scripture, and experience—makes this project idiosyncratic. That blend of epistemic commitments also makes this book atypical, oscillating between narrative, Scriptural reflection, personal testimony from victims of displacement, and a wide range of empirical and theoretical social-scientific research. Looking back, we can identify the seeds of this unconventional research even in the early days of our explorations, drinking miserably burnt coffee while we picked the brain of a twenty-something Colombian sociologist and heard testimonies from

35. Watkins, "Particularity and Unity," 152.
36. Watkins speaks of a "radical commitment to particularity as theologically authoritative;" Watkins, "Particularity and Unity," 152.
37. Watkins, "Particularity and Unity," 152–53.

local Christian leaders. But, at the time we had no inkling of where the Spirit would blow.

## Descent from the Balcony to the Road

We spent eight months studying the displacement crisis in 2014 before holding our big conference with the unwieldy title "Migration, Exile, Displacement, and Violence." We read articles by social scientists and reports by nongovernmental organizations (NGOs). We talked with local leaders of Christian ministries to IDPs. But we never left the seminary campus while conducting our research. We never visited an IDP settlement. We never interviewed a displaced person.

In retrospect, having now logged hundreds of hours in interviews and focus groups, and having made dozens of trips to all corners of Colombia, I writhe with discomfort at the hubris of holding an academic conference on displacement without conversing face-to-face with displaced people. But at the time, it seemed perfectly normal. After all, I was a biblical scholar, and for a biblical scholar even to venture topically beyond the second century was already to swerve off-piste. Electing to work on a twenty-first-century humanitarian disaster through the lens of Latin American social sciences was already enough to earn hearty claps on the back at the Society of Biblical Literature conference. Nobody could reasonably expect you to venture into hot zones of Colombia to conduct firsthand interviews; biblical scholars do not run focus groups! So we convened our conference on displacement without personally interviewing a single IDP, and we had no sense that doing so was deficient.

From an academic perspective, the conference was a success. A contingent of four researchers from Fuller Theological Seminary contributed presentations, making the event FUSBC's first international academic conference. Most of the papers were strong. The discussion was lively. We even published the proceedings, *in Spanish*, with a North American theological press[38]—an endeavor that remains almost unheard of.[39] Academic readers would see the work as a laudable engagement of theological

---

38. Oscar García-Johnson and Milton Acosta, eds., *Conversaciones teológicas del sur global americano: violencia, desplazamiento y fe* (Eugene, OR: Puertas Abiertas, 2016).

39. When North American theological presses publish a book in Spanish, it is almost always a translation of a text written originally in English for a North Atlantic audience.

scholarship with urgent contemporary issues in ways that seemed (to the guild) concrete and practical. We had done what we had set out to do, which was a big win for a little Latin American seminary. We could have just wrapped things up then and there. Right? But there were whispers telling us not to stop.

The whispers came in two ways. In the months leading up to the conference, as the enormity of the travesty of displacement became increasingly clear to us, a few of us grew uncomfortable with the plan to conclude our work following the conference and the book. We felt that the Holy Spirit was pulling on our hearts.[40] I began to think that, if we let this work drop after sending the final draft of the conference proceedings to press, we would be sinning.

The second set of whispers emerged at the conference itself. A great many practitioners attended the event, most of whom made approving noises throughout the conference. But at the edges of the event, during coffee breaks and on the way to lunch, people pulled some of us aside. After appreciative preambles about how much they enjoyed the learned papers, attendees expressed, almost apologetically, that they were still not quite sure *what to do* with what we had said. Yes, they agreed that the Christian faith demanded that we act in the face of the tragedy of displacement. Yes, they agreed that economic justice and psychological care were vital parts of the church's ideal engagement with IDPs. But these practitioners had been working with IDPs for some time, and the problems they confronted felt intractable in ways that our papers did not address. They needed more specific guidance with particular cases of poverty or trauma or government ineptitude, and they were hoping the seminary could provide it. But at that point, we did not know what to do about that sort of thing.

Trying my best not to sound defensive, I explained (defensively) that this was an academic theological conference, that academic theologians do not deal with those sorts of nitty-gritty details. "Ah, okay, of course," they responded. "Thanks so much. Really, this was a great conference. Blessings." And as they walked away, I knew that something remained seriously deficient in my theologizing.

---

40. Now you understand why the previous section of this chapter included a methodological preamble on the legitimacy of subjective experience as a source of theological insight.

Latin Americans sometimes distinguish between *teología del balcón* and *teología del camino*, "theology of the Balcony" and "theology of the Road." Notwithstanding their widespread purchase in Latin American theology, the expressions were actually coined by a Scottish missionary to Latin America, named John (Juan) Mackay. Born in 1889, Mackay spent a decade in missionary service before moving to the United States in 1936 to become the president of Princeton Theological Seminary and, in 1940, penning his staggering little book *A Preface to Christian Theology*.

When I first heard of theology of the Balcony, I understood it as being equivalent to "ivory tower theology," in contrast to "street" theology. Mackay, however, intended a different nuance. The Balcony, in many Latin American cities, is a small platform from the second or third floor of a house that hangs out over the street, from which one can observe passersby, well above the fray. "There the family may gather . . . to gaze spectator-wise upon the street beneath. . . . The Balcony thus conceived is . . . the symbol of the perfect spectator, for whom life and the universe are permanent objects of study and contemplation."[41]

Theology of the *camino*, by contrast, implies not merely something "down to earth," but something en route, *en marcha*, theology that is going somewhere; indeed, a theologian who is going somewhere. "By the Road I mean a place where life is tensely lived, where thought has its birth in conflict and concern, where choices are made and decisions are carried out. It is the place of action, of pilgrimage, . . . where concern is never absent from the wayfarer's heart. On the Road a goal is sought, dangers are faced, life is poured out. . . ."[42]

While the term "concern" sounds potentially tepid to twenty-first-century ears, for Mackay it carried a weighty referent: justice. In his account, that concern for justice requires the submission and action of the human will.

> What is that concern, and what is that commitment which lead to a true knowledge of God and His will? Our answer is: a concern about righteousness and a commitment to righteousness [*el interés por la justicia, la completa*

41. John A. Mackay, *A Preface to Christian Theology* (New York: Macmillan, 1941), 29.
42. Mackay, *Preface*, 30.

*adhesión a la justicia*[43]. . . . As righteousness means the secret of right relations between God and man, and between man and man, it can never be
adequately apprehended as an idea. To be known it must be intensely desired
and submitted to. . . . Truth, as it relates to God, is always existential in
character, involving a consent of the will as well as an assent of the understanding. Assent may be given on the Balcony, but consent is inseparable
from the Road.[44]

A theology of the Road entails that the theologian recognize that they
cannot speak genuine truth from the sidelines, but that any truth worthy
of the name will entail the personal, active, and existential involvement
of the theologian.

The Road is the symbol of a first-hand experience of reality where thought,
born of a living concern, issues in decision and action. When a man squarely
faces the challenge of existence, a vital concern is aroused within him. He
puts to himself the question, what must I do? . . . How can a better order be
established than that which now exists? . . . There can be no true knowledge
of ultimate things, that is to say of God and man, of duty and destiny, that is
not born in a concern and perfected in a commitment; which is the same as
saying that religious truth is obtained only on the Road.[45]

The gentle prodding of the practitioner conference attendees made
clear to us that we were doing spectator theology: watching, analyzing,
grieving even . . . but we were not getting personally involved, not risk-
ing ourselves, not exposing our theology and proposals to the peril of
falsification that comes when the theory is landed in practice. It was not
enough. So we decided to climb down from the Balcony to the Road. The
rest of the book explains where the *camino* led.

43. This Spanish translation is from Juan A. Mackay, *Prefacio a la teología cristiana*,
trans. Gonzalo Báez-Camargo, 3rd ed. (México, D.F.: Casa Unida de Publicaciones,
1984), 58.
44. Mackay, *Preface*, 50.
45. Mackay, *Preface*, 44–45.

# María Fernanda

From the outside, the Iglesia El Redil, situated in a lower-class neighborhood of Bogotá, looks like just any other *iglesia de garaje*.[46] An Assemblies of God congregation, the church's entrance is indeed a garage door. It looks out onto a highway and is flanked by a dirt lot where truckers have their tires replaced. What you cannot tell from its humble facade is that the upper floor of this unassuming edifice houses a beautiful ministry to disadvantaged local children, the Fundación CreativaMente.[47] One December evening in 2016, the foundation opened its doors for us and convened local IDPs for a series of interviews with us. And, as dusk fell, in limped María Fernanda.

Years in the sun make it difficult to discern the age of many campesinos, but María Fernanda was perhaps in her late fifties, with graying hair and close-clipped nails. Clad in an ankle-length skirt and a pill-covered gray sweater, she leaned on a cane and pulled at the handrail to get up the narrow stairs to the Fundación CreativaMente. Hobbled by an injury that had healed poorly, she moved like a woman ten or twenty years her senior.

She joined Milton Acosta for an interview in the pastor's office, while I was busy conducting a focus group on economic issues. Per his interview

---

46. A "garage church," to use a disparaging term sometimes foisted upon small evangelical or Pentecostal communities.

47. The pastor of El Redil is David López Amaya, an ordained minister of the Assemblies of God who also has a PhD in political science and consults with the Colombian Ministry of the Interior on religious affairs. The Fundación CreativaMente is run by Stefanía Castro, a whip-smart lawyer with a heart of gold. David was a member of our public sector interaction team; Stefanía was a coresearcher of Faith and Displacement.

protocol, Milton was supposed to ask her about the issues that most affected her current community. Nonetheless, María Fernanda quickly shifted conversation to the topic of her own displacement from the department of Córdoba. So, Milton just listened while she told her story of loss after awful loss in what she called *esta guerra sin fin* . . . this war without end.

> They did not just take from me what I owned. Rather, they also took from me the life of my son. My father died because he couldn't handle the loss of my son, at the age of twenty-one. That's life. It's left me quickly.
>
> When we moved to Montería[48] [from the campo], in a week's time I got work washing clothes, cooking. We got a little place there. One day, my son went to work. He left at 4:30 a.m. with four other people. They worked until 11:00 a.m. [and then he was taken]. Out of [the four people in] that car, they only took my son, but from our neighborhood they took a total of fourteen people that day. I held out hope that my son would come back or that he had been with his father, because [his father] didn't live with me. (Sixteen days after my daughter was born, he went to be with another woman, and I was left alone.)
>
> In total, eighteen boys were lost. I believe my son was the eldest of the young men that were lost, because my son was already twenty-one years old but the others hadn't even made it to eighteen.
>
> They returned eight bodies to us with letters written in their own blood, in which they said to the boys' mothers, "There's your dog. The frog[49] dies. Whatever is useless, is thrown away."

At this point, Pastor David interrupted the interview, bringing María Fernanda something to eat. On the recording, you can hear him pray over the snack. Thereafter, Milton gently tried to steer the conversation back to the questions on the interview protocol (which have nothing to do with her traumatic past), but in a couple of minutes, María Fernanda

---

48. Montería is the capital of the department of Córdoba, part of the Caribbean coastal region of the country. As such, María Fernanda was a *costeña*, a cultural group very different from the *cachacos* and *rolos* that inhabited the national capital city of Bogotá.

49. "Frog" is a derogatory term for an informant, akin to "rat" in English. The implication is that the young people were killed on suspicion of having collaborated with an enemy group.

picked up her narrative thread again, almost abruptly. And just as abruptly, tears overtook her.

> Losing my son wasn't easy, it wasn't easy for me. They made me understand that I had to let him rest, that I had to leave him in peace. It's not easy for mother to lose her son, it's not easy. Even at the age of twenty, he was taking care of me. He said, "Mami, all that I want is for you not to have to work. I want you to help raise my little niece"—my daughter had been raped, she had a baby as a result of that rape—"that's all that I want." But I would wait until he would go to work, then I would take the girl to preschool, and I would go to work part-time. I worked part-time with a teacher, and it was great. And all of a sudden, someone called me at work to tell me that my son had been taken. One day he was working until 11:00 a.m. and they took him, never again, never again, never again. I have not gotten any more news, right up until today's sun. Since 2012, when they took my son, until today, nobody has said why.

Fearing for her own safety, María Fernanda fled to Bogotá, eventually to be joined by her granddaughter. But after being displaced, her troubles had only just begun: "I got here to Bogotá and I spent almost five months sleeping in the parking lot of a car wash, cold, with cardboard boxes. I became friends with this lady, and she told me, 'Do you want to work in the house of a family?' I said, "'Well, of course.' She said, 'There's a lady where I work who needs a housekeeper during the days, let's go tomorrow. But when you are there, don't tell her that you're a *desplazada* or anything.'"[50]

Trying to address some of the questions in his interview protocol, at this point Milton inquired about whether María Fernanda had found sanctuary or peace in any Christian communities. She replied,

> I was the sort of person who would say, "The Christian churches . . . they do it to make money." I didn't understand, I thought it was like that. You could see how they were. From one to the next they became pastors and began to exploit the people, going into the *veredas*,[51] covering themselves with the

---

50. This off-handed comment reveals the suspicion with which displaced persons are often regarded by the non-displaced, especially in larger cities.

51. A *vereda* is a small rural settlement, smaller than a village.

Bible, saying that they were sons of God. They would come to your house and say, "I'm your pastor. I have come here because the Lord has revealed to me that you have to hand that pig over to me," and the people handed it over because that is supposedly what the Lord had revealed to him. They were loaded with things that they would bring from the *veredas*, from the villages where they would deceive people. So I would say, "Well, why would God permit this?" And I would say, "No, I'll never become a Christian," because you would see so many things.

But when I met this pastor [David], I would tell him all these things and he would say to me, "Do you know what, sister? Do you know why these things happen? These are not sons of God. These are sons of the demon." And from then on, I started to realize that was true.

Here in Bogotá, I attended a lot of churches, but I'd never heard of a Christian church that was with the victims. The first one is here with the *hermano* pastor. It's the first one that I've heard of that is trying to work among the victims.

[Before coming here] I was going to a church nearby, behind the Catholic church. And one day I got to church, they were collecting the offerings, and I said to the girl that was collected the offerings, "I don't have money. But I am taking some of this love that I have here in my heart and I'll put it in [the basket]." When I said those words, the pastor turned to look at me and he said that people who came to his house to occupy a chair and not to tithe or give offerings, well, it was better if they didn't come anymore. I got up from the chair, and discreetly I left. As I was leaving, a girl outside said to me, "Do you have to go?" And I said to her "Do you know why I'm leaving? Because I'm not welcome in this church, because I don't have money and people who don't have money are not welcome at this church. Since I don't have money, well, God told me to go."

After gaining employment as a housekeeper, María Fernanda also managed to secure a room for herself and her granddaughter in the home of another family, in exchange for housekeeping. The man of the house treated her poorly. She did not have a bed to sleep on, but at least she had a place to stay.

After I got a job in that family's house, things went well for me. One day, my boss told me, "Come early tomorrow." If you tell me to come early, then I'm going to arrive at 6:00 a.m. So the next day I got up, took a shower and I went to wait for the bus, but the bus never came. When it got to be 6:40 and the bus hadn't come, I hailed a taxi.

No less than a block away from where we were heading, [the driver] turned around and he knocked me out. But I was protected by our Lord Jesus Christ because, in spite of whatever he gave me, or stuck me with or made me smell—I don't know, I don't remember anything—I opened my eyes and I realized that I was in a pasture, way up high. I said, "My God, what am I doing here?" And that man said to me, "Either you pay me fourteen thousand *pesos*[52] or you have to be with me."

Holy Virgin, I launched myself at [the driver]. I got him with my nails, I almost snapped off this finger with my teeth. When he went to hit me, he pulled me by the hair, put this finger in my mouth, and he was pulling my hair and I was biting his finger all the more and I drew blood, I had blood all over here. He let me go let me go because I almost bit off his finger. I got out of the car, but I had forgotten my bag in the taxi and turned around to grab my bag and that was my mistake. I turned around, and he came at me and he kicked me in the knee. I fell to my knees beside the taxi. He came at me and broke my ankle and burst a vein. After that people told me that the man was gonna' hit me with something that he took out of the taxi.

I don't remember anything, but some *muchachos* saved me. They tried to take a photo of the taxi [as he left] — but you can't see the [license plate]. The police didn't do anything. I told the police, "This blood that I have here [on my face], it isn't mine, it's his. I bit his finger. I don't know if I bit it off." I said that to the police, but the police didn't do anything.[53]

The fight with her attacker left María Fernanda with a badly broken leg, internal bleeding, and an eventual infection.

I had been working for five months when this thing happened with my leg. My boss fired me. They almost cut off my leg in the hospital. The doctor told me that they had to cut it off because gangrene was setting in. But the man who owned the car wash [where María used to live] didn't let them cut off the leg. He said, "She does not have a family. But you can't do with her

52. About seven US dollars at the time.
53. Later in her interview, María Fernanda revealed that she had previously been sexually assaulted three other times, at the ages of eleven, seventeen, and twenty-three.

whatever you want just because she doesn't have a family. You can operate on her, but I'm not going to let you cut off her leg."

Thanks to a doctor in the hospital there who takes care of the victims, they gave me a bed [for my apartment] with a fluffy bedspread and everything, and I no longer had to sleep on the floor. I slept with my girl [the granddaughter] because there was only one bed.

One day, [Family Welfare] arrived to visit me. I heard a knock on the door, and the lady from the floor below said, "They need you down here because they say you have a girl at risk." "A girl at risk?! My God, why? What risk does my girl have? I've got her in school, what's the risk?" So the ladies from Family Welfare came up. One talked with me and the other talked with the girl in the back. She says to me, "We've come to take the girl, we are from Family Welfare." Believe me, that day my sky came crashing down and I didn't know what to do. Pain took me over. I was only twelve days post-op. The girl started to cry, and I told her, "Don't cry, don't cry, *mi'ja*." The little thing got scared because they were going to take her and leave me alone. I told her, "They're not going to take you, *mi'jita*." So I had to take her out [of school] and I took her to Montería [to be with my daughter]. Thank God, my daughter went to Usme and she's there, and the children are studying there.

The interview went on far longer than expected. It was getting late for a woman in María Fernanda's condition to be out. In closing, Milton inquired one final thing of her: "What is your dream for your future?"

What's my dream? The same dream that I never ceased to dream. I hope to have—not a farm, not anymore because I'm afraid—but, yeah, a little piece of land, two or three hectares, to live off that. I hope that God might allow me to live in *Planeta Rica*,[54] and to find a way to live my final days, months, years—I don't know, until God says, "Up to here," and then takes me. And, *hermano* pastor, whenever you go to Córdoba, well, the doors of my apartment or my house, whatever God gives me, will be open.

I finished my focus group long before Milton wrapped up his interview with María Fernanda. Gathering my things, I thanked the people who had

---

54. Planeta Rica is small municipality in Córdoba, near Montería. It is the same town from which our coresearcher, Deiner Espitia, was displaced some years earlier; see vignette 5.

come out to talk with me and then began to transfer the day's files from my digital recorder to my laptop. When they finally emerged from the pastor's office, I watched from the far side of the room as Milton clasped María Fernanda's hand and bid her good night. After she left, I hoisted my bag over my shoulder and crossed the space to meet him, only then noticing his red eyes, still glistening.

CHAPTER 2

# Getting Off the *Balcón*

In the weeks after that first academic conference, an uneasy conscience harassed me and my Fundación Universitaria Seminario Bíblico de Colombia (FUSBC) colleagues. Like a mosquito bite on your ankle that you keep trying to scratch with your heel during a meeting, we couldn't stop thinking that a conference and a book simply weren't *enough*. Somehow, we needed to do more. We needed to get off the *balcón* and onto the *camino*.

But what could a seminary do? After all, we were a fistful of theologians, nerds working at an underfunded Majority World institution. The seminary did not even have a budget to provision its faculty with sticky notes or pens, let alone to fund an as-yet-undefined project in response to a catastrophic and intractable humanitarian crisis.

That same summer, by happenstance, I found myself giving a wee presentation in a science-and-religion conference back in Oxford. I ended up enjoying a Sunday lunch with Dr. Andrew Briggs, a professor of nano-materials, a committed believer, and the director of the Templeton World Charity Foundation, Inc. (TWCF). As we sipped elderflower cordial under the elusive English summer sun, the smell of fresh-cut grass floating on the breeze, Andrew off-handedly queried me about our research on displacement. After I summarized some of our early findings, he suggested that the TWCF might entertain a research proposal that had something to do with Christian theology and forced migration. Doing my level best to play it cool, I probed Andrew for guidance on the proposal process. Then he said something staggering, something that missionaries and Majority World scholars never hear: "Don't be overly timid in your budget projections. Figure out what it would cost to do it right."

After a Lufthansa 747 had carried me back across the Atlantic and Caribbean, I hurriedly set up a meeting with the seminary's administration and related what had transpired over elderflower cordial. The bosses were cautious. "Once bitten, twice shy," the saying goes, and the seminary had heard many ambitious speeches about funding possibilities which never came to fruition.

While sympathetic, the administration was reticent. The seminary had to be faithful to its own institutional mission: to train pastors. All academic institutions, but especially those in the Global South, have to prioritize teaching and administrative needs. Universities do not exist for social causes (as many an idealistic undergraduate has found out when wanting to launch a revolution from her dorm room). On top of that, we had to contend with the perception, held by some institutional stakeholders, that theology and missions are primarily spiritual rather than social affairs.

So, we needed to find a way to thread the needle, creating a proposal that would (a) address the burden we felt for the displaced, (b) fit with the missional raison d'être of the seminary, and (c) capture the interest of an elite academic grant-making organization. We had no road map showing us the route from academic research through theological education and into real humanitarian impact. But our consciences told us that if we could not find a way to traverse that route, then there was something seriously amiss in our theology.

## The Holistic Mission of the Jerusalem Church (Acts 2:41–47)

The earliest Christians would probably not have had much sympathy for our uncertainty about how to integrate gospel proclamation with care for the vulnerable and the needy. And if ever there were an argument to be made for focusing on spiritual and theological matters rather than social matters, it would have stalked Jerusalem in the 30s.

Following the death of the Messiah, the risen Christ commissioned his followers to be his "witnesses, in Jerusalem, in all Judea and Samaria, and to the ends of the earth" (Acts 1:8). That first-century ragtag band of nobodies was so underqualified and underfunded (see Acts 3:6; 4:13) for the task of global missions that they made our skimpy faculty in Medellín look like a cadre of premier intellectuals backed by a nine-figure endowment. The biggest thing they had going for them was the (admittedly, vague) promise "You will receive power when the Holy Spirit has come upon you." So, when the Holy Spirit was poured out on them and gave rise to fabulous miracles (Acts 2:1–13; 3:1–10; 5:12–16; 6:8), anointed preaching

(2:14–36; 3:11–26; 4:31; 6:15–7:53), and mass conversions (2:37–41; 4:4; 6:7), one could be excused for assuming that the apostles would lean into the evangelistic and charismatic side of their ministry, leaving other aspects of community life to the side. Such an assumption, however, could not be further from the truth.

Acts reveals that, following the mass baptism of three thousand new believers on the day of Pentecost (2:41), the Jerusalem community established a practice of community life that today we would call "holistic mission." This mission certainly entailed both evangelism and *spiritual* formation. The early believers were devoted to prayer and to worship in the Jerusalem temple (2:42, 46). They also placed emphasis on *intellectual* formation in the framework of the apostles' teachings (2:42). But their tasks did not end there.

Luke also highlights the earliest community's commitment to providing for people's *material* needs. Daily nutritional requirements were met through shared meals in the homes of the more affluent believers (2:42, 46), on top of which, community members with land or homes would even liquidate some of those immovable assets whenever the poverty of community members required a "capital infusion" (2:44–45; 4:32–37).[1] Furthermore, the believers were marked by *emotional well-being*: they had "glad and generous hearts" (2:46: more literally, "with rejoicing and simplicity of heart"). Likewise, the community cultivated *social* unity within the family of faith. Luke says they were of a unified will (2:46; *homothumadon*), that they were devoted to fellowship (2:42), that they spent time together (2:44), in the temple and as smaller groups gathering in one another's homes (2:46). They even enjoyed warm *relations with those outside their religious collective* (2:47: "having the goodwill of all the people").

In brief, Luke describes the activities of the earliest believers in decidedly holistic terms: they brooked no separation between the spiritual, intellectual, social, material, emotional, or public aspects of their faith.[2] For the apostles, spiritual conversion and social conviction, supernatural

---

1. On which, see Christopher M. Hays, *Renouncing Everything: Money and Discipleship in Luke* (Mahwah, NJ: Paulist, 2016), 56–62.

2. Notice that these features of the church's activities map over the areas of inquiry of the Faith and Displacement project, described below: missiology, pedagogy, sociology, economics, psychology, and public sector interaction.

outpouring and psychological well-being, were all part and parcel of the mission of the church.

Some scholars have objected that this rosy depiction of the Jerusalem community smacks of utopian romantic idealization and that Luke must therefore be playing fast and loose with history, despite the fact that Luke does little to hide the warts of those early believers (consider, e.g., the embezzlement and summary execution of Ananias and Sapphira in 5:1–10, or the prejudiced discrimination against Hellenistic widows in 6:1–2, on which see further, chapter 4). But even if there is some distance between Luke's description of the Jerusalem church in Acts 2:41–47 and the real historical facts (now largely inaccessible to us), the key point is that Luke and the apostles understood that, in the dawning kingdom of God, the responsibility of the church encompassed the entirety of the human person: spiritual, intellectual, material, social, and emotional.

This basic ecclesial insight offered the seminary a way to respond to any stakeholders who worried that attention to forced displacement might augur a slow drift away from our institutional mission. If the mission of the Jerusalem church was holistic in nature, then why should a seminary limit its attention exclusively to the intellectual and spiritual training of pastors? Insofar as biblical Christianity brooks no fissure between the spiritual or intellectual aspects of discipleship and its emotional, economic, and social entailments, the seminary was able to overcome the concern that forced migration was somehow a "social issue" discontiguous with its own mission to train Christian leaders. Indeed, this is a lesson that Latin Americans began to teach the North Atlantic evangelical world some fifty years ago. Our Latin American predecessors did not, however, use the language "holistic ministry;" rather, they spoke of *misión integral*, integral mission.

## Integral Missiology

The concept of *misión integral* was birthed in Latin America in the 1960s and spread worldwide in the ensuing decades. It denotes an orientation toward Christian mission that affirms God's reign over both the spiritual and the physical dimensions of humanity. It functions as a corrective to forms of Christian theology that prioritize spirituality but neglect people's material and social needs, as well as to theologies that prioritize social realities over biblical truth. Integral missiology (i.e., the theological theory underpinning the integral mission movement) aims to mobilize Christians in the pursuit of both healthy *doctrine* and *practice*. As such, integral missiology entails an imperative to stimulate "integral" or complete human development in both physical and spiritual senses. Without intending to give a history of the movement, I should at least briefly sketch the historical context of integral missiology (including its key interlocutor, liberation theology) and as well its crucial commitments. In what follows, I place special emphasis on the writings of René Padilla, arguably the most important theorist of the movement. Padilla stands out as the most direct inspiration for our own work.

### Liberation Theology as a Key Interlocutor for Integral Mission

It would be useful to begin with some Catholic context since Roman Catholicism has long been (and remains) the dominant form of Christianity in Latin America. In August 1968, the Conference of Latin American Bishops met in Medellín to consider how to apply the concepts of the Second Vatican Council in the Latin American context, in response to *Ad gentes* (Vatican II's decree on the mission of the church in the modern world) and Pope John XXII's exhortation, *à la* Matthew 16:3, to read "the signs of the times" (*Humanae salutis* 4). Applying their missiological analysis to topics of justice, peace, education, and youth in Latin America, the Latin American bishops concluded that, "the church was not to be centered on itself nor on its own concerns, but on its mission in the very concrete world of Latin American reality; mission was conceived not only as the proclamation of the gospel but as a commitment to justice, genuine development and liberation. This was a turning point, not just in the Latin American church but in the church at large, for it marks the beginning of what would become liberation theology."[3]

In 1971, Peruvian theologian Gustavo Gutiérrez published *A Theology of Liberation*, one of the first and surely best-known treatises on liberation theology. Liberation theology attempts both to understand the realities of poverty and to work toward liberation from oppression and sin (personal and structural).[4] Liberation theologians also called for the instantiation of

3. Stephen B. Bevans and Roger P. Schroeder, *Constants in Context: A Theology of Mission for Today* (Maryknoll, NY: Orbis, 2004), 312.

4. Gustavo Gutiérrez, *A Theology of Liberation: History, Politics, and Salvation*, trans. Sister Caridad Inda and John Eagleson, rev. ed. (Maryknoll, NY: Orbis, 1973), 27–37.

God's kingdom of justice through social revolution—specifically, *Marxist* revolution. These scholars engaged seriously with Marxist political analysis and thereupon constructed formidable theoretical edifices that they hoped would contribute to human flourishing.[5] Their political hopes were disappointed, in no small part because they tied their expectations of liberation to an economic system that has not proved successful in their context. Nevertheless, this Catholic movement became a crucial interlocutor for the next decades of Protestantism in Latin America.

## The Emergence of Integral Mission

Beginning in the 1960s, Protestant evangelicals in Latin America brought about a similar theological renaissance within their own tradition, developing an approach which they subsequently brought into dialogue with liberation theology.[6] Over the course of the 1970s and '80s, the Latin evangelicals criticized elements of liberation theology's Marxist analysis and its occasional tendency toward soteriological universalism (inter alia). Nonetheless, they wanted to affirm with the liberationists that the God of the Bible was indeed concerned about both spiritual and social realities.[7] Thus, a Latin American evangelical alternative to liberation theology emerged under the name "integral mission." The term "integral" focuses on the fact that humans are not just spiritual beings, but are conjointly physical, spiritual, psychological, and social. According to the conviction that God's kingdom entails dominion over all of creation, and not just souls, integral missiology argues that the church must give attention to the whole human person in her integrality.

---

5. Key works include Gutiérrez, *Theology of Liberation*; José Míguez Bonino, *Doing Theology in a Revolutionary Situation*, Confrontation Books (Philadelphia: Fortress, 1975); José Míguez Bonino, *Christians and Marxists: The Mutual Challenge to Revolution* (Grand Rapids: Eerdmans, 1976); and Leonardo Boff, *Jesus Christ Liberator: A Critical Christology for Our Time*, trans. Patrick Hughes (Maryknoll, NY: Orbis, 1978).

6. Samuel Escobar, "Doing Theology on Christ's Road," in *Global Theology in Evangelical Perspective: Exploring the Contextual Nature of Theology and Mission*, ed. Jeffrey P. Greenman and Gene L. Green (Downer's Grove, IL: Intervarsity, 2012), 67–85; and Ruth Irene Padilla DeBorst, "Integral Mission Formation in Abya Yala (Latin America): A Study of the *Centro de Estudios Teológicos Interdisciplinarios* (1982–2002) and Radical *Evangélicos*" (PhD dissertation, Boston University, 2016), 125–30.

7. As, for example, in the 1988 *Declaración de Medellín*, drafted by the *Confederación evangélica de Colombia* and the *Seminario Bíblico de Colombia*.

Integral mission was not, in the first place, an academic movement.[8] It grew out of a concern for missions and evangelism, specifically emphasizing that contemporary missions should address people's physical needs as well as their spiritual ones. While this concern had begun to percolate in the minds of key theological figures in previous decades,[9] it thrust itself onto the wider evangelical stage in the 1974 International Congress on World Evangelization, held in Lausanne, Switzerland.[10] The Lausanne Covenant stated that "The results of evangelism include obedience to Christ, incorporation into His church, and responsible service in the world. . . . Evangelism and socio-political involvement are both part of our Christian duty. . . . When people receive Christ they are born again into his kingdom and must seek not only to exhibit, but also to spread, righteousness in the midst of an unrighteous world. The Salvation we claim should be transforming us in the totality of our personal and social responsibilities."[11]

Two young Latin American scholars came to the forefront of the proceedings at Lausanne, arguing that evangelism cannot be disconnected from Christian social responsibility. Those academics were theologian Samuel Escobar and biblical scholar René Padilla.[12]

8. For a more detailed history of the movement, see C. René Padilla, "La trayectoria histórica de la misión integral," in *Justicia, misericordia y humildad: la misión integral y los pobres*, ed. Tim Chester (Buenos Aires: Kairós, 2008), 55–80.

9. See Brian Stanley, *The Global Diffusion of Evangelicalism: The Age of Billy Graham and John Stott*, A History of Evangelicalism, vol. 5 (Downer's Grove, IL: IVP Academic, 2013), 151–55.

10. From the conference emerged the *Lausanne Covenant*, of which section 5 "On Christian Social Responsibility" was in its moment the most revolutionary. For a key exposition of the *Covenant*, see C. René Padilla, ed. *The New Face of Evangelicalism: An International Symposium on the Lausanne Covenant* (Downer's Grove, IL: InterVarsity, 1976).

11. Lausanne Covenant §5, cited in John Stott, *The Lausanne Covenant: Complete Text with Study Guide*, Didasko files (Peabody, MA: Hendrickson, 2009), 28.

12. For a robust account of the role of Padilla and Escobar in Lausanne, see J. Daniel Salinas, *Latin American Evangelical Theology in the 1970's: The Golden Decade*, Religion on the Americas (Leiden: Brill, 2009), 121–61; and Stanley, *Global Diffusion of Evangelicalism*, 158–60, 163–73, 177–79.

## Seminal Works and Key Commitments

Padilla and Escobar were founding members of the Fraternidad Teológica Latinoamericana (FTL; English: Latin American Theological Fellowship), a scholarly society of Latin American evangelicals that continues to this day.[13] The FTL has been the incubator of integral missiology,[14] but no one scholar was so influential in catalyzing the movement as was Padilla.[15] A talented essayist, Padilla's seminal book was *Misión integral: ensayos sobre el Reino y la iglesia* (1986), which collected his groundbreaking essays from 1974 to 1984. The volume begins with Padilla's 1974 Lausanne address ("El evangelio y la evangelización" ["The Gospel and Evangelization"]),[16] and then fills in the picture with eight other essays. Two chapters merit special attention here, as they represent key lineaments of integral missiology.

The book's eponymous chapter, "Misión integral,"[17] makes three key arguments that would define the movement thereafter:

1. Latin America had been baptized but had not been discipled away from animism.
2. North Atlantic missions remained heavily colonial, and Majority World churches needed to grow into mature and mutual relationships with the denominations of Europe and North America.

---

13. For more on the history of the FTL, see Salinas, *Latin American Evangelical Theology*, 83–119; J. Daniel Salinas, *Taking Up the Mantle: Latin American Evangelical Theology in the 20th Century*, Global Perspective (Carlisle, UK: Langham Global Library, 2017), 101–7; and Brian Stanley, *A World History of Christianity in the Twentieth Century*, Princeton History of Christianity (Princeton: Princeton University Press, 2018), 210–15.

14. Although the FTL predominately uses the language of "integral mission" rather than "integral missiology," one of its key contributions was to develop the missiological theory that fostered the mission movement. The present chapter focuses primarily on the missiological theory.

15. For more on Padilla's biography and formation, see David C. Kirkpatrick, "C. René Padilla and the Origins of Integral Mission in Post-War Latin America," *Journal of Ecclesiastical History* 67, 2 (2016): 351–57; and cf. David R. Swartz, "Embodying the Global South: Internationalism and the American Evangelical Left," *Religions* 3 (2012): 892–94.

16. C. René Padilla, *Misión integral: ensayos sobre el Reino y la iglesia* (Grand Rapids/Buenos Aires: Eerdmans/Nueva Creación, 1986), 1–44.

17. Padilla, *Misión integral*, 123–35; this essay was originally written in 1978.

3. Attention to justice and development needed to be central components of Christian mission.[18]

This third point is further elaborated in "Perspectivas neotestamentarias para un estilo de vida sencillo (New Testament Perspectives for a Simple Lifestyle),"[19] another of the volume's key essays. Here Padilla (a New Testament scholar who earned his PhD under F. F. Bruce) elaborates his convictions about justice for the poor. In agreement with liberation theology, Padilla confirms the New Testament's central concern for the poor and echoes Jesus's call to self-sacrificial care for the needy. The essay emphasizes the virtues of simplicity and generosity, implicitly in contradistinction to the liberationist thesis that the poor would be saved through communism.

Another key publication to emerge from the FTL was *Biblical Bases of Mission: Latin American Perspectives*.[20] Authored by an array of leading FTL members, the volume includes eleven chapters detailing how different biblical books contribute to the vision of integral mission. Additionally, in a final section of thematic studies, the volume showcases essays on suffering,[21] laypersons,[22] and corruption.[23] The collection thus brings to the fore integral missiology's profound commitments to

---

18. The Faith and Displacement project has, in various ways, taken on board each of Padilla's arguments. (1) Our approach emphasizes the discipleship of believers into greater participation in the church's integral mission. (2) Our research team combines North Atlantic and Latin American scholars in mutually enriching collaborations. (3) The entire focus of the project is to advance the mission of the church in pursuit of justice and personal development for marginalized populations.

19. Padilla, *Misión integral*, 164–79; this essay was originally composed in 1980.

20. C. René Padilla, ed. *Bases bíblicas de la misión: perspectivas latinoamericanas* (Buenos Aires: Kairós, 1998).

21. Nancy Elizabeth Bedford, "La misión en el sufrimiento y ante el sufrimiento," in *Bases bíblicas de la misión: perspectivas latinoamericanas*, ed. C. René Padilla (Buenos Aires: Kairós, 1998), 383–403.

22. Catalina F. de Padilla, "Los 'laicos' en la misión en el Nuevo Testamento," in *Bases bíblicas de la misión: perspectivas latinoamericanas*, ed. C. René Padilla (Buenos Aires: Kairós, 1998), 405–35.

23. Arnoldo Wiens, "La misión cristiana en un contexto de corrupción," in *Bases bíblicas de la misión: perspectivas latinoamericanas*, ed. C. René Padilla (Buenos Aires: Kairós, 1998), 437–64.

- the role of the *Bible* in doing theology,
- the *social realities* of the Latin American contexts, and
- *lay participation* in the work of the church.

These three commitments of integral missiology would eventually prove formative for the approach of Faith and Displacement, so they merit further delineation here.

### Biblically Rooted Theology

Upon perusing the seminal works of both liberation theology and the FTL from the 1970s and '80s, one thing that jumps out at the reader is the massive difference between the sources appealed to by the liberationist (Catholic) and the FTL (Protestant) authors, respectively. While both groups do theology from similar social locations and come to many similar conclusions, the Catholic authors appeal heavily to ecclesial proclamations and systematic theologians, whereas the Protestants primarily invoke Scriptural texts and, disproportionately, the works of biblical scholars, even when they are not "doing" Bible, but missiology or theology. As mentioned above, eleven of the chapters of *Bases bíblicas de la misión* are examinations of how different portions of the biblical corpus contribute to a Christian understanding of the church's mission. It might come as a surprise, then, that several of the contributing authors (Escobar, Bedford, Davies, Rooy, Saracco) are theologians, missiologists, and church historians, rather than biblical scholars.

Various factors account for this phenomenon. Naturally, Protestantism places proportionally greater emphasis on Scripture vis-à-vis tradition and doctrine than does Catholicism. So also, the general paucity of academically credentialed Protestant theologians in Latin America has meant that Scripture courses in seminaries are taught by faculty of all specialties. The aforementioned theologians would have certainly also taught many Bible courses.

But one other factor merits highlighting: Latin American Protestantism has long exhibited a certain coolness—at times manifest as reticence or even suspicion—to tradition and doctrine, in contradistinction to the movement's signature fervor for the Bible. This is not to say that Latin evangelicals (be they academics or pastors) care little for systematization, only that they prefer to generate schema and structures in direct and immediate conversation with the Scripture. While they may appeal to theologians or the history of the church along the way, notionally their goal is to elaborate their theology primarily on the basis of the Bible. The FTL was and remains no exception to this broader Protestant tendency. Indeed, the explicitly biblical nature of their argumentation has doubtless been a key factor in their success. It warrants flagging this point now, for as our own project unfolded, we also followed this pattern of perpetually connecting our proposals and curricula not necessarily to systematic theological categories, but always to Scriptural texts.

### Attention to Concrete Social Realities

A second key commitment of integral missiology is to respond to the real suffering of discrete geographic and cultural contexts, as opposed to proclaiming a primarily spiritual or doctrinal gospel. Padilla's definition of the church's mission emphasizes a multifaceted holism, identifying this as a demand of the Scriptural witness itself. "Missions only do justice to the biblical teaching and the concrete reality when they are *integral*, in other words, when there is a crossing of borders (not only geographical, but also cultural, racial, economic, social, political, etc.) with the purpose of transforming human life in all its dimensions."[24]

Jesus's ministry was irreducibly practical and concretely oriented in ways that integral missiology contends are paradigmatic for Jesus's followers.[25] Padilla affirms, "The disciple's mission would not be limited to making converts in order to increase the number of church members. It would be directed, rather, to making disciples in whose lifestyle the example of Jesus Christ would be reproduced: an example of unconditional love for God and neighbor, of humble service and solidarity with the poor."[26]

### Centrality of Lay Participation

Just as integral missiology brooks no division between the spiritual and material aspects of the church's mission, so also does it reject the

24. C. René Padilla, "Hacia una definición de la misión integral," in *El proyecto de Dios y las necesidades humanas*, ed. Tetsunao Yamamori and C. René Padilla (Buenos Aires: Kairós, 2000), 31.

25. Cf. Ricardo Gómez, *The Mission of God in Latin America* (Lexington, KY: Emeth, 2010), 186.

26. C. René Padilla, "Introduction: An Ecclesiology for Integral Mission," in *The Local Church, Agent of Transformation*, ed. Tetsunao Yamamori and C. René Padilla (Buenos Aires: Kairós, 2004), 31.

vocational dichotomy between the individual Christian's spiritual and professional lives, as well as the ecclesial bifurcation between pastors (who putatively "do" the ministry) and laity (who receive or support the ministry).[27] Instead, "the practice of integral mission assumes that the church and *each of its members* will give absolute priority to following Jesus in terms of a missionary lifestyle: a way of life modeled on Jesus for the purpose of bearing witness, by word and action, to Jesus Christ the Lord."[28]

Padilla summons churches to help members reflect the sovereignty of Christ into all spheres of life. In such churches, disciples "learn obedience to their Lord in all the circumstances of daily existence, private and public, personal and social, spiritual and material. The call of the gospel is the call to a total transformation that reflects God's purpose to redeem human life in all its dimensions."[29]

The implementation of this mission does not depend primarily upon academically trained theological "professionals." Instead, "integral mission demands the 'declericalization' of ministries and a 'laicization' of the clergy. In other words, it requires recognition of the apostolic nature of the whole church."[30] This theology invites laity to actualize their own calling and mobilize their gifts for the purpose of serving others.

It is safe to say that integral missiology has been the most significant contribution of Latin American evangelicalism to global theology.[31] The impact of integral mission on evangelical Christianity well beyond Latin America is evidenced by the three Lausanne Conferences and five Congreso Latinoamericano de Evangelización (CLADE) conferences, as well as the Micah Network, whose mission is "to motivate and equip a global community of Christians to embrace and practice integral mission."[32] To date the Micah Network has over six hundred members, including major faith-based organizations (FBOs) such as Compassion International, Tearfund, and World Vision.

---

27. Padilla DeBorst, "Integral Mission Formation," 67–69.

28. Padilla, "Ecclesiology," 33, emphasis added.

29. Padilla, "Ecclesiology," 30.

30. Padilla, "Ecclesiology," 45.

31. Padilla DeBorst, "Integral Mission Formation," 134–41.

32. Micah Network, "Vision and Mission," https://www.micahnetwork.org /visionmission/.

The three hallmarks of integral missiology began to give shape to a project that enabled the seminary to engage even more deeply with the reality of forced displacement. We decided to interpret the gospel *for* our own contextual reality, in response to the defining crisis of our nation. We committed to doing such theology with a robustly biblical vision, in accordance not only with the approach of the FTL but also in fidelity to our own identity as the *Biblical* Seminary of Colombia. Finally and crucially, we decided early on that, however we went about this work, it would have to issue in the equipping of the members of local churches. In that way, we were being faithful to our institutional vision of service to both the church and society. With integral mission as our guiding theological framework, the seminary as a whole committed to make this *the* primary research project of the entire institution. We decided to call it Faith and Displacement.

## Integral Mission and Interdisciplinarity

Integral missiology provided us a theological framework within which to undertake further work on displacement. But like all productive doctrinal theories, integral missiology had potential for further development, development which we came to see would be necessary if we were to make effective headway in our work. The first such area with potential for development had to do with interdisciplinary rigor. (The second area will be discussed in chapter 3.)

As mentioned in chapter 1, we realized almost immediately that we would need non-theologians to help us understand the realia of the crisis. For this reason, we hired Laura Cadavid Valencia, a sociologist. Our colleagues at Fuller Theological Seminary looped in Lisseth Rojas-Flores, a Colombian-American psychologist whose father actually taught in our seminary when Lisseth was a little girl. In our first conference and book, the benefits of their expertise were manifest. (We were all very impressed by the way social scientists could use numbers for more than literary citations!) But in conversations with local community leaders, we learned that the suffering of the displaced peoples was not exclusively spiritual, emotional, or social; it also had economic, political, and educational ramifications. If, therefore, we were to venture a truly *integral* response to the displacement crisis, we were going to need to increase the number of social scientists in our "stable" even further. It was a moment for recalling the advice Professor Briggs offered me over elderflower cordial: "Don't be overly timid in your budget projections. Figure out what it would cost to do it right."

After taking a few deep breaths and reviewing what local leaders had shared with us in the previous months, we concluded audaciously that we would need to create six teams in order to give attention to the multidimensional nature of internally displaced person (IDP) suffering:

- economics
- sociology
- psychology
- pedagogy
- public sector interaction[33]
- missiology

Perhaps at a full-scale university, this would have been a simple task. One could just stroll over to the pertinent department and buy coffees for a few colleagues and sell them on the idea of teaming up. But at a seminary, recruiting a team of social scientists was no simple task. So we began to look both at home and abroad, and found some truly remarkable colleagues, people like Lina Marcela Cardona Sosa, an economist from the Colombian National Bank (Banco de la República); Elisabet LeRoux, a sexual violence researcher from South Africa; and Duberney Rojas Seguro, a political scientist working on his doctorate in Germany, even though he himself grew up in our barrio and was converted in the seminary's soccer ministry after climbing over the seminary's walls to steal mangos from our trees! Slowly, steadily, God drew international scholars to this project. But then the question emerged: What exactly should we *do* with them?

We knew that the social scientists had knowledge we needed. That much had become clear back in 2014. Still, notwithstanding the benefits that Laura and Lisseth had provided that first year, we had not figured

---

33. Led by diplomat-turned-theologian Guillermo Mejía Castillo, the public sector interaction team focused on issues relating to engagement with the state, whether in pursuit of government aid or as part of political activism. Nonetheless, in certain evangelical circles "politics" is a dirty word, so we opted for terminology that would not prematurely shut down people's interest.

out how to harness their skills for our missional project nor how to integrate their social-scientific knowledge with our theological inquiry. They wrote like a sociologist and a psychologist, and we wrote like theologians. I worried that we might end up being ships passing in the night.

Unfortunately, our academic predecessors in integral missiology did not provide much guidance on this matter either. Admittedly, liberation theology had distinguished itself with a vigorous interdisciplinary synthesis of theology and Marxist political analysis. But liberation theology's level of constructive interdisciplinary engagement with the social sciences has not, by and large, been matched by integral missiology. This is not to deny that there have been some bright moments of fusion. For example, a 1988 edition of the FTL's journal *Boletín teológico* focused on the importance of relating theology to the social sciences.[34] Likewise, Padilla wrote works addressing the intersections of theology, economics, and ecology.[35] Still, most of these interdisciplinary forays have been brief and nonsystematic. They derive from the brilliance of a theologian like Padilla and his commitment to bringing himself up to speed on other fields of knowledge, as opposed to getting a more mediocre theologian (like me) to work synthetically and constructively with a social scientist (such as economist Lina Cardona Sosa).

In principle, I believed ardently that "all truth is God's truth,"[36] such that any genuine special revelation must de facto be compatible with and complemented by the insights of general revelation (from e.g., the natural or social sciences). Accordingly, it seemed only logical that the fundamental commitments of integral missiology to serve the will of God in all spheres of life entailed that integral missiology could be well served by a research program that is equally attentive to the interrelated aspects of human existence. I reasoned that the holistic nature of the church's integral missional practice should be undergirded by systematically interdisciplinary missiological research, continuing to enrich

34. Rubén Paredes, "Fe cristiana, antropología y ciencias sociales," *Boletín teológico* 20, no. 31 (1988): 215–30; and C. René Padilla, "Ciencias sociales y compromiso cristiano," *Boletín teológico* 20, no. 31 (1988): 247–51.

35. C. René Padilla, "Economía y plenitud de vida," in *Economía humana y economía del Reino de Dios* (Buenos Aires: Kairós, 2002), 73–99; and C. René Padilla, "Globalization, Ecology and Poverty," in *Creation in Crisis: Christian Perspectives on Sustainability*, ed. Robert S. White (London: SPCK, 2009), 175–91.

36. So Arthur F. Holmes, *All Truth Is God's Truth* (Grand Rapids: Eerdmans, 1977).

the holistic ministry of the church with the most recent advances in social-scientific knowledge.[37] It stood to reason that, if theology and the social sciences could each support the flourishing of displaced persons in their own ways, then operating together they should be able to have a greater impact than operating independently. Right?

It all seemed very plausible in theory. But it remained, at that point, unclear precisely how to put the theory into practice.

My initial, less-than-elegant strategy was simply to smash the social scientists together into small groups with theologians, lock them in a room together with coffee and empanadas, and hope that they would come up with new insights on how to care for IDPs. Nonetheless, I came to worry that we might end up with the sort of floppy interdisciplinarity that is all too common in religious scholarship: a theologian or biblical scholar adopting a fistful of social-scientific terms and "translating" their theological ideas into the language of another discipline, in hopes that the terminological do-si-do might create a veneer of erudition adequate to secure publication in an unsuspecting journal.

More methodological rigor was needed, to take integral missiology to the next level, and to help ensure that our collaboration between social scientists and theologians really could generate strategies to aid IDPs that went beyond what either set of disciplines had been achieving by operating independently.

---

37. This is not to deny the interdisciplinary advances of missiological researchers in other contexts and schools of thought. The focus here is on ways to foster such interdisciplinary work in the context especially of the Latin American integral mission.

# Pedro Ramón González Yanes

The afternoon heat in the town of Tierralta (Córdoba) bears down on you like a lead blanket, smothering your breath, rendering the livestock and even the insects strangely subdued. If feels as if the entire countryside has agreed that, between lunch and the cool reprieve of dusk, slow-moving silence is the only way to survive. You learn to slink from one shady spot to the next, knowing that the paint-peeling rays of the sun have little mercy upon the squinting souls baking under their pitiless barrage.

One day in 1996, a bedraggled and heartbroken parade of parched campesinos shuffled into town and collapsed onto the concrete of the town plaza, seeking some meager protection beneath the handful of scraggly trees that dot what is otherwise a large concrete slab with a few benches and desiccated planter beds. They had just completed a forty-kilometer journey from the remote mountain *vereda* of Batata, accompanied by children, dogs, and whatever small livestock they could draw along as they fled from guerrilla militia.

I learned about this mass displacement from our coresearcher, Pedro Ramón González Yanes,[38] on a muggy Monday afternoon in January of 2017. I sat down with Pastor Ramón and a church elder named Leonardo López González, who had been among the company that had descended from the mountains to Tierralta two decades earlier. Señor López recalled that a total of sixty-five families fled from Batata at that time. Ramón nodded: *309 people.*

---

38. Ramón had himself been displaced from Santa Fe de Ralito to Tierralta in 1985.

Leonardo narrated how a young leader named Pedro Acosta[39] had seen them languishing in the town plaza and so invited them to take refuge inside the doors of Cristo el Rey, an evangelical church just a few blocks away. The senior pastor was in a meeting when he got a word that Pedro had let in the *desplazados*.[40] By the time he made it back to the church, the exiles from Batata had settled themselves into the sanctuary, surrounded by their chickens and overwhelmed by their trauma. The pastor decided to let them stay.

The church had become, overnight, a refugee camp. Sunday services were suspended, to the chagrin of some congregants. Ramón explained: "That broke with the vision [of the church] that some brothers had. They would say, 'No, how can we suspend services to bring people here like that?' So, God gave wisdom to those who were [in charge. They said,] 'Brothers, but what's more important, having our services or looking after our brothers? What's more important to God?' So, the people gave in, [some] with gritted teeth."

"Here in the church, they had a school," Leonardo added. I nodded, suppressing a smile, since we were conducting the interview in one of the school classrooms. "They paralyzed the school in order to give shelter to all the families they received here."

Suddenly overwhelmed by the memory of those heartbreaking days, tears overtook Ramón, but he pushed ahead with his narrative. "It is hard to hear people say that they didn't lack anything in their *vereda*, to have to talk to them [after they have lost everything], and tell them, 'Brother, God hasn't abandoned you. We don't understand. [But] God is with you.'"

"For weeks, our worship was simply to sit with them, and hear their stories, and weep."

Ramón spoke of how the church began to grasp the scope of the social and emotional damage caused by displacement. "When they are displaced, a person suffers disintegration. They feel less than other people, not valued. Here in Tierralta [some] people came to see the displaced

39. Pedro Acosta is now the director of Corporación Social Comunitaria (CORSOC), mentioned below as the social ministry founded by Cristo el Rey in 1992. He has become one of the Christian leaders in Colombia who best understands the armed conflict and has assisted in peace talks, mediations, and disarmaments for decades.

40. When we first met in 2017, Ramón had been the pastor of the church Cristo el Rey for four years, but the day the IDPs had arrived from Batata, he was just a lay leader.

as a plague, like an infected person. This caused many people to abandon the faith. Many homes were broken, many families were torn apart. Many of those children that were displaced went on to swell the ranks of armed groups. Many girls got pregnant at a young age. Some ended up in prostitution."

To make matters worse, the townspeople often abused the IDPs' financial desperation, paying them well below even the paltry minimum wage. "They would hire a *desplazado*, but they would pay them something insignificant. They would say to the person who wanted to bring home sustenance for his family, 'Here is work, what I have to pay you is this,' and the person had to [do it]. Many people suffered that sort of humiliation."

Fortunately, a few years earlier, the church had created a foundation called CORSOC (Corporación Social Comunitaria), for the purpose of executing the congregation's social initiatives. When the IDPs flooded into Tierralta, CORSOC leapt into the fray, addressing the material needs of the IDPs housed within the walls of Cristo el Rey, and advocating with them before the government, to expedite their access to state funds and support. In this way, "the church sought [to make them feel] that their dignity had been restored, accepting them, loving them, making them feel important in our community."

As people eventually got settled in new homes, the church's school continued to serve the displaced children. Ramón explained, "The school began to offer support for the education of the [displaced] brothers, subsidizing them with projects and things like school supplies and fees."

In the year 2000, men from the displaced community began to return tentatively to Batata. Slowly but surely, they made progress recovering the fields that the jungle had rapidly begun to swallow. Nonetheless, in 2008 the violence resumed, this time perpetrated by paramilitary groups. A second mass displacement from Batata to Tierralta resulted. Once again, Cristo el Rey was there to receive the victims, to help them resettle and recover.

A few years later, the people ventured a second return to Batata, this time to stay. On the occasion of this second return into the mountains, they were accompanied by a new pastor. His name was Pedro Ramón González Yanes.

# CHAPTER 3

# Missional Action Research

It was the kind of problem that made my chest tighten and my jaw lock down: I needed to identify a rigorous, empirical field research method that could be applied across several different fields of the social sciences as well as in different theological subdisciplines, all without unduly constraining the sort of field research that could be done by the project's social scientists. This was not the sort of thing covered as part of my graduate theological formation and it made me feel like an academic poser. My TMD (temporomandibular disorder) flared up so badly that I had to stop drinking my habitual twelve cups of coffee a day. I cut down to two, which hardly enhanced my mental acuity. (On the upside, I saved money on Splenda.)

To make matters worse, I was becoming more keenly aware of my own distance from the reality of Colombian internally displaced persons (IDPs) (in spite of living in a lower-class, gang-controlled barrio of a notoriously violent city). So, in addition to needing to ascend higher in the academic stratosphere to ensure the methodological rigor of the project, I also had to get more grounded to assure our practical efficacy.

### Facing Up to Realities and the Probability of Failures

This latter point was thrust upon me rather indelicately in a brewery. Medellín is home to Tres Cordilleras, a line of surprisingly tolerable beers (considering that Colombia is, well, not Germany). On Thursday nights, for twenty thousand pesos (eight dollars) Tres Cordilleras offered brewery tours, a flight of beers, and live music from a band whose lead singer had such amazing pipes that she could cover everyone from Aerosmith to Adele. I had planned to go there with a British expat buddy of mine, but he showed up with his boss, Leonardo Ramírez, the director of a Christian foundation (Fundación Vive) that works with IDP children.

Leonardo was no academic and was not impressed with my being one. He had an undergraduate degree and a whole lot of experience working with the children of deeply impoverished displaced persons in "hot" regions of Colombia. He had been to our theological conference a couple months earlier, after which he compiled a long mental list of reasons why the tactics that we were envisioning to help IDPs would probably be a huge waste of time. Leonardo pulled a tall chair up next to mine and began to recite his litany of "observations" for me. The fact that I was grimacing my way through a pint of something called "rosé pale ale" did not make his criticism any more palatable.

As the overamplified singer belted out "Roxanne," Leonardo leaned close to my ear and yelled into it that academic publications and curricula would not mean much to a population that by and large had not finished primary school and was in great measure illiterate. I countered that we could try to communicate key messages through things like video.

He laughed. "How is that going to work for communities without TVs, with people who may not even have electricity or whose electricity might be intermittent because they're pirating it from the power company?"

Before I could respond, he pressed ahead, pointing out that it was not a given that the communities could be expected to engage activities that would require them to have things like blank paper or soccer balls on hand. What's more, why would I suppose that they would have time or interest in hearing my thoughts about poverty or justice when many of them make just enough money in a given day to buy a single serving of rice, beans, and plantains?

The singer switched to a *vallenato* tune by Carlos Vives.[1] I hurried through the last swallow of my ghastly rosé ale, pushed my stool back from our teetering table, and stalked to the bar to order a porter and get some space from Leonardo's barrage of naysaying. I felt overwhelmed by my ever-increasing apprehension of the challenge we were confronting, irritated by the criticism, and guilty for having spent eight dollars on beer and music when the people I was hoping to help might not even make that much after a whole day's hard labor. I fumed, rationalized, and finally admitted to myself that Leonardo was right: I had no idea how to connect effectively with, and serve, the IDPs.

---

1. An immensely popular folk musical genre from the Caribbean coastal region of Colombia, often fused with pop or rock features. I hate *vallenato*.

But Leonardo did. So I asked if he would join the project, whether he'd agree to help us communicate, contextualize, and generally not waste our time. He agreed.

That evening at the brewery was a turning point, as I accepted that the insights of academics would need help if they were ever to land effectively in IDP communities. We needed professionals to work with us. Thus, as we continued to form our teams, we ensured that each one of them included a member who was not an academic, but a professional in the field pertinent to the team. This approach was coherent with the emphasis that integral missiology placed on the participation of laity in the mission of the church (see chapter 2). The work of the kingdom of God is not incumbent only upon the pastor or the scholar, but on all members of the body. "The eye cannot say to the hand, 'I have no need of you' nor again the head to the feet, 'I have no need of you'" (1 Cor. 12:21).

## Inspiration for an Empirical Research Methodology

Progress was being made in the process of finding ways to connect effectively with IDP communities. But I was still casting about for an overarching research methodology that could structure the interdisciplinary collaborations of our diverse teams. I reached out to some sociologist friends—Laura Cadavid Valencia and Ivón Cuervo—to ask if they had any suggestions regarding a broad-spectrum research method that was compatible with the sort of project we were undertaking, could be applied in various fields, and would be pertinent to a Latin American context. They pointed me to an approach called Participatory Action Research (PAR) and shot me a packet of essays to get my feet wet.

I was hooked.

### Action Research

The phrase "action research" was coined by a psychologist named Kurt Lewin in a 1946 article in the *Journal of Social Issues*.[2] Lewin, who was at that time studying interracial relations in the United States, proposed that research on such a poignant topic could not terminate in academic literature, but should generate social action. Although Lewin was a

---

2. Kurt Lewin, "Action Research and Minority Problems," *Journal of Social Issues* 2, no. 4 (1946): 34–46.

psychologist, he argued that such action research ought to encompass various social scientific disciplines.[3] He suggested that scholars from different fields should collaborate in the developing of theories, proposing interventions to test their theories, and thereafter evaluating the effectiveness of their intervention in order to model a larger-scale plan.[4]

Action research has drawn criticism for its divergence from more "disinterested" forms of social-scientific research, which seek to describe social phenomena in generalizable fashions while preserving an objective distance from the phenomena in question. Action research, by contrast, begins with a problem—even an injustice or a "wound"[5]—and gets close to that problem or wound at a local level. Action research begins by saying, as it were, "Tell me where it hurts" and listens to people's answers. Then, rather than providing a mere descriptive characterization of what they have heard, action researchers endeavor to *do something about the pain* by creating an intervention to ameliorate the problem. In this sense, research is not just a prerequisite for helping people; helping people is an intrinsic component of the research. As William Foote Whyte puts matters,

> Although no mainstream behavioral scientist would argue that research in his or her field is entirely devoid of a practical significance, the prevailing view—supported by common practice—is to assume that it is up to the behavioral scientist to discover the basic facts and relationships, and it is up to others to somehow make use of what social researchers discover. . . . The mainstream researcher nevertheless assumes that good science must eventually lead to improved practice. Here the important word is eventually. How long must we wait before what mainstream researchers discover eventually gets implemented in practice?[6]

## Participatory Action Research

Action research sank roots into Latin American soil in the 1960s and '70s. Far from simply reproducing Lewin's model, Latin American social

3. Lewin, "Action Research," 36.
4. Lewin, "Action Research," 38.
5. To crib from Mary McClintock Fulkerson, *Places of Redemption: Theology for a Worldly Church* (Oxford: Oxford University Press, 2007), 12, who characterizes theology as "a response to a wound."
6. William Foote Whyte, "Introduction," in *Participatory Action Research*, ed. William Foote Whyte (London: Sage, 1991), 8.

scientists took action research to the next level by increasing the emphasis on the *participation of base communities* in social scientific research. The 1977 International Symposium in Cartagena proved a watershed event in the theory's development, affixing the term "Participatory" to "Action Research"[7] and thereby affirming that subject participation had become a distinctive feature of (what was now called) Participatory Action Research (PAR).

Latin American PAR developed most strongly in two social-scientific disciplines: sociology and pedagogy.[8] The seminal sociological theorist was the Colombian Orlando Fals Borda, one of the conveners of the 1977 Cartagena Symposium. Fals Borda—along with priest-sociologist-turned-guerrilla-revolutionary Camilo Torres Restrepo[9]—founded the first Colombian department of sociology at the Universidad Nacional and became one of Colombia's leading intellectual lights. The key pedagogical theorist of PAR was the Brazilian Paolo Freire.[10] It was Freire who "most famously inspired researchers to involve their participants directly in knowledge production and turn research into the means of social transformation."[11] While PAR has spread far and wide on the global

7. Orlando Fals Borda, "Orígenes universales y retos actuales de la IAP," *Análisis político* 38 (1999): 84; Eduardo Leal, "La investigación acción participativa, un aporte al conocimiento y la transformación de Latinoamérica, en permanente movimiento," *Revista de investigación* 67, no. 33 (2009): 23.

8. Ana Mercedes Colmenares E., "Investigación-acción participativa: una metodología integradora del conocimiento y la acción," *Voces y silencios: revista latinoamericana de educación* 3, no. 1 (2012): 103-5.

9. Camilo Torres was a member of the Ejercito de Liberación Nacional (ELN), a Marxist guerrilla group. Apparently, however, priests make lousy guerrillas, because he was killed in his first armed confrontation. Nonetheless, Torres became something of a patron saint of the ELN, to the degree that they even changed their name to include him in it. Their official moniker is the Ejercito de Liberación Nacional-Unión Camilista. Try convincing your conservative evangelical Colombian seminary to use a theory associated with a famous Catholic guerrilla . . . not easy.

10. Particularly owing to his groundbreaking book *Pedagogy of the Oppressed*; Paulo Freire, *Pedagogy of the Oppressed*, trans. Myra Bergman Ramos, 30th anniversary ed. (New York: Continuum International, 2000).

11. S. Kindon, R. Pain, and M. Kesby, "Participatory Action Research," in *International Encyclopedia of Human Geography*, ed. Rob Kitchin and Nigel Thrift (Amsterdam: Elsevier, 2009), 90.

scene, the hallmarks of the theory continue to bear the impress of these two foundational Latin American theorists.

While a great deal of ink has been spilled in the description of PAR, four features of the methodology bear special emphasis:

- the integral role of an action, that is, an intervention, in PAR
- the cyclical nature of PAR
- the irreducible necessity of nonacademic community participation in PAR
- returning knowledge to the community in generically diverse fashions

## Action

Preserving the seminal impulse of Kurt Lewin, Orlando Fals Borda rejected the notion of academic investigatory neutrality and argued that good research should be oriented toward social action. "The principle criterion of the research should be to obtain knowledge useful for the promotion of just causes."[12] Eschewing the notion of objective, disinterested, or emotionally unmoved study, Fals Borda contended that "science, properly understood, requires the possession of a moral conscience, and reason should be enriched—not dominated—by emotions. Head and heart would have to work together, addressing challenges that cannot be faced except with ethical postures that seek to balance that which is ideal with that which is possible by means of the application of a holistic epistemology."[13] Given integration of head and heart in the PAR process, Fals Borda concluded that social action—praxis—was the litmus test of any theory.[14]

---

12. Fals Borda, "Orígenes universales," 75. This sentiment rather calls to mind Augustine's hermeneutical dictum that a good biblical interpretation is one that builds up love of God and neighbor. "Whoever, then, thinks that he understands the Holy Scriptures, or any part of them, but puts such an interpretation upon them as does not tend to build up this twofold love of God and our neighbour, does not yet understand them as he ought" (Augustine, *Christian Instruction* 1.36.40).

13. Fals Borda, "Orígenes universales," 76.

14. Orlando Fals Borda, *El problema de como investigar la realidad para transformala por la praxis*, 7th ed. (Bogotá: Tercer mundo, 1997), 28. The resonances with the praxiological primacy of Latin American liberation theology are unmistakable, and not coincidental, as the two movements were mutually informing.

Accordingly, action research not only hypothesizes about social problems but also creates "intervention experiments." These intervention experiments serve on the one hand to test the hypothesis, and on the other hand to generate a social benefit. The two components cannot be separated, because the social benefit generated is precisely the evidence that confirms or falsifies the hypothesis.[15]

## Cyclicality

A second key feature of PAR is its cyclical nature. As was the case with Lewin's action research, PAR theorists understood concrete social intervention to be an integral part of the research process, by which one experimentally tested one's analysis of reality. But PAR took a step beyond Lewin's formulations and proposed that the research process be characterized by a *cycle or rhythm of reflection and action.*[16] By this token, one begins by reflecting on reality, and on that basis proposes an intervention to test that reflection. Thereafter, one analyzes the impact of that intervention precisely in order to refine and retest. This cyclical approach reflects PAR's comfort with the provisional nature of knowledge. Far from presuming to produce pristine analyses, PAR remains suspicious of polished theories that sometimes take a Procrustean approach to interpreting reality, stretching the facts and lopping off inconvenient bits that do not fit the theory.[17]

More schematically, PAR projects tend to be divided into various repeating phases:[18]

---

15. Chris Argyris and Donald Schön, "Participatory Action Research and Action Science Compared: A Commentary," in *Participatory Action Research*, ed. William Foote Whyte (London: Sage, 1991), 86; and Ernest T. Stringer, *Action Research*, 3rd ed. (Los Angeles: Sage, 2007), 12.

16. Fals Borda, "Orígenes universales," 78.

17. Fals Borda, *Por la praxis*, 22–24; and Mariane Krause, "Investigación-acción-participativa: una metodología para el desarrollo de la autoayuda, participación y empoderamiento," in *Experiencias y metodología de la investigación participativa*, ed. John Durston and Francisca Miranda, *Políticas sociales* (Santiago, Chile: Naciones Unidas, 2002), 49.

18. Colmenares E., "Investigación-acción participativa," 107–8; Fabricio E. Balcazar, "Investigación acción participativa (iap): aspectos conceptuales y dificultades de implementación," *Fundamentos en humanidades* 4, no. 1/2 (2003): 62–63; and Fals Borda, *Por la praxis*, 24–25.

1. Initial research
2. Construction of an action/intervention
3. Execution of the intervention[19]
4. Systematic evaluation of the intervention in order to continue the research cycle by
5. Adjusting the diagnosis or intervention, and re-execution (potentially on a larger scale)

These steps are all conducted in the same local contexts, believing that optimal precision will result from having direct continuity between the community in which the preliminary diagnosis was conducted and the one in which the intervention is implemented. While other social sciences emphasize generalizability of results, PAR is wary of hastening to generalization, recognizing that local communities are all different, and that greater degrees of generalization are likely to dilute the efficacy of an intervention.[20]

Notionally, the cyclical nature of PAR could allow the spiral to repeat ad infinitum, since adjusted reinterventions might continue to suggest further revisions with substantial benefits. But when a refined intervention achieves a reasonable level of efficacy, it can be diffused on a larger scale.[21] Of course, sensitivity to the slippage between the original contexts in which an intervention was developed and the other contexts to which it is extended require that the diffusion of the intervention also be systematically evaluated to take into account variances between the earlier and later target communities.

The PAR diagnosis and reflection processes tend to use qualitative rather than quantitative research tools, with a special preference for interviews and focus groups.[22] This is not a matter of strict necessity, but qualitative methods, by dint of being open-ended, are less likely to prejudice the reactions of local respondents. In addition, quantitative

19. These first three steps of PAR bear a marked similarity in relation to the "see, judge, act" methods of liberationist base communities.

20. So Stringer, *Action Research*, 5.

21. Jan Irgens Karlsen, "Action Research as Method: Reflections from a Program for Developing Methods and Competence," in *Participatory Action Research*, ed. William Foote Whyte (London: Sage, 1991), 151.

22. Jarg Bergold and Stefan Thomas, "Participatory Research Methods: A Methodological Approach in Motion," *Forum Qualitative Sozialforschung* 13, no. 1 (2012): §§66–70.

methods tend to be less effective at eliciting the active participation of base community members. This brings us to the third and arguably most complicated feature of PAR.

### Nonacademic Community Participation

The trademark feature of PAR, highlighted in the 1977 Cartagena Symposium, is the *participation* of nonacademics in the research process. Fals Borda emphasized the value of the knowledge of "common peoples."[23] By "common peoples," Fals Borda meant more than simply working with nonacademicians who are professionals (as when I recruited Leonardo Ramírez). He meant working with the very people one seeks to benefit with PAR: the vulnerable and disenfranchised. Resisting the tendency to reduce marginalized communities to the objects of research, placing them (as it were) on a glass slide under the researcher's microscope, PAR views nonacademic community members as "coresearchers" who peer down the microscope at their own situation and work alongside academics in the cycles of reflection and action.

Seeking to overcome the polarization between the expert and the client, PAR recognizes that both parties are *sentipensantes*,[24] "feeling thinkers." This attentiveness to the affective component of knowledge derives, according to Fals Borda, from "Pascal's dictum in his *Thoughts*: 'the heart has its *reasons* which reason itself does not at all perceive.'"[25] That is to say, there often exist excellent reasons for holding a view, even if one is not at a given moment able to articulate the logic of that conviction. Sometimes, the academic researcher can help make explicit the "tacit knowledge" of the nonacademic, who herself is likely to possess the most lucid apprehension of her own situation.[26]

Given the effort academics invest in learning to think like an academic, it is not easy to overcome a suspicion (or outright disdain) for the tacit knowledge of marginalized communities. Similarly, it is not uncommon

23. Fals Borda, "Orígenes universales," 74.

24. Fals Borda, "Orígenes universales," 78.

25. Orlando Fals Borda, "Remaking Knowledge," in *Action and Knowledge: Breaking the Monopoly with Participatory Action Research*, ed. Orlando Fals Borda and Muhammad Anisur Rahman (New York: Apex, 1991), 150.

26. Elaine Graham, "Is Practical Theology a Form of 'Action Research'?," *International Journal of Practical Theology* 17, no. 1 (2013): 152.

for base communities to brush aside academic perspectives, especially if presented in a recondite fashion opaque to the nonacademic.

Conversely, it is possible for people to lionize the knowledge of the other and to disparage their own views. This happens most commonly among marginalized communities, who have grown to despair of their own efficacy and intelligence. But it can also transpire among academics whose sensitization to postcolonial dynamics can cause a lopsided elevation of the perspicacity of the poor. None of these extremes is optimal.

Although the academic researcher and nonacademic coresearcher hail from different backgrounds and possess divergent ways of thinking (academic as opposed to experiential), in their collaborative research they commit themselves to mutual, empathetic listening, working together to seek convergences between popular and academic knowledge in order to achieve real social transformation.[27] "The sum of knowledge from both types of agents . . . makes it possible to acquire a much more accurate and correct picture of the reality that is being transformed. Therefore academic knowledge combined with popular knowledge and wisdom may result in total scientific knowledge of a revolutionary nature which destroys the previous unjust class monopoly."[28]

In an ideal scenario, PAR involves local actors in all stages of the research process: the identification of the problem/topic to be researched, the identification of information to be sought out, the elaboration of research tools to be applied, the collection and analysis of data, the design of an intervention, and the reflection on its effectiveness.[29]

Furthermore, the participatory nature of an ideal PAR project goes beyond thoroughgoing involvement of marginalized communities. PAR seeks to maximize the cooperation of all actors pertinent to the problem, not just victims but any number of adjacent entities (nongovernmental organizations [NGOs], nonvictimized populations, religious groups,

27. Fals Borda, "Orígenes universales," 75, 80.

28. Fals Borda, "Some Basic Ingredients," in *Action and Knowledge: Breaking the Monopoly with Participatory Action Research*, ed. Orlando Fals Borda and Muhammad Anisur Rahman (New York: Apex, 1991), 4; and cf. Fals Borda, "Remaking Knowledge," 152.

29. Colmenares E., "Investigación-acción participativa," 106–8; Rodrigo Contreras O., "La investigación acción participativa (IAP): revisandos sus metodologías y potencialidades," in *Experiencias y metodología de la investigación participativa*, ed. John Durston and Francisca Miranda, Políticas sociales (Santiago, Chile: Naciones Unidas, 2002), 10–12; and Leal, "Investigación acción participativa," 25.

government groups). This tendency toward inclusivity also aims to address all pertinent facets of a problem (economic, social, political, religious, etc.) and accordingly to mobilize all pertinent forms of expertise (academic and experiential) on the team of researchers and coresearchers, recognizing that, when the only tool you have is a hammer, every problem looks like a nail.

From an academic perspective, the benefits of such an approach are obvious:

1. Local coresearchers possess firsthand and nuanced knowledge of their circumstances, such that
   a. they diagnose their own situation in endogenous terms,[30] and
   b. they can troubleshoot potential interventions, taking into account dynamics that would be opaque to outsiders.
2. Involving local coresearchers increases community ownership and proactivity, generating more nuanced data and more contextually viable interventions.
3. All of this leads to a higher community buy-in to intervention, which in turn increases the probability of the intervention's success.

Nonetheless, the academic benefits of PAR should not overshadow the fact that, following the commitments of Paolo Freire, the Latin American version of action research aims to build critical consciousness (*conscientização*) among the nonacademic researchers and to support them with knowledge and skills so that they can defend their own interests and alter their own circumstances.[31]

### Returning Knowledge to the Community

For this reason, essential to PAR's *participatory* character is the commitment to *return knowledge* to the local communities.[32] Rather than the research process being purely extractive, PAR aims to generate knowledge

30. See, e.g., the argument of Robert Chambers about the differences between how poverty is understood by people from the Majority World in contrast with the paradigms of researchers from the North Atlantic; Robert Chambers, "Poverty and Livelihoods: Whose Reality Counts?," *Environment and Urbanization* 7, 1 (1995): 173–204. Chambers is a pioneer of Participatory Rural Appraisal, a methodological cousin of PAR.
31. Freire, *Pedagogy of the Oppressed*, 65–69; and Fals Borda, "Orígenes universales," 76.
32. Fals Borda, "Some Basic Ingredients," 9.

conjointly with nonacademic coresearchers and to circulate that knowledge back to the wider community. This entails the development of non-academic means of communication. "We had to modify our customary ways of informing the public [of our findings] so that they would understand well the data and messages reported. We developed a differentiated approach to communication according to their levels of literacy. . . . We developed stories on cassette tape, illustrated pamphlets, protest *vallenatos* and *salsas*,[33] spoken portraits and cultural maps."[34]

The importance of diffusing information in multiple genres and to multiple audiences cannot be overstated. This is not to deny the necessity of academic publication in the view of PAR practitioners (Fals Borda was a prolific academic), only to undermine the "monopoly of the written word." Fals Borda urged researchers to undertake multiple levels of communication simultaneously, depending on the public to which the knowledge is being diffused. "A good PAR researcher should learn to address all . . . levels with the same message in the different styles required if he is to be really effective."[35]

Similarly, Ernest Stringer (an educationalist who worked extensively with Aboriginal people in Australia) encourages action researchers to widen their generic repertoire as writers, learning to incorporate strategies used by, for example, journalists and fiction writers. Doing so presents facts with interpretative lucidity and rhetorical verve to facilitate the apprehension of what data means, not only abstractly but also personally, practically, and politically. He encourages authors to experiment with genre, voice, and style, since these "will provide more effective ways of knowing, other ways of feeling our way into the experiences of others. Such writing . . . will reveal the meaning of events given by interacting individuals, focusing on experience that is deeply embedded in and derived from local cultural contexts that will include homes, offices, schools, streets, factories, clinics, hotels, and so on."[36]

---

33. *Vallenato* and *salsa* are popular styles of music and dance in Colombia. I like salsa music a lot. Did I mention that I loathe *vallenato*?

34. Fals Borda, "Orígenes universales," 79; cf. Fals Borda, *Por la praxis*, 39–40; and Kindon, Pain, and Kesby, "Participatory Action Research," 94.

35. Fals Borda, "Some Basic Ingredients," 9.

36. Stringer, *Action Research*, 207.

This insight fits very much with the PAR sensitivity to participants as *sentipensantes*, "feeling thinkers" whose knowledge is interpreted and expressed through emotions and in concrete circumstances. If PAR reports its aim to be faithful to the sorts of data contributed by coresearchers, they cannot be exclusively dispassionate, abstract treatises. "They must be empathetic, evocative accounts that embody the significant experiences embedded in the taken-for-granted world of people's everyday lives. They must record the agonies, pains, tragedies, triumphs, actions, behaviors, and deeply felt emotions—love, pride, dignity, honor, hate, and envy—that constitute the real world of human experience."[37]

It bears adding that the incorporation of emotionally evocative renderings of data is not of exclusive pertinence to nonacademic audiences, as if the latter groups' lack of academic training requires the condescension of the scholar to communicate in affectively poignant fashions. If a scholarly audience is to understand the knowledge of the nonacademic coresearchers, they too will have to engage their empathy. The tendency of academics toward purely cerebral knowing is not a strength, but a deficiency, for truth is not merely a matter of rational data. Moreover, if the scholarly audience is going to be *changed* by the PAR project (bearing in mind that the impact of a PAR project need not be limited to the local participants), they will need to be reached at both the intellectual and emotional levels. In short, the participatory approach entails benefits for both the emic quality of the research and the dissemination of findings in and beyond academic circles.

## Finding the Answers I Was Looking For

I blitzed through the first tranche of PAR essays Laura and Ivón sent me as if I were a fantasy fiction fan reading an eighth Harry Potter novel. Orlando Fals Borda was offering solutions to the challenges that Leonardo had hollered into my ear at the brewery.

I had been anxious about how to bridge the massive cultural gap between our research teams and the displaced (as well as the recipient communities). Fals Borda responded: make the displaced and local leaders part of your project. Make them coresearchers.

37. Stringer, *Action Research*, 208.

I had worried about how to ensure that an academic project could generate real, immediate impact in community lives. But PAR offered a method in which generating impact was an irreducible component of the academic research. I had feared that the research we gathered would languish in a library, or, if expressed in accessible fashions, be too "popular" to publish in scholarly venues. Nevertheless, Fals Borda cajoled us to issue findings for diverse audiences at distinct registers and in distinct genres (written and otherwise). I was fretting that our efforts at interdisciplinary collaboration would founder upon methodological ambiguity, or that the premature imposition of a research method would stifle the collaborations of individual teams. Action research, however, not only countenanced the possibility of interdisciplinary research; it also saw interdisciplinarity as vital to responding to the multifaceted realia of the problems being addressed. Moreover, it provided a methodological cycle sufficiently clear to guide the research of each team, without straightjacketing the questions that could be asked or the interventions that might be created.

But could action research work for a seminary? More pointedly, could it serve a project structured around integral missiology? We ventured to think that it might.

## The Compatibility of Action Research and Integral Missiology

Although PAR and integral missiology emerged within different academic disciplines, the fundamental commitments of both methods make them natural allies. As delineated in chapter 2, the three major components of integral missiology are

- the central role of the Bible in doing theology,
- a commitment to respond to the concrete social realities of the Latin American contexts, and
- the prioritization of lay participation in the mission of the church.

So also, the vital commitments of PAR laid out above are

- the creation of an *action*, an intervention, in response to a real-world problem,

- the *cyclical* nature of reflection, intervention, and evaluation,
- the necessity of *nonacademic community participation* in the research process, and
- returning knowledge to the community in diverse fashions.

Two of each theory's critical commitments have counterparts in the other theory. Integral missiology's commitment to respond concretely to the social realities of the church finds its counterpart in PAR's commitment to create an intervention in response to the problems it confronts. Likewise, the emphasis of integral missiology on lay participation in mission fits hand in glove with PAR's concern to emphasize nonacademic participation in the research processes. In sum, *both movements seek to respond concretely to real social problems by combining the efforts of traditional leaders with the contributions of nonspecialists.*

The remaining commitments of the two theories do not obstruct their mutual compatibility. For example, there is nothing incompatible between integral missiology and PAR's cyclical approach to research, nor between PAR and integral missiology's emphasis on the role of the Bible in the church's pursuit of its mission. One could *hypothetically* imagine a missiological biblicism short-circuiting collaboration with the social sciences, if the Scriptures were viewed as the *exclusive* source of knowledge about the concrete realities to which the church responds. But such epistemological reductionism has been soundly rejected by integral missiologists. The 1988 Fraternidad Teológica Latinoamericana (FTL) conference "Fe cristiana y las ciencias sociales en América Latina hoy (Christian Faith and the Social Sciences in Latin America Today)" in Santiago de Chilé explicitly decried such obscurantism. Likewise, the Comunidad de Estudios Teológicos Interdisciplinarios (CETI; Community of Interdisciplinary Theological Studies)—founded by the Kairós Community[38]—emphasizes the importance of interdisciplinarity in both the title of the school and

---

38. The Kairós Community is a key practitioner of integral mission and something of a daughter of the FTL.

their curricular design.[39] René Padilla himself repeatedly incorporated social-scientific analysis into his theological reflection.[40]

Although PAR has no religious commitments (and has been applied especially by nonreligious scholars, in accordance with the dominant environment of the social science faculties in Latin America), there exists no intrinsic incompatibility between a Christian commitment and the PAR method. On the contrary, consider the founding Latin American theoreticians of PAR in the sociological guild: Camilo Torres was a Catholic priest; Fals Borda began his work as a Presbyterian and, in spite of eventually ceasing to identify as a Christian, his work continued to be marked by Christian features.[41] In specific relation to integral missiology, it is worth highlighting that the pedagogical theory of Paulo Freire was key in the curricular design of CETI[42] and prominent in the famous Lausanne address of FTL member Orlando Costa.[43] It therefore seems reasonable to conclude that integral missiology can be enriched through the application of PAR, without imperiling its own fundamental commitments.

## The Definition and Advantages of Missional Action Research

Being convinced of both the benefits that action research could bring to our work and of the essential compatibility of action research with integral missiology, we decided to synthesize the two into what we called "A Participatory Action Approach to Integral Missiology."

39. Padilla DeBorst, "Integral Mission Formation in Abya Yala (Latin America): A Study of the *Centro de Estudios Teológicos Interdisciplinarios* (1982–2002) and Radical *Evangélicos*" (PhD dissertation, Boston University, 2016), 236–55.

40. C. René Padilla, "Ciencias sociales y compromiso cristiano," *Boletín teológico* 20, no. 31 (1988): 247–52; C. René Padilla, *Economía humana y economía del Reino de Dios* (Buenos Aires: Kairós, 2002); and C. René Padilla, "Globalization, Ecology and Poverty," in *Creation in Crisis: Christian Perspectives on Sustainability*, ed. Robert S. White (London: SPCK, 2009), 175–91.

41. Gabriel Restrepo, "Seguir los pasos de Orlando Fals Borda: religión, música, mundos de la vida y carnaval," *Investigación y desarrollo* 24, no. 2 (2016): 199–239; and Nancy Milena Contreras Lara and José Daniel Gutiérrez Rodríguez, "La parte religiosa e ignorada de Orlando Fals Borda" (Corporación Universitaria Minuto de Dios, 2012).

42. Padilla DeBorst, "Integral Mission Formation," 295–99.

43. Brian Stanley, *Global Diffusion of Evangelicalism: The Age of Billy Graham and John Stott*, A History of Evangelicalism, vol. 5 (Downer's Grove, IL: IVP Academic, 2013), 167.

Doesn't really slide off the tongue, does it? So, in the interest of concision, we eventually opted for the name Missional Action Research (MAR).[44] Its features are laid out in the following definition.

### Defining Missional Action Research

Missional Action Research (1) responds to a real-world problem by means of undertaking a project that (2) generates a concrete intervention (3) implemented according to the PAR sequence (4) through the mobilization of local Christian communities. (5) Missional Action Research incorporates diverse participants (drawn from those directly affected by the problem as well as from both academics and professionals, both clergy and laity), (6) gives deep attention to religious sources of knowledge, especially the Bible, (7) fusing them with nonreligious sources of knowledge and (8) returning that knowledge to the affected communities as well as to the academy via generically diverse media.

Each of these points will be elaborated in turn.

(1) Missional Action Research is not interested in merely theoretical or academic research; it is (to invoke Mary McClintock Fulkerson again) "a response to a wound." Although it is genuinely academic research, MAR confronts *concrete problems*, as an expression of the integral mission of the church.

(2) Intrinsic to the MAR effort is the creation and implementation of an *intervention* designed to respond to the loss, hurt, or injustice being confronted. While MAR is deeply interested in enriching theology via engagement with the affected population, refined theological understanding is ancillary to the primary goal of advancing the kingdom of God through the mission of the church. Indeed, the evaluation of a MAR project hangs upon this latter criterion.

(3) Missional Action Research follows the *sequence* of PAR elaborated above. It begins by (a) *initial research on the problem,* applying the tools (literature, surveys, interviews, focus groups, etc.) of social-scientific research and sources of knowledge (theological, sociological, experiential) of all stakeholders to provide a full-orbed explication of the problem. On the basis of that preliminary diagnosis, the MAR team (b) *constructs an ecclesially based intervention* designed to respond to the "wound." All parties cooperate to (c) *execute that intervention* in real-life communities,

---

44. MAR is also a much better acronym that PAAIM.

ideally the ones in which the preliminary diagnosis was realized. Thereafter, the team (d) *analyzes the impact of their intervention*, assessing its efficacy and identifying how it might be improved. On that basis they (e) *revise the diagnosis or intervention*, and (f) *re-implement the intervention*, potentially on a larger scale if the initial efficacy of the intervention so warranted. As appropriate, the MAR process could be continued cyclically to further sharpen the intervention.

(4) A component of MAR that is not directly envisaged by PAR is the *mobilization of Christian churches*. As the "M" in the acronym indicates, MAR seeks to serve the mission of the church. Without denying the value of seminaries and parachurch organizations within the body of Christ, the primary agent of the kingdom is the church, which, notwithstanding its universal nature, exists and operates especially as local communities of faith. As such, MAR seeks to cooperate with, learn from, resource, and support local Christian churches in their missional work, rather than engaging in its own missional endeavor parallel to that of the local church.

(5) The mobilization of Christian faith communities is pertinent to the MAR incorporation of various *participants*. Following the lead of integral missiology, MAR works both with church leaders and church laity, recognizing the unique giftedness of different parts of the body. Following the lead of PAR, MAR incorporates members of the population directly affected by the problem being confronted—alongside academics, church leaders, and professionals.

Missional Action Research also draws on and cultivates both (6) *religious* and (7) *nonreligious sources of knowledge*. Believing that "all truth is God's truth,"[45] that both general and special revelation derive from the same source, MAR spares no intellectual expense in learning how best to advance the mission of the church in response to and against the pain in creation. All forms of knowledge—be they scientific, social-scientific, or humanist; be they religious or otherwise; be they academic or experiential—need to be explored. Practitioners of MAR thus recur both to scholarly literature and to field research. However, per the commitments of integral mission the Bible is given special attention, serving as a source of both truth and inspiration for participants. This is not to deny the other mediations of special revelation (traditional, charismatic, experiential), but rather to recognize that in the Protestant contexts of the Americas

---

45. Again, Arthur F. Holmes, *All Truth Is God's Truth* (Grand Rapids: Eerdmans, 1977).

the Bible is of irreducible importance in engaging the hearts and hands of Christian communities.

(8) Finally, and per PAR, MAR commits itself to the *return of knowledge*, first to the immediately affected communities, and second to the wider academic and ecclesial world. To foster the mission of the church (and to ensure that academic careers are not advanced simply by narrating the suffering of others), MAR prioritizes the distribution of knowledge to those immediately affected by the problem confronted, and as a second priority disseminates that information to unaffected (e.g., academic and ecclesial) audiences. This runs contrary to the typical priorities of academic research, and as such requires an atypical approach to knowledge distribution. Missional Action Research thus pursues pedagogical efficacy and innovation to ensure that knowledge putatively "returned" to the community is not just made notionally available but is effectively imparted to and thereafter implemented by the community.

## Advantages of Missional Action Research

The MAR approach offers numerous benefits for theologians and missional communities.[46] In the first place, MAR creates a structure for interdisciplinary collaboration between theologians and social scientists. They work together to decide what concepts (theological and social scientific) they want to explore with their target population. The social scientists can guide the process of creating field research protocols (which is not a skill that theologians typically possess) and together with the theologians they analyze the data, taking into account the immanent and transcendent features of their findings. In turn, with the aid of the social scientists, the theologians can incorporate salient aspects of social-scientific thought without themselves needing to become experts in those fields. Likewise, believing social scientists are helped by the theologians to explore the transcendent aspects of their research without lapsing to biblical proof-texting or theological reductionism.

In addition to structuring interdisciplinary collaborations, MAR facilitates theologians' concrete application of their theological reflections in ecclesial practice. Although missiology is among the most "application oriented" of the theological subdisciplines (much more so than,

---

46. Which is to say, MAR is a *useful* tool, not that it is somehow the *best* tool for missiological or practical theological research.

say, biblical studies or philosophical theology), because application and cyclical reevaluation are intrinsic to MAR, a thoroughgoing analysis of the ramifications of new theories is part and parcel of MAR inquiry. The fact that the development of an intervention is "built in" to MAR should be particularly amenable to integral missiologists, who have long emphasized the importance of practical applications of missional theory.

Beyond creating and implementing an intervention, MAR enables theologians to evaluate the effectiveness of their interventions empirically and multidimensionally. This facilitates the revision of the interventions in ways that go beyond the impressionistic adjustments typically made by practitioners (without the input of the academic who initially postulated their theory), which in turn heightens the efficacy of the intervention in future applications.

Furthermore, the empiricism of MAR increases the possibilities of securing funding for missiological research and for the dissemination of the interventions designed. Theological disciplines frequently experience difficulties securing research funding from non-theological grant-making bodies precisely because they operate according to methodological and epistemological canons that differ from those of most grant-making bodies. Nonetheless, the empirical structure provided by MAR as well as a collaboration with social scientists gives theologians access to other sources of funding for research and larger-scale implementation.

Finally, MAR brings academic researchers closer to the affected community. By doing field studies in conjunction with local coresearchers, the academics gain deep insights into the gritty realities of the community. Likewise, the imperative to return knowledge to local communities prevents the tendency of academics to secure the data they need for academic publication and then disappear back to their universities.

## Drawing Close to the Problem with Pilot Communities and Coresearchers

Once the MAR method had been established, it allowed us to create a detailed sequential plan of action for our project (the course of which is laid out in the following chapters). Additionally, MAR obligated us to go out and find the flesh-and-blood people with whom we would work: the IDP communities in which we would conduct our MAR work as well as the locals who would serve as our coresearchers. This was slightly daunting, since New Testament scholars do not typically do field research. I had lived in Colombia for fewer than two years and thus had a very limited network. To be honest, I had a painfully superficial understanding of the basic geography of the country! Thankfully, after more than seventy years of embedded ministry, the seminary's network was ample.

## Pilot Communities

To begin, we set our minds to finding two or three sites where we could conduct our preliminary diagnosis and beta test our intervention. We called these "pilot communities," revealing that we were cautiously hopeful about doing a large-scale implementation someday, should our findings prove useful. We elaborated criteria for our pilot communities of IDPs, focusing on "receptor sites," that is, communities *to which* people arrived after having been displaced, not the communities *from which* they were displaced (since by definition IDPs depart those locations).

Since Colombia is a nation of huge cultural diversity, we needed some geographic diversity (at least one community from the Caribbean coast, one from the central Andean region of the country, and one from the less densely populated southern regions of Colombia). Further, we sought to balance urban, semi-urban, and rural sites. Ethnic diversity was also key; we would need a mixture of mestizo,[47] Afro-Colombian, and indigenous IDPs.[48] At that point we realized that two or three pilot communities would simply not be enough!

---

47. Race is a complex theme in Colombia. The majority of Colombians are the descendants of some combination of Native American and Spanish colonist ancestry. Additionally, a large slave population was trafficked to Colombia during the colonial period. Racism continues to be a prominent force in the country, with a preference for lighter skin. A wide range of terms exists to describe different degrees of combinations of indigenous, Spanish, and African ancestry, but for the purposes of simplicity, I will use the term "mestizo" as a catchall for people with a mixture of indigenous and Spanish ancestry, by far the largest ethnic group in the country.

48. Afro-Colombian and indigenous people are disproportionately targeted by the armed conflict and represent unique cultural subgroups. See Marco Romero Silva, Fabio Alberto Lozano, et al. ("La crisis humanitaria en Colombia persiste: El pacífico en disputa: Informe de desplazamiento forzado en 2012"), interview with Consultoría para los Derechos Humanos y el Desplazamiento, Bogotá, 2013. "Afro-Colombian" is a broad term that includes people of predominantly African heritage, as well as those of mixed African and European heritage (*mulato*) and mixed African and indigenous heritage (*zambo*).

Another vital factor was the presence of a church or parachurch organization with an established ministry with IDPs that was, at least in one facet, exemplary or insightful. We hoped to learn from local practitioners, not only under the influence of PAR but also because the preliminary stages of our research had already been tremendously enriched by conversations with local practitioners. Additionally, we knew that the amount of time spent in each pilot community would not be sufficient to establish trust with the IDPs from the ground up. We needed trusted brokers, people who had already gained the confidence of the IDP community and could extend their reputation to us, thus helping to recruit participants and foster candid conversations.

Also, notwithstanding the logic of working primarily in receptor sites, it was suggested that we find a community that had returned, following displacement, to the location from which it had originally been displaced. Such communities are extremely scarce, since the violence of contested territories tends not simply to disappear after people are displaced. The conflict between armed groups of different ideologies ebbs and flows over the course of years. Nonetheless, given the government's hopes of establishing a peace accord and plans for land restitution, if we could find a community of IDP "returnees," there might be a great deal to learn from them.

In the end, then, we settled on a total of six pilot communities, in which ministries from five different denominations[49] were present:

- El Granizal,[50] on the border of Medellín and the neighboring municipality of Bello, in the department[51] of Antioquia. El Granizal is the second largest IDP settlement in all of Colombia, with over 27,000 inhabitants.

---

49. The denominations included the Assemblies of God, the Denominación de Iglesias Evangélicas del Caribe (AIEC), the Christian and Missionary Alliance, the Iglesia Cristiana Evangélica Nasa, and the Federación de Iglesias del Pacto Evangélico de Colombia (FIPEC).

50. Literally meaning "hail," because the settlement is set so high on the mountain ridge surrounding the Aburrá Valley that the precipitation sometimes falls as hail (not a common thing on the equator).

51. Colombian *departamentos* are basically equivalent to US states.

- La Granja,[52] an IDP settlement on the outskirts of the municipality Puerto Libertador, in the department of Córdoba.
- Santa Viviana and Santa Cecilia Alta, neighborhoods at the margins of Bogotá with high populations of IDPs.
- La Grandeza de Dios,[53] a settlement of IDPs from the Nasa indigenous near the town of Piendamó, in the Cauca department.
- Nelson Mandela,[54] originally a *barrio de invasión*[55] created by IDPs in the city of Cartagena.
- Batata,[56] a small town in the mountains forty km from the municipality of Tierralta, in the department of Córdoba. Batata has been at the epicenter of prolonged conflict between guerrilla and paramilitary groups. This resulted in multiple forced displacements, after which many members of the population voluntarily returned to their homes.

## Coresearchers

In each community, we aimed to select two coresearchers. The coresearchers were people with extensive experience working in that pilot community, whether as a member of the community or as a leader of the Christian ministry among the IDPs. These coresearchers provided us with on-the-ground local knowledge, extensive lived experience, and updates on the security situation (which became massively important in 2018 when the armed conflict intensified sharply in Córdoba, generating new waves of IDPs arriving in Puerto Libertador). They also shared with us the benefits of their good reputation, facilitating our interactions with the IDP populations and helping assemble people for our surveys, interviews, and focus groups. Additionally, these coresearchers went on to help lead the application of our intervention among the IDPs and the impact analysis of the same.

52. "The Farm."

53. "The Greatness of God" was the name that the fifty Nasa families gave their eight-hectare settlement at the end of a country road outside Piendamó.

54. Yeah, it is what it sounds like.

55. Literally an "invasion neighborhood," this is a common term which refers to settlements formed on the edges of formal municipalities without documentation, proper zoning, legal recognition, or infrastructural access.

56. "Sweet potato." They grow a lot of tubers there.

The coresearchers were also invited to develop their own research topics to feed into the larger project. Once the topic of research was identified, the coresearchers were paired with academic members of the team, who supported the coresearchers to facilitate the successful development of their projects.

In retrospect, I can see that undertaking this work without the partnership of coresearchers would have doomed it to failure. Apart from their advocacy and local leadership, the preliminary research never would have happened, let alone the implementation and analysis of the intervention. They are truly extraordinary people, which is why I include many of their stories between the chapters of this monograph. It is the local coresearcher, far more than the academic researcher, who assures that a MAR project results in tangible kingdom change.

## The Migrant Ministry of the Jerusalem Church (Acts 6:1–7)

I'm embarrassed to admit that I had to read a ream of PAR research before realizing the necessity of including local and IDP leadership in our project. I should have picked up on it earlier, given that my niche in New Testament studies is in the Lukan writings. You see, the book of Acts reveals that devolving leadership responsibility to migrants has been part of the church's leadership strategy since its very earliest days.

As described in chapter 2, the explosive post-Pentecost growth of the Jerusalem community (Acts 1–5) was marked by extraordinary solidarity between believers, especially expressed in the voluntary redistribution of possessions (Acts 2:44–45; 4:32–37) and meal sharing (2:42, 46). Luke specifies that a regular distribution of food was directed toward poor widows (6:1), who, alongside orphans, were the most vulnerable demographic in Jewish society (Deut. 27:19; Exod. 22:22; Isa. 1:23; 10:2; Ps. 68:5; James 1:27; *T. Mos.* 7.6–7; *Ps. Sol.* 4.10–13). But even in those early and, in some senses, idyllic days, prejudice reared its head, specifically toward a group of Jewish believers referred to as the "Hellenists."[57]

---

57. Further on this passage, see Christopher M. Hays, "What Is the Place of My Rest? Being Migrant People(s) of the God of All the Earth," *Open Theology* 7, no. 2 (2021): 152–53; and Christopher M. Hays, *Luke's Wealth Ethics: A Study in Their Coherence and Character,*

The Hellenists were, it bears stressing, not Gentiles. If they were Gentiles, Luke would have just called them that, and, as becomes clear when reading the account of the conversion of Cornelius in Acts 10–11, the conversion of an actual Gentile was a matter of no small controversy. The Hellenists were, rather, Greek-speaking Jews living in Jerusalem. During the first century, it was relatively common for Diaspora Jews— those living outside the holy land—to relocate to the holy land later in life and basically "retire" near the Temple.[58] These diaspora Jews, having been born and raised abroad, spoke Greek rather than Aramaic (which was the dominant language of Jews in Judea and Galilee). As such, when they migrated to Jerusalem, they had to confront the fact that they were linguistic and cultural outsiders, notwithstanding their shared Jewish ethnicity and religion.

It was also not uncommon that, after some time, the Hellenist husband would die, leaving his wife a widow and therefore subject to all the financial vulnerabilities that a normal Judean widow would confront. But on top of the conventional challenges the Hellenistic widow faced as both husbandless and Hellenist, she also frequently had to make her way without the support of male children, who very often would not have migrated to Jerusalem with their parents.[59] As such, the Hellenistic widow was triply vulnerable in first-century Jerusalem: widow, migrant, and functionally childless.

This is the social backdrop to the rather galling admission made in Acts 6 that the Aramaic-speaking Jewish believers (referred to by Luke as the "Hebrews") were skipping the Hellenist widows when making their daily distribution of food. Even among the earliest Christians, the very people swept up in the post-Pentecost wave of the Spirit, anti-immigrant prejudice resulted in the neglect of the most vulnerable.

---

Wissenschaftliche Untersuchungen zum Neuen Testament II, vol. 275 (Tübingen: Mohr Siebeck, 2010), 225–32.

58. Ernst Haenchen, *Die Apostelgeschichte*, 7th ed., vol. 3, Kritisch-exegetischer Kommentar über das Neue Testament (Göttingen: Vandenhoeck & Ruprecht, 1977), 255; and Hans-Joachim Degenhardt, *Lukas, Evangelist der Armen: Besitz und Besitzverzicht in den lukanischen Schriften: eine traditions- und redaktionsgeschichtliche Untersuchung* (Stuttgart: Katholisches Bibelwerk, 1965), 172.

59. F. Scott Spencer, "Neglected Widows in Acts 6:1–7," *Catholic Biblical Quarterly* 56 (1994): 728.

Fortunately, when that scandalous situation was brought to the attention of the apostles, they acted quickly, creating a team of "seven men of good standing, full of the Spirit and of wisdom, whom we may appoint to this task" (6:3) of administering the daily distribution to the widows: "Stephen, a man full of faith and the Holy Spirit, together with Philip, Prochorus, Nicanor, Timon, Parmenas, and Nicolaus, a proselyte of Antioch" (6:5).

The eyes of most modern readers glaze over when falling upon a list of names in the Bible, which is unfortunate in this case because it is precisely in the names that the most exciting component of this passage comes to light. The thing that no first-century reader of Acts would overlook is that each name on this list of Jewish people in Jerusalem is Greek; none of those names are Aramaic! In the context of a narrative about conflict between Greek-speaking and Aramaic-speaking Jews, Luke implies that the team appointed to care for all the believing widows—Aramaic and Greek-speaking alike—was in fact comprised entirely of Greek-speakers: Hellenistic Jews and one "proselyte" (which is to say, a Gentile convert to Judaism who subsequently joined the Jerusalem community of believers). Or, put in different terms, when a conflict arose between migrant and nonmigrant believers, the apostles commissioned a team of migrant believers, those closest to the problem, to be the ones to solve the problem. Naturally, these migrants were part of the affected community, enjoyed the trust of that community, and could therefore be counted on to remain alert to the best interests of the Hellenistic widows. While the apostles were not conducting a MAR project in Acts 6, they understood the practical and indeed moral value of participant community leadership in community life.

As leaders of the Jerusalem community, the apostles (mostly Aramaic-speaking men) were the most powerful actors in this scenario. Yet they recognized their own limits as well as the fact that their calling was especially to "serving the word" (Acts 6:4; cf. v. 2). They were not, consequently, in a promising position to handle this important responsibility. But they had the good sense to entrust a significant component of the success of their enterprise into the hands of the group that was less powerful, that was more vulnerable. In addition, by highlighting the need to appoint people "full of the Spirit and of wisdom," the apostles recognized that migrant people, who might have a different accent or language or be culturally less than adept, can nevertheless possess great wisdom. What is more, the Spirit of God can work among and through them.

Appointing coresearchers was a novel idea for me. If the apostles were academics, it would not have been so for them.

# Olger Emilio González Padilla

Pastor Olger González is a neat man. He wears square-framed glasses and has closely trimmed curly hair, probably bespeaking a Zambo heritage.[60] A bit gangly even in his early fifties, I have only ever seen him wearing a carefully pressed, short-sleeved *guayabera*.[61] Rather the opposite of the stereotypical *costeño* (known for their big personalities), Olger is soft-spoken and self-effacing.

Subdued demeanor notwithstanding, Olger pastors El Libertador, which is now "the big church" in the little town of Puerto Libertador, Córdoba. Barely a mile from an open-pit mining operation with a surface area as large as the town itself, Puerto Libertador is also the closest municipality to the east of the huge Jaramillo National Nature Preserve. This makes it a common destination for IDPs fleeing armed groups in the mountains.

Olger grew up in El Libertador, the son of the community's pastor. Initially, he had no intention of going into "the family business." Instead, upon graduating from high school, he decided to get a *técnica* (the Colombian equivalent to an associate's degree) in mining. It was a good way for a smart kid to make a secure life for himself in Puerto Libertador, and he spent a decade working in mining. Then the first wave of *desplazados* arrived. That's where he started his story during our first conversation, on a Saturday morning, the second week of Advent in 2016.

---

60. "Zambo" refers to Latins whose ancestry combines both indigenous persons and people of African descent.

61. A loose-fitting, pleated linen shirt, popular around the Caribbean. Although worn untucked, it is considered an elegant garment, even appropriate for formal occasions.

I'll start in the '80s. I was a young man in the church. I had finished the *técnica* in mining. . . . At that time, I was perhaps the most intellectual one in the community. A *técnica* was a big deal, there were not many professionals. But then the first displacements happened.

[At that time] the church, well, it was rather humble. There were still no paved streets. The first desplazados arrived and they came straight to the church. I was young, I didn't have much vision. But as a church we succeeded in establishing a partnership with World Vision and we ministered to about two hundred families.

In the 1980s, forced displacement was not yet the rampant phenomenon it would become a decade later. Perhaps the community thought this would be a one-off problem. Nonetheless, because Puerto Libertador is situated at the edge of one of the most persistently contested parts of the country, they have ended up receiving numerous waves of IDPs over the course of the armed conflict. When the second large influx of IDPs began arriving, El Libertador did not respond immediately. "Again, in the '90s and the year 2000, there was a second displacement, in which the people did not come directly to the church, rather they went to the peripheries [of town]. For the most part, well, displaced people go to the peripheries. They don't come here [to El Libertador] anymore, because the [road in front of] the sanctuary, it's already paved. Now we are the center. . . . The *desplazado* goes the periphery, right? To the edges of town."

*Everything is relative*, I thought wryly. The paved road in front of the church was badly deteriorated, as was literally every street in town. We were conducting this interview behind the church building, on a dirt pad, seated at a rough, handmade wooden table. But Olger was right: the sanctuary of the church was tiled, and El Libertador stood in the center of town, the biggest town around for miles. To a campesino fleeing from the Jaramillo Nature Preserve, El Libertador must have seemed downright cosmopolitan.

It was Olger's appointment as pastor of El Libertador that renewed the church's ministry with IDPs.

I started to work as the pastor in the 2004. So, that year, we went to the barrio Ramón Rubio, to attend the vulnerable population there. We went there, where they were, preaching the gospel, discipling. We started to form a group of believers and a [new] church started coming together. In 2005, we formed the church Elim, with [those] vulnerable people. From 2005 onward, we started to get help from JUCUM.[62] We brought potable water to that vulnerable neighborhood and we would do *brigadas*[63] with them. It was way for the church to interact with the vulnerable society, bringing potable water, buying pipes, and doing work projects with the community and all that. It was marvelous. When Elim became an established church, we brought them pastors and paid them until the church grew and became independent.

It was at this point I knew that I liked Olger a lot. Elim was literally one mile away from El Libertador. Olger could easily have justified folding that community into the ranks of his own congregation and thereby bolstered his own community's income. Instead, he did the opposite: he used his own congregation's funds to help salary a pastoral staff for Elim until Elim became self-sufficient. Then, the mother and daughter churches began to work together to serve a new IDP community, when a third massive wave of displaced people came to Puerto Libertador and created new *barrios de invasión*. "In 2014, the barrio La Granja began to form. We would go in to evangelize. There, we formed the [church] group, and we did it conjointly with Elim. As mother church and daughter church, we formed another church in La Granja."

After a while, the daughter church Elim had to pull back from La Granja. Taking a page from the El Libertador playbook, they established a partnership with Compassion International in order to allow them to invest more substantially in their own (still vulnerable) neighborhood of Ramón Rubio. Olger followed suit. "We [in El Libertador] also established a partnership with Compassion International. Now we are serving three hundred kids [in La Granja]. Elim is also attending over two hundred children [in the barrio Ramón Rubio]."

At that point, I marveled that El Libertador had managed to establish partnerships with three major international faith-based organizations (FBOs)—World Vision, YWAM, and Compassion International—and thereby funded ministries to hundreds of people in three different barrios. I later came to understand why those FBOs leapt at the chance to fund the work of El Libertador: they needed reliable partners, an honest

62. Juventud Con Una Misión, or, in English, YWAM, "Youth with a Mission."
63. Literally meaning "brigades," *brigadas* are one- or two-day charitable events held in marginal communities, often offering medical attention.

community with a proven track record that could help them hire and supervise people of integrity to work with the IDPs, day in and day out.

Of course, Olger could not do all the work on his own. A major part of his own pastoral strategy consists of discipling people from his community so that they can take responsibility for diverse aspects of the church (on which, see further chapter 5). He also knew to look directly to the IDP population when seeking workers to minister among the displaced. And one day, he made a brilliant decision when he tapped a displaced man named Deiner Espitia to head up the new ministry in La Granja. Deiner's story will have to wait for vignette 5.

CHAPTER 4

# Interdisciplinary Field Research

Research projects tend to have a short honeymoon phase. We were of course all ecstatic that our audacious grant proposal got funded. But we knew that the initial thrill would wear off, as does the euphoria of nuptial bliss when confronted with the realities of dirty laundry, burnt dinners, and visiting in-laws. Indeed, our honeymoon did not last long. It turned out that the audacity of the proposal was also its vulnerability: when running an interdisciplinary endeavor comprised of twenty-five scholars from four continents, the very diversity of perspectives intended to energize the work could just as easily derail it.

After the official launch in July 2016, the six teams that we had created—economics, sociology, psychology, pedagogy, public sector interaction, and missiology—spent a few months getting the new members up to speed and defining their research goals. But at Halloween time (a holiday firmly eschewed by Colombian evangelicals, such that my wife and I would sneak our costumed kids over to missionary houses for covert trick-or-treating), we flew all the project researchers to Medellín for our first intensive collaboration session. We packed a week's worth of activity into just a couple days: teams shared their nascent ideas with one another in plenary sessions and hunkered down in small groups to draft research protocols. Evening excursions were planned to cemeteries and museums that memorialized the conflict in Medellín, both to put the foreign researchers in more vivid contact with the realities of the violence in Colombia and to nourish the social tissue we knew that our multiyear endeavor would strain.

Overall, the intensive collaboration session proved hugely effective, setting us up to undertake field research by the beginning of Advent. But that first session of face-to-face interaction also revealed the beginnings of challenges that would accompany us for the rest of the project.

Once the teams actually scooted their chairs around a single table, we began to gain a deeper appreciation for how difficult it would be to pull this collaboration off, for reasons that ranged from personal to cultural to disciplinary to methodological. In the personal sense, some researchers were simply unprepared for the speed at which the project would have to advance to complete a full cycle of MAR inside of three years (per the limits of our grant funding). They had to be encouraged, coaxed, and coerced into meeting their deadlines.

Sometimes, our disagreements involved the intersection of cultural and disciplinary factors, a point which became most starkly clear to me one morning when our field research coordinator, Laura Cadavid, showed up to talk to my economics team about our research protocols. She sat down flustered, distracted, and after fumbling through part of our meeting, tears began to rim her eyes. I hastily suggested that the rest of the team break early for lunch and produced a box of tissues just in time for Laura to break down and relate to me a series of difficult interactions she had just concluded with some more senior researchers from different countries. A talented field researcher and sociologist, Laura was strong but young, with respectable but limited English and no doctorate. In Colombia, where there are far fewer graduate degrees per capita, people holding a single master's degree often serve as university faculty and researchers for governmental agencies and nongovernmental agencies (NGOs), and many people (like Laura) perform those jobs in exemplary fashion. But since that is not the norm in, for example, North Atlantic institutions, some of the international researchers were rather condescending to Laura and disinclined to follow her guidance on best practices for participatory field research with displaced persons. The differences between research methods from one social-scientific field to the next charged the interactions even further. Parties on all sides ended up feeling aggrieved, angry, and wounded. Subsequent conversations were convened to explore the frustrations and salve wounds. Still, it became clear in the subsequent years that, even though the parties involved were able to work and publish together productively, those wounds never healed completely. I came to understand that directing a large-scale project requires a great deal of emotional care;[1] addressing interpersonal conflict is every bit as essential to success as are clear protocols and reasonable timelines. As a contribution to my own development as a leader, I learned never to do collaborative research without a box of tissues close at hand.

1. For the record, I have the emotional quotient of a sea cucumber.

The interdisciplinarity of the project made for some bumpy inter-actions as well. The social scientists were perplexed by the theologians' ignorance of empirical scholarship and research ethics, especially in rela-tion to vulnerable populations. In fact, the seminary had no committee for research ethics and had to establish one for the project![2] Conversely, some members of the seminary were discomfited by aspects of the aca-demic discourse that prevailed among the social scientists. Colombian social science is heavily influenced by Marxist theory, whereas Colombian evangelicalism is patently anti-Marxist (in no small part, owing to the role of Marxist ideology among the guerrilla groups). For similar reasons, more conservative members of the seminary administration cringed at the ways in which some team members hoped to draw on insights and techniques from liberation theology, such as *lectura comunitaria de la Biblia* (community reading of the Bible), which in previous decades had been used to generate critical consciousness and sometimes revolutionary action among Catholic base communities.

Beyond these personal, cultural, and disciplinary challenges, our over-arching MAR method ended up demanding continuous reflection, as we evaluated the fit of components of PAR with aspects of the research of different teams and with the realia of the project as a whole. However much PAR had captured my attention and inspired major components of our MAR approach, the PAR method is not without its detractors and serious drawbacks.

## Challenges and Criticisms of PAR

Notwithstanding the advantages of PAR enumerated in the previous chapter, the methodology is not without its drawbacks. Some of these limitations are intrinsic, while others are only vulnerabilities given the dominant research climate of the academy. But, intrinsic or contextual, we definitely felt their pinch. In what follows, I will delineate several of the challenges and criticisms that PAR projects present and will indicate how we shaped Faith and Displacement in response to each.

---

2. We had our most sensitive field research approved by the Institutional Review Board of Fuller Theological Seminary.

## Methodological Rigor

To begin, PAR projects have often come under fire for their perceived lack of methodological controls. The PAR preference for qualitative methods, and the frequent execution of research by nonprofessionals, cause some to doubt the reliability of some PAR findings.[3] Furthermore, the goal of creating and implementing an intervention intended to substantially benefit a target population entails that researchers seldom control for one variable at a time in the ways that practitioners of the scientific method traditionally prefer. As such, the researcher is often caught on the horns of a dilemma: create an intervention that has the best chance of generating a positive change, or create an intervention that ensures assiduous methodological rigor. Action researchers

> are faced with a fundamental choice that hinges on a dilemma of rigor or relevance. If social scientists tilt towards the rigor of normal science that currently dominates departments of social science in American universities, they risk becoming irrelevant to practitioners' demands for usable knowledge. If they tilt towards the relevance of action research, they risk falling short of prevailing disciplinary standards of rigor. . . . The challenge is to find and meet the standards of appropriate rigor without sacrificing relevance.[4]

Swinging to the opposite extreme, one needs to be wary of the tendency (of action researchers!) to applaud PAR at the expense of delegitimizing conventional research methods. Even Fals Borda appreciated that "PAR techniques do not exclude a flexible use of other practices deriving from sociological and anthropological tradition, such as the open interview (avoiding any excessively rigid structure), census or simple survey, direct systematic observation."[5] Local community knowledge, however valuable,

---

3. Fabricio E. Balcazar, "Investigación acción participativa (iap): aspectos conceptuales y dificultades de implementación," Fundamentos en humanidades 4, no. 1/2 (2003): 70; and Jarg Bergold and Stefan Thomas, "Participatory Research Methods: A Methodological Approach in Motion," Forum Qualitative Sozialforschung 13, no. 1 (2012): $78.

4. Chris Argyris and Donald Schön, "Participatory Action Research and Action Science Compared: A Commentary," in Participatory Action Research, ed. William Foote Whyte (London: Sage, 1991), 86; and Ernest T. Stringer, Action Research, 3rd ed. (Los Angeles: Sage, 2007), 85.

5. Fals Borda, "Some Basic Ingredients," in Action and Knowledge: Breaking the Monopoly with Participatory Action Research, ed. Orlando Fals Borda and Muhammad Anisur Rahman (New York: Apex, 1991), 10.

should not be romanticized or absolutized, and of course not all local stakeholders will agree on what problems exist or how those problems can be addressed. Even in participatory approaches, one must recognize that different sorts of partners bring different strengths to the table, lest the contributions of formally trained researchers be cavalierly dismissed. "Action research does not mean that the researcher should or can relinquish his or her specific professional contribution and responsibility by becoming victim to some misunderstood 'democracy' in thinking that everyone must take part equally in every step of the research process."[6]

Furthermore, one needs to acknowledge that certain topics are not optimal candidates for participatory research. For example, studies oriented toward certain psychosocial problems can only with great difficulty incorporate participatory approaches, given the way that the problems in question affect potential participants.[7]

In Faith and Displacement, I felt torn between the clear methodological and indeed moral benefits of PAR approaches, and an appreciation of the advantages of the nonparticipatory approaches which my classically trained social-scientific colleagues remained keen to use. It took a while to decide that the project should not be defined by purity of adherence to either methodological canon, but by the criterion of what (in the team's judgment) would most effectively help us to serve the IDP communities.

This meant that various portions of our research were conducted in nonparticipatory fashion, such as the study of sexual violence among IDP and religious communities undertaken by our psychology team: the need for sensitivity and anonymity meant that the data from those interviews and focus groups were only evaluated by a select few researchers and were never shown even to coresearchers. Likewise, as part of a diverse suite of research tools, the economics team administered traditional surveys, with specific "closed" questions, to gather numerical data on, for example, reserve wages.

Other research protocols, by contrast, used highly participatory methods. For example, the economics team started its focus group by inviting participants to draw economic maps of a community, because doing so allowed the IDPs to tell us what aspects of their economic lives

6. Jan Irgens Karlsen, "Action Research as Method: Reflections from a Program for Developing Methods and Competence," in *Participatory Action Research*, ed. William Foote Whyte (London: Sage, 1991), 148.

7. Balcazar, "Investigación acción participativa," 70.

they perceived to be most poignant, without us determining the topics in advance. The sociology and public sector interaction teams included protocols that focused on reading Scripture with IDPs and then dialoguing about, for example, politics or poverty or forgiveness on that basis. This approach created space for the IDPs to explain how they understood the connections between their spirituality and their present lived reality. In aggregate, our research protocols were heavily participatory. But we did not shy away from applying traditional tools if they were necessitated by best standards of care for participants and by the sort of information that would be most helpful in creating the project's intervention.

## Time

A second drawback of PAR is its general incompatibility with the timelines and output orientation of most universities and funding bodies. After all, if a project is highly participatory, then it is by definition methodologically inappropriate to establish a fixed timeline along which it must unfold. Participatory Action Research also typically affirms that the topics of study be collaboratively agreed upon by participants, which means that research questions and hypotheses can only emerge gradually. Similarly, the cyclical nature of PAR implies that the problem may never be considered solved.[8]

In abstract, this all may sound well and good. Universities, however, conventionally require their researchers to adhere to preestablished timelines and funding bodies expect researchers to establish a topic and timeline *before* extending funding to scholars. Therefore, it is difficult to develop a proposal for research funding in a fully participatory fashion.[9] Likewise, although PAR ideally values the freedom to alter the path of a project in accordance with the interests of a community, funding limitations and the features of grant-making bodies' charters often do not allow radical redirection of projects.[10]

In our project, we did not have the luxury of flexibility in relation to timelines. Our grant-making body required a clear statement of topic

8. Maggie Walter, "Participatory Action Research," in *Social Research Methods*, ed. Maggie Walter (Oxford: Oxford University Press, 2010), 6–7; and Bergold and Thomas, "Participatory Research Methods," §§78, 83.

9. Bergold and Thomas, "Participatory Research Methods," §82.

10. Andrea Cornwall and Rachel Jewkes, "What Is Participatory Research?," *Social Science & Medicine* 41, no. 12 (1995): 1674.

and method in advance of deciding on funding, and we needed to get through a full cycle of action research within the scope of the three-year grant. The constraint was not ideal for protecting the participatory power of nonacademic stakeholders, but it was prerequisite to the financial viability of the project. Methodological purity does not matter much if the pristine project cannot be implemented! This meant that we had to delineate our timelines and our basic method within our leadership team, without discussing the method of the project alongside our coresearchers. Likewise, we decided that the academic researchers would analyze the findings of our field research on our own, and then discuss our analysis with the coresearchers, rather than attempting a joint analysis which would have been unrealistic given the project calendar and, frankly, the level of availability of our coresearchers.

Since our coresearchers were selected in part because they occupied key positions of local community leadership, they were also busy people. As the first year of the project unfolded, we realized that some had bitten off more than they could chew. One coresearcher ghosted us entirely after he came to appreciate the sort of collaboration that we were inviting him into. Others were, in principle, happy to share greater levels of responsibility but struggled with the frequency of back-and-forth communication entailed by a more robustly participatory collaboration. We had to pare back what we asked of coresearchers in order to respect the amount of time that they could offer. In the end, diminishing the participatory load helped *preserve* our relationship with some coresearchers, who had begun to feel overburdened by the research we were *inviting* them to do. Full-fledged forms of participation can be a gift to those who want them, but the researcher should not impose this on a coresearcher simply to satisfy the methodological purism of fellow academics.

## Impediments to Large-Scale PAR Projects

Participatory Action Research presents additional difficulties for researchers tackling larger-scale projects, for example, ones that involve hundreds of people, the intersection of multiple different systems, or diverse stakeholders with unaligned visions and goals.[11] Such projects entail major challenges for project design, processes, and final decision-making. "No

---

11. Geoff Mead, "Muddling Through: Facing the Challenges of Managing a Large-Scale Action Research Project," in *The SAGE Handbook of Action Research: Participative*

matter how broadly stakeholders are involved in planning and considering alternatives in large-scale change, the complexity of the system means the action research project may evolve in unpredictable ways."[12] Large-scale projects require the development of processes that engage multiple perspectives in accordance with the complexity of the project, but even with such processes, final harmony cannot be guaranteed. It is often impossible to achieve a consensus, and in some circumstances many stakeholders are excluded from the final decision-making process, even if the decision-makers strive to consider the input of all stakeholders. Ann Martin grasps the nettle of large action research projects when she says, "In the attempt to make sense of decision-making in a large system I have been unable to see that large groups of stakeholders can actually *decide* to move ahead with change. . . . Formal consensus, an ideal in participatory decision-making, is not possible with so many actors. The best we can hope for is some groundswell of agreement on what is most important."[13]

In short, there exists an inverse correlation between the size of a project and the extent of community participation that is feasible. Action research projects that venture larger-scale engagements should be realistic about the nature of participation that they can plausibly integrate into their design, especially when timelines and funding considerations are in play.

Faith and Displacement was a *big* project, including actors from several fields, multiple cultural contexts and languages, and a diversity of IDP communities with varying levels of access to internet and cellular communication. Yes, the project could have been imagined on a smaller scale, but what would have been lost would far outweigh what was gained. For example, we could have chosen to include fewer interdisciplinary teams. But we selected precisely the six teams we had in response to what initial research and community leaders voiced as being the most poignant and interrelated challenges. Diminishing the number of teams would have blunted the efficacy of the intervention. Alternatively, we could have reduced the number of pilot communities. But we selected

*Inquiry and Practice*, ed. Peter Reason and Hilary Bradbury (Los Angeles: SAGE, 2008), 637–39.

12. Ann W. Martin, "Action Research on a Large Scale: Issues and Practices," in *The SAGE Handbook of Action Research: Participative Inquiry and Practice*, ed. Peter Reason and Hilary Bradbury (Los Angeles: SAGE, 2008), 398.

13. Martin, "Large Scale," 399.

six pilot communities to ensure a representative sampling of ethnicities, geographic locations, ecclesial affiliations, and urban-rural balance. We could not have cut back the number of pilot communities without damaging our ability to create an intervention sufficiently flexible as to respond to the diversity of IDP communities in the nation. In other words, the project was big for good reason. But as a consequence of being so multifaceted, it became clear that various decisions would need to be taken by the teams, insofar as robust discussion of each issue by all stakeholders would be nearly impossible.

## PAR and Marxism

Shifting from logistical to ideological challenges, I would be remiss not to highlight the fact that much Latin American PAR carries a distinctively Marxist flavor, in no small part under the influences of Paolo Freire and Orlando Fals Borda.[14] These Marxist underpinnings manifest themselves in the affirmation that PAR seeks to change power dynamics in favor of the marginalized.[15] Fals Borda explained, "In [the course of] the active investigation, we work to arm the social classes of society ideologically and intellectually, so that they might consciously assume their roles as actors in history. This is the ultimate destiny of the knowledge [acquired in the research], one which validates the praxis and fulfills the revolutionary commitment."[16]

While I share a number of the values that these Marxist underpinnings of PAR seek to promote, some research projects aim at ends other than building critical consciousness in marginalized groups. Certain goals of action research can be achieved through conventional research methods. For example, to the degree to which a marginalized group is suffering, not simply because of oppression, but because of psychological, religious, familial, or environmental difficulties, the central Marxist

---

14. Marxist features are apparent in, e.g., Paulo Freire, *Pedagogy of the Oppressed*, trans. Myra Bergman Ramos, 30th anniversary ed. (New York: Continuum International, 2000), 48–57, and in Orlando Fals Borda, *El problema de como investigar la realidad para transformala por la praxis*, 7th ed. (Bogotá: Tercer mundo, 1997), 27–32, 42–46, 49.

15. See, e.g., Balcazar, "Investigación acción participativa," 67–69; and Leal, "La investigación acción participativa, un aporte al conocimiento y la transformación de Latinoamérica, en permanente movimiento," *Revista de investigación* 67, no. 33 (2009): 25.

16. Fals Borda, *Por la praxis*, 37.

preoccupation with political power dynamics should not be allowed to wag the action-research dog.

This is not to say that PAR is only useful for fostering critical consciousness. Quite to the contrary, it has benefits for all sorts of other outcomes (especially insofar as it corrects exogenous suppositions and cultivates local buy-in to research interventions). But PAR is not the only apt tool for fomenting such outcomes. As such, project designs should carefully consider to what degree the desired outcomes might be optimally supported through a mixed-methods approach that combines features of PAR with more conventional strategies.

In relation to the Faith and Displacement project, it bears noting that IDPs have been victims of violence, but their current suffering cannot be reduced to inequity qua political disenfranchisement or to lack of access to means of production. Their suffering is the result of a combination of factors, including emotional and spiritual challenges, psychological traumas, lack of professional skills appropriate to their arrival sites, and so forth. Thus, without excluding the role of the power dynamics conventionally highlighted by Marxist analysis, we sought to avoid any reductionism which might have caused us to marginalize conventional research in favor of a purely participatory approach. The conscientization goals of PAR—while laudable and valuable—were not the *summum bonum* of Faith and Displacement. Rather, fostering holistic IDP flourishing holds that privileged place. Thus, our MAR project combined elements of the participatory approach with traditional research methodologies, in order to optimize our support of holistic IDP flourishing. While IDPs' increased sense of conscientization and enfranchisement can be legitimately construed as an important aspect of their flourishing and thus one desirable outcome of participatory research, and while participatory research can provide excellent information to complement traditional research methods AND increase community buy-in to the intervention processes, we needed to acknowledge the limits of the PAR method, so as not to allow PAR ideology to hamstring our MAR project's multifaceted intervention.

## How Participatory Is Participatory?

The PAR emphasis on conscientization helps explain one of the largest debates in discourse about participatory methods: just *how* participatory does a method have to be in order to call itself "participatory"? As PAR has grown in popularity, there has been a corresponding increase in inquiry regarding what sorts of nonacademic involvement in a research endeavor are sufficient to qualify a project as *participatory*.[17]

Researchers using the PAR method are sometimes so ideologically vociferous about the importance of participation that one can feel deficient for engaging in work that is less than fully participatory. As one textbook on action research revealed, "Almost all researchers using PAR expressed doubts about the 'purity' of their projects, but it is important to remember that all research has limitations. Honesty is the best policy in such cases, but it is also necessary to explain why these limitations are not fatal to the study."[18]

Psychologist Fabricio Balcazar has provided a helpful taxonomy of participation that articulates the different modes of participation by non-academics, in accordance with the various degrees of *control, collaboration*, and *commitment* in and to the project.[19] According to Balcazar:

- In non-PAR projects, the nonacademic participants are objects of research without any control over the research. They engage in minimal degrees of collaboration and have no personal commitment to the project.
- In PAR projects with low levels of participation, nonacademic participants do not control the research, but can offer feedback on it. They serve as a committee of advisors to the academic researchers but have minimal levels of commitment to the project.
- In PAR projects with medium levels of participation, nonacademic participants have a significant level of control over the project, bearing responsibility for oversight of the project and attending team meetings. They act variously as consultants or contracted supervisors and have a real sense of belonging and commitment to the project.

---

17. Balcazar, "Investigación acción participativa," 66, notes that most PAR projects actually entail rather low levels of participation by nonacademic participants.

18. Kathryn Herr and Gary L. Anderson, *The Action Research Dissertation: A Guide for Students and Faculty* (Thousand Oaks, CA: Sage, 2012), 92.

19. Balcazar, "Investigación acción participativa," 66. The following is my translation of Balcazar's work.

- In PAR projects with high levels of participation, the
  nonacademic participants have high levels of control, either as
  equal partners in the endeavor or as leaders with the capacity
  to contract the academic researchers. They collaborate as active
  coresearchers or leaders of the research and have a sense of total
  commitment to and ownership of the research process.

Balcazar clarifies that the degree of control borne by the nonacademics might not always align with their degrees of collaboration or
commitment. For example, a high level of collaboration might coexist
with a low or medium level of participant control. Therefore, within his
framework, the researcher needs to evaluate in which of these senses
and to what degrees nonacademics are participating in a given research
project. Indeed, I would argue that coresearcher commitment should be
a factor in determining their degree of control.

Nonetheless, the major limitation of this approach is that it treats
the research project as a nonsequential whole rather than assessing the
discrete stages of the project. Nonacademics' forms of participation will
vary in different moments of the research process, and diverse community
actors will participate in diverse ways. As such, it is helpful to specify
*which actors* participate *in different moments of the process,* and in what
*different ways* that participation takes place.[20] As a matter of necessity or
design, it may be wisest for levels of participation to oscillate in different
stages of the project.

In sensitivity to the problems entailed by monolithic construals of
participatory research, Andrea Cornwall and Rachel Jewkes describe
the different ways in which participatory and conventional modes of
research might fluctuate in relation to distinct elements of the research
process. They explain that, according to an unnecessarily binary opposition between participatory and traditional approaches, conventional
research is done for the benefit of enriching scholarly understanding,
prioritizing academic knowledge, utilizing typical disciplinary conventions, and selecting topics that align with the researchers' professional
or institutional agendas. Topic selection, data collection, interpretation,

---

20. Bergold and Thomas, "Participatory Research Methods," §33; and Hella von
Unger, "Partizipative Gesundheitsforschung: Wer partizipiert woran?," *Forum: Qualitative
Sozialforschung* 13, no. 1 (2012): §31.

and analysis are done by the researchers, and no action is taken by the researcher on the basis of what was learned. By contrast, it is supposedly only in participatory projects that research is done for the purpose of taking action for local people, prioritizing local forms of knowledge, utilizing methods designed for local empowerment, and selecting topics based on local priorities. Topic selection, data collection, interpretation, and analysis are putatively done by local people and action is taken by locals as an integral part of the project.[21]

Notwithstanding this extreme binary construal of participatory research over against conventional research, Cornwall and Jewkes point out that many projects do not fall neatly into one category or the other. "In practice there is a considerable degree of fluctuation between poles, which suggests that the difference between modes of research may be more one of degree than of kind in some instances. Frequently the relationship between the two approaches takes the form of a zig-zag pathway with greater or less participation at various stages, rather than vertically following either one."[22]

Cornwall and Jewkes's "zig-zag" model permits a more nuanced description of the ways in which Faith and Displacement oscillated between conventional research approaches and participatory ones. For example, our emphases on the creation of an action and the prioritization of local people's interests and benefits are all typical of *participatory* research. By contrast, the processes of data collection and interpretation were undertaken in ways more typical of *conventional* research. And in some relations (such as the sort of knowledge that is considered valid and the audiences to whom the findings are presented), the project straddled *both conventional and participatory* methods. Cornwall and Jewkes's approach thus enabled me to think sequentially about our MAR project and to make cooler decisions about whether participatory or conventional approaches were more apt in a specific relation, given the unique contours and goals of the project.

It was the matter of participation that caused me the greatest anxiety in relation to this project's method (especially since this foray into the social sciences sent my typically low-grade imposter syndrome into overdrive). Over the course of a few years, I came slowly to appreciate

---

21. Taken from Cornwall and Jewkes, "What Is Participatory Research?," 1669.
22. Cornwall and Jewkes, "What Is Participatory Research?," 1668.

that participation itself should not be elevated to supremacy in project design; this is part of the reason that our approach is called Missional Action Research. We omitted the term "Participatory," given the hegemonic force the term has exerted in so much social-scientific literature on research methods in the past decades (notwithstanding the genuine disadvantages and liabilities that PAR entails). Since the goal of Faith and Displacement was to foster holistic IDP flourishing, and since we were working within the parameters of real chronological, institutional, and financial constraints, I had to step back and ask repeatedly whether participatory or nonparticipatory methods would be most beneficial at each stage of our undertaking[23] and for each individual team.

## Off the Beaten Path and into Broken Places

After much methodological wrangling and innumerable messages back and forth with coresearchers, we headed off to the IDP communities and the adjunct Christian churches from which our coresearchers hailed. From November 2016 through February 2017, our cadre of field researchers (selected to ensure that a representative of each of the six disciplinary teams was present in each pilot community) began to crisscross the country. We jangled our brains in buses careening down cratered rural highways, squeezed two or three helmetless people at a time onto rickety motorcycles, stuffed sweaty legs into 4×4s that crawled along treacherous mountain roads (being stopped a couple of times by groups of machete-wielding strangers in the jungle who hitched a ride from one village to the next). After bouncing along for miles in the back of a truck bed, I on occasion arrived at a remote IDP village covered head to toe in thick dust, only to have that dust later turn to slime as the ride back from the settlement coincided with a tropical deluge punctuated by tooth-rattling thunderclaps.

My boots trailed bits of mud behind me as I traipsed incongruously across the sparkling floors of El Dorado Airport in Bogotá, and I grew accustomed to the feel of the plastic-wrapped mattresses we'd enjoy at our eight-dollar-a-night motels, the nights punctuated by the nasal cries of drivers summoning travelers onto overnight buses. Sometimes things became surreal, as on the occasion of an obscure local festival in cattle

---

23. So also Karlsen, "Action Research as Method," 149.

country, when explosions of fireworks erupted at 2 a.m. and the streets were suddenly invaded by dozens of *vaqueros* (cowboys) on horseback; or when we first reached a recently founded indigenous IDP settlement, cut into rainforest so virgin that we literally bounced along the springy humous soil that sparkled with iron pyrite in the morning sun.

Upon arriving at each locale, we would hunker down with our core-searchers to hash out the details of when, where, and with whom we would hold our interviews, focus groups, and Bible studies over the coming days. Then, sometimes en masse and sometimes in drips and drabs, people would start to show up.

With time, it became clear that the participation of the members of the displaced community was a gift, because being with us meant that men were not in the fields and that women were not (generally) with their kids. Most people came in their Sunday best, the ladies nervously smoothing their skirts and men slouching down in chairs with their arms folded across their chests attempting to feign ease. I initially attributed people's nervousness to the presence of outsiders (especially one foreign outsider), but I soon realized that more was at play. Since they did not know what precisely we wanted to discuss with them, they feared that we might delve into details of the violent events that precipitated their displacement, putting them at risk of drawing the attention of the groups that had already ruined their lives once.[24] Sometimes, the presence of a local *muchacho* (a euphemism for a gangbanger) hovering outside a window would drive home the delicacy of the situation our presence created.[25]

Ensuring genuinely informed consent was also delicate, as we did not want to railroad anyone into conversing with us (perhaps agreeing to participate out of fear that they would disappoint the pastor or local leader who was our coresearcher). It took time to put people at ease and ensure that they possessed clarity about what we wanted to explore with them, especially when low levels of education or literacy complicated matters. I

24. We assiduously avoided asking about the displacement events themselves in our research groups, focusing instead on their experiences after displacement, as part of our commitment to preserve the safety of the participants.

25. We secured private locations for all but the most mundane of inquiries and in developing the field research protocols we had steered well clear of topics that could put participants at risk. On the one occasion that the psychology and sociology teams spoke with victims of sexual violence—the most sensitive topic of the project—we took participants to a secure tertiary location outside of their settlements, to ensure safety and privacy.

quickly realized that the apology "I have weak eyes" was a face-saving way to avoid saying "I can't read." I learned that for many IDPs it was confusing to be asked to print their name on one line of a consent form and then "sign" the next one, since they only knew how to write their name in one way, and in some cases, could write nothing more than their name. We had to create a special informed consent protocol to work with the Nasa indigenous people, as our first afternoon with the community made it clear that their limited knowledge of Spanish (most people there spoke Nasa Yuwe) meant that their capacity to understand even our simplified explanations was questionable. We returned to the nearby town to get cell reception, and a few of us crowded together in the narrow hallway of our motel, consulting over the phone with anthropologists from public Colombian universities about how to ensure that we honored the Nasa participants in the research process.[26]

Since the research was all part of a larger project to foster IDP flourishing, we wanted to ensure that the participants felt respected and cared for in our engagements. So we had meals together (typically hiring local women to cook for the participants), would join them for Sunday worship (generally preaching, sometimes at multiple sites in a given morning), and I did my level best to resist the urge to let the schedule of events hurry us from one thing to another (no small challenge for a type-A control freak like me). We also were sure to have a psychologist with us on every trip (either Francis Alexis Pineda or Josephine Hwang) to provide emotional care to anyone who became troubled by the topics of our inquiries.

I did not initially appreciate how vital the presence of Alexis and Josi would be . . . until I helped provide support to the first focus group run by the psychology team, up in El Granizal, on the northern border of Medellín. A group of eight women had assembled (ages ranging from 30 to 65) and the questions that Alexis asked were (I thought) gentle to the point of being innocuous ("After you were displaced, who provided you support? What sort of support would you like to have received? Did you receive support from your church?" etc.). But for a number of

---

26. Given the patriarchal nature of the Nasa tribe, it was agreed (and approved by the ethics committee) that the community leaders could give informed consent on behalf of the members of the community, providing an oral explanation of our researching in Nasa Yuwe to the members of the tribe and clarifying that they could opt out of participation at any point.

participants, even the first question called forth tears. By the second focus group, this time in the semirural settlement of La Granja, I knew that my most important job was to distribute tissues as quickly as possible.

Subsequent to the conclusion of that first group, after Alexis had spent 20 minutes counseling an older participant, I asked him about the strikingly quick reaction people had to the questions—indeed, the ladies seemed to have been surprised by their own tears. Alexis nodded soberly and explained that most of the participants had never been afforded space to process the sorrow of their displacement (and the violence that caused it). Their grief had never been given voice, so it became necrotic, an infected emotional wound that was now breaking open years after their forced migration, because today, perhaps for the first time, someone had asked how they wished that they had been cared for.

The psychology team did more than just cushion the experience of the IDP participants in the research. They ended up providing pastoral care for us field researchers. As hundreds of people uncovered their sorrows and shared their sufferings with us, we found that we held those stories, not just during the interviews, but in days and weeks thereafter. Even though most of our research tools avoided direct inquiry into traumatic events, many participants wanted, needed, someone to know about their pain. So Juan Ignacio in Batata spoke of drowning in despair after discovering that, in the town of Tierralta, literally everything you ingested—even something so simple as a banana that he could normally have plucked from any number of trees around his village—cost money, such that he eventually attempted to take his life with an electric cattle prod. Santiago in Piendamó recounted how members of his community had been tortured, hung upside down for hours with their shins levered under wooden beams, until sometimes their legs broke. And even when words were not spoken, the message came across. One indigenous pastor noticed me looking at a deep scar that sliced all the way around his thick forearm; tugging at his sleeve he muttered something about *aquellos tiempos*, "those times," and looked relieved when I changed the subject. The accumulation of exposures to so many people's stories of suffering began to weigh on us as researchers. Like lead in our stomachs, a fist in our chest, or the persistent pressure of tears at the bottom of our eye sockets, sorrow insisted on being recognized. So, we developed an evening liturgy, typically led by Alexis, of sharing something that we had heard that day that was nagging at us, tugging at us, following us. And in so doing, grief was given its due and despair was kept at bay.

## Select Discoveries

The goal of that time in the field was to understand better the diverse facets of IDP experience and to identify best practices for fostering their recovery, so that we could in turn develop church-based interventions to support the holistic flourishing of the IDPs. We were not disappointed. A detailed account of our findings exceeds the scope of this chapter many times over, but it is worth offering a taste of the findings from the field research of a few of the teams, to illustrate how the work with pilot communities gave shape to our intervention.[27]

### Missiology

The missiology team applied two tools in the field: a semi-structured key-informant interview with leaders of the Christian congregations that ministered to the IDPs,[28] and a survey responded to by 170 professional persons within those congregations. The combined results of this research were illuminating.[29]

The surveys began by asking whether congregants would be willing to apply their professional skills to serve the IDP community, as part of the mission of the church. Ninety percent of respondents answered in the affirmative (2 percent said no, and 8 percent did not respond). In stark contrast, only 29 percent of respondents claimed that they were actually serving with the IDPs.[30] We complemented these figures with the estimates of their own leaders regarding the number of participants in their current ministries in comparison to congregation size (see table). In brief, we observed a huge gap between the 90 percent of survey respondents who claimed to be willing to participate in ministries to IDPs, and those who actually are doing so.

---

27. A summary of the findings of the psychology, sociology, and public sector interactions teams is available in appendix 2.

28. Applied thirteen times, to a total of fifty people, insofar as we conducted group interviews in certain locations.

29. For a more detailed account of the missiology team's field research, see Christopher M. Hays, "El equipo de Misiología," in *Fe y Desplazamiento: la investigación-acción misional ante la crisis colombiana del desplazamiento forzoso,* ed. Christopher M. Hays and Milton Acosta (Eugene, OR: Wipf & Stock, 2022), 56–63.

30. Bear in mind that these surveys were conducted in congregations that we chose to study because they already had an impressive ministry with IDPs.

Participation of congregants in ministries to IDPs (according to pastors)

| Church | Approximate number of participants | Approximate number of congregants (excluding children) | Percent of congregant participation |
|---|---|---|---|
| El Encuentro | 25 | 430 | 5.8% |
| El Redil | 5 | 250 | 2% |
| El Libertador | 20 | 280 | 7.1% |
| Centro Evangélico Blas de Lezo | 10 | 300 | 3.3% |
| Comunidad Cristiana El Shalom | 13 | 70 | 18.6% |
| **Totals** | **73** | **1330** | **5.5%** |

We then asked what people would need to start working with IDPs, in the event that they were not already doing so (see chart below). The question was open-ended, but people's answers clustered around the themes of time, conditions (e.g., space, infrastructure, pastoral authorization), opportunities (i.e., a ministerial event or structure in which they could take part), and training/support materials. While I had guessed that time would be a primary consideration, respondents were more than twice as likely to express the need for ministerial opportunities, and more than three times as likely to say they needed training to be able to undertake service to IDPs.

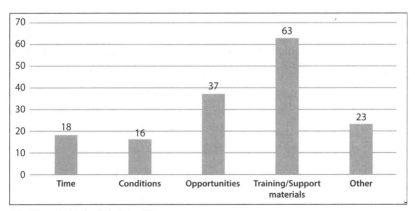

**What is needed to begin helping IDPs**

The combination of these findings indicated that local churches possessed a huge amount of untapped professional human capital, people willing (in principle) to serve the IDP population, even though they were not currently doing so. The research suggested that any intervention designed to mobilize members of Christian congregations would need to prioritize the provision of high-quality training and the creation of ministerial opportunities in which congregants could participate . . . an insight which only compounded our appreciation of the importance of our pedagogy team.

## Pedagogy

Throughout the first year of Faith and Displacement, the pedagogy team held focus groups with IDPs, conducted interviews with experienced teachers of IDPs, queried leaders of adult discipleship programs in local churches, and piloted a preliminary curriculum to test their initial approaches to education.[31] Precious little pedagogical research had previously been done on how forced displacement affects learning. The pedagogy team found, however, that IDP learning is dramatically inhibited by the traumatic experiences they have undergone, the social stigma they endure as victims of displacement, and the fact that the forms of knowledge (typically, agricultural) on which their lives relied are not appreciated or apparently beneficial in their arrival sites. Moreover, their minimal formal education prior to displacement exacerbates their difficulties in learning in their new contexts, especially when teaching is attempted in abstract or theoretical fashions, or when training sessions last multiple hours.

The team concluded, therefore, that IDP education would require the creation of trusting relationships, in order to overcome the obstacles presented by social stigmas and prior trauma. They identified that pedagogical approaches dependent upon literacy and numeracy would need to be replaced by interactive, dialogical, and practical training. In particular, the team showed that the arts could be especially potent for IDP adult education, especially when incorporating artistic forms (music,

---

31. See further Saskia Alexandra Donner, "El equipo de Pedagogía," in *Fe y Desplazamiento: la investigación-acción misional ante la crisis colombiana del desplazamiento forzoso*, ed. Christopher M. Hays and Milton Acosta (Eugene, OR: Wipf & Stock, 2022), 84–95.

handcrafts, etc.) that are traditional to their communities and predate their experience of displacement.

As a result, the pedagogy team set out to ensure that all educational materials that Faith and Displacement created for IDP participants would be highly practical and dialogical, and that emphasis would be placed on fostering the creation of long-term relationships of mutual respect between IDPs and the curricula facilitators. Activities involving literacy and numeracy were avoided in most curricula,[32] and artistic dynamics (dramas, drawing, collages, music) came to play a prominent role. This attention to IDP learning would eventually assure that the research conducted by the other project teams had its desired impact among the IDP communities rather than allowing good ideas to flounder due to clumsy pedagogy.

## Economics

The economics team applied four tools: a key-informant interview with local leaders, a focus group with IDPs, a survey for IDP participants in the focus groups, and a survey for Christian businesspeople and entrepreneurs. This combination of tools generated numerous insights.[33] For example, the focus groups with IDPs fostered dialogues about the pros and cons of different forms of income generation: creation of one's own business, working as an employee in the business of a third party, working in domestic service, and performing agricultural labor. The responses revealed a marked enthusiasm for agricultural labor and for the creation of one's own business, and significant antipathy toward the prospects of formal employment in a business or domestic service, both of which were frequently described as "enslaving."

These IDP perspectives stood in significant tension with our interviews and literature-based research. Interviewees revealed that very few IDP microenterprises succeed (less so even than businesses established by members of other vulnerable populations), and that it is difficult for IDP

32. The material on creating microenterprises did require basic numeracy, and the material on formal employment assumed basic literacy.

33. See further Christopher M. Hays, "El equipo de Economía," in *Fe y Desplazamiento: la investigación-acción misional ante la crisis colombiana del desplazamiento forzoso*, ed. Christopher M. Hays and Milton Acosta (Eugene, OR: Wipf & Stock, 2022), 131–43; and cf. Christopher M. Hays, "Collaboration with Criminal Organisations in Colombia: An Obstacle to Economic Recovery," *Forced Migration Review* 58 (2018): 26–28.

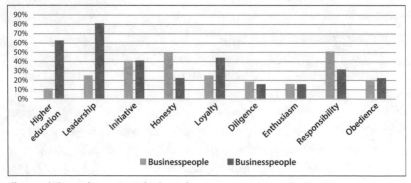

**Characteristics employers most value in employees**

farmers to make more than a subsistence living through their agricultural endeavors. By contrast, formal employment offers the sort of stability and participation in insurance and retirement structures that foster trajectories out of poverty, even though securing formal employment is no small challenge for IDPs.

Intriguing results also emerged when comparing answers to the surveys applied to IDPs and to Christian businesspeople (see chart above). For example, both groups were asked about which characteristics they most valued in employees. IDPs had exaggerated beliefs about the importance of higher education and leadership qualities to prospective employers (which perhaps indicates that they might self-exclude from the labor market because of their low levels of education); they also significantly underestimated how much ethical qualities such as honesty and responsibility matter to employers.

On the basis of these findings, the economics team concluded that it would be vital to accompany IDPs in a process of appreciating the advantages and disadvantages of different forms of income generation, as well as the benefits of formalization in both employment and the creation of new businesses, *before* making decisions about which avenue of income generation to pursue. It was clear that strategies and trainings would need to be generated to heighten the odds of success of IDP microenterprises and of those seeking formal employment, and that it would be wise to propose approaches to increase the financial viability of agriculturally based projects. We also concluded that our trainings would need to emphasize the importance of virtues like honesty and responsibility, alongside the typical hard and soft skills of training for income generation.

## Interdisciplinary Crossover in Findings

One unique advantage of this project was its trenchantly multidisciplinary character, which meant that findings that straddled different fields needed not to be overlooked or reduced to the lens of a single discipline. For example, in the early months of the project, we agreed that we could not skirt the issue of sexual violence, however delicate the matter was. Instead, we combined the skills of our sociologists (Elisabeth Le Roux and Laura Cadavid), who had experience working with victims of sexual violence, and the insights of our psychologists (Lisseth Rojas-Flores and Joseph Currier), who were experts on issues of trauma. Their social-scientific understanding could then be interwoven with the theological contributions from biblical scholars like Tommy Givens in order to think more holistically about how Christian leaders can provide better care to victims of sexual trauma.

Similarly, one of the most interesting observations from the economics team crossed over into the field of sociology. The very first activity in which the economics focus group invited IDPs to participate was the creation of an "economic map" of the community. IDP groups were given paper, markers, colored pencils, and pens, and were asked to work together to draw a map of their neighborhood or settlement, indicating thereupon each location of financial significance (where they bought groceries, sold goods, borrowed money, paid their utilities, etc.). The results were fascinating, not only on a case-by-case basis, but also when comparing one community's economic map to another.

The Nasa economic map, from the settlement La Grandeza de Dios, stood at one extreme. It was highly sophisticated, including the home of each of the fifty families in the community and differentiating between the houses that had been upgraded from bamboo to brick as part of a systematic initiative to improve the community. The map was drawn very nearly to scale and included details of the diverse crops cultivated by each family in their respective garden, as well as the aloe field and tomato greenhouses the community farms together. Many crops and livestock were drawn with great precision, a point made all the more impressive when one bears in mind the extremely low level of education of participants.

When invited to explain their map, the participants recounted that, just three years earlier, they had moved to this land and agreed jointly on the design of the settlement (complete with the traditional town plaza centered on the church, a school, a football pitch, and a combination of communal and non-communal parcels). They described how families cultivate their own choice of crops in their own parcels (though the produce of their parcels is available to those in need) and how the community labors together on their shared crops of aloe and tomatoes, which are sold as a source of external income. They highlighted that the leadership of the settlement's governor, Ananías Cuetumbo, and the community coordinator, Marco Tulio Cuspián, facilitated their productivity (see vignette 4).

As it happened, Marco Tulio had been present in the focus group, and took the lead in creating the map. After sketching some basic parameters on the map on his own, he passed a pencil to the next oldest man in the group, whom he instructed to contribute to a portion of the map. He repeated this procedure sequentially, moving from the most to the least senior of the men, and then from the most to the least senior of the women. This gave us a fascinating glimpse of how an indigenous patriarchal organization could operate, in ways that did indeed engage the contributions and creativity of all members of the group, under the guidance of a senior male leader.

At this point it bears noting that, of all the communities in which we conducted our field research, nowhere did we see such a rapid trajectory of economic advancement as among the Nasa at La Grandeza de Dios. In the course of a mere three years after arriving at that site, they had achieved nutritional self-sufficiency. They had initially built rustic huts for each of fifty families and then renovated the majority of them in cooperation with a Christian NGO. They had received three microloans (one to build greenhouses for tomatoes, and two to open small stores), acquired a water filtration system, and founded a school. What made this accomplishment doubly extraordinary is the fact that they did so without having been legally recognized by the government as IDPs, meaning that they received no government aid to help them along in this process.

None of the other IDP communities we studied exhibited anything akin to the social cohesion of the Nasa believers in Piendamó. In Cartagena, for example, we spent time in the community of Nelson Mandela, which emerged some twenty-five years previously as a *barrio de invasion* on the outskirts of the city. The neighborhood was highly visible (thanks both to its geographic location and the advocacy of various community leaders, such as our coresearchers Rachel Caraballo and Maribel Colina).

The community had therefore received a great deal of government aid, especially in the form of infrastructural development (roads, water, electricity, etc.). But the participants in the economics focus group in Nelson Mandela exhibited nothing like the economic dynamism on display in La Grandeza de Dios. Additionally, they proved incapable of cooperating in the creation of a coherent economic map. In spite of the instructions and coaxing of Alexis Pineda (whom I had asked to facilitate the group to avoid the cultural awkwardness of an affluent White American inquiring into the financial practices of a group of displaced Afro-Colombian women), instead of drawing a single, integrated map, each participant doodled in her own corner of the butcher paper we had provided, sketching out two or three items of economic import to her personally. The four pictures were in no way interconnected, in spite of the fact that the women all knew each other (two were related) and all sent their children to the same Christian school (where we conducted the focus group).

Obviously, diverse factors contribute to the economic dynamics of a community, but social cohesion and cooperation play key roles (much more so among impoverished IDP communities than in middle-class neighborhoods). Colombian researchers have established that IDPs, as a consequence of their prior traumatic experiences, evince a strong preference for low-risk, low-reward economic behaviors,[34] which entails that few are emotionally capable of undertaking the sort of risky and emotionally demanding entrepreneurial endeavors (like founding a new business or attempting to work in a field in which they have no prior experience or cultural affinity) that are vital for economic recuperation after displacement. It is our perception that the Nasa succeeded in overcoming their individual limitations and traumas in no small part because of their atypical and intense social cohesion (generated by their tribal identity, their minority religious identity, and their experience of being collectively displaced), especially under the centralized patriarchal leadership of a person like Marco Tulio who was uniquely gifted in conceiving and implementing action plans for the community. This suggested to us that

---

34. Andrés Moya, "Violence, Emotional Distress and Induced Changes in Risk Aversion among the Displaced Population in Colombia," Working Paper No. 105, Programas dinámicas territoriales rurales (Rimisp - Centro Latinoamericano para el Desarrollo Rural, 2013).

conventional forms of financial training could be complemented by initiatives to strengthen IDP social tissue, both within the IDP community and between them and non-IDPs.

Other tools ended up confirming this impression. For example, our key-informant interviews highlighted time and again that personal, holistic accompaniment was vital for the success of IDP microenterprises. Similarly, our surveys of IDP focus-group participants revealed that 94 percent of them would be interested in receiving professional mentoring, in the forms of consultations (88%), educational talks (81%), and support in bureaucratic processes such as formalization (66%) and registration (56%) of their businesses, and market analysis (53%). This highlights the degree to which they feel that the accompaniment of another person would nourish their financial advancement.

Happily, the interdisciplinary approach of our project meant that the initiatives that our sociology team created to cultivate social capital in the IDP communities would also provide spillover benefits for the economic advancement of the community. Alongside the sociology team, however, the economics team decided to work these findings into our own intervention. As it happened, 88 percent of the Christian entrepreneurs surveyed also expressed that they would be willing to mentor an IDP. Accordingly, we established that one of our key priorities in our intervention would be the development of long-term relationships of mutual respect between the IDPs and local Christian businesspeople, in addition to the creation of dynamics to establish mentoring relationships between them.

Three things bear stressing at this juncture. First, we did not go looking for information on social cohesion and economic flourishing. But because we were using open-ended participatory research tools (in this case, economic mapping), unexpected dimensions of the IDP experience surfaced. Nonetheless, and second, our findings were nonsystematic and anecdotal, lacking the methodological rigor that a conventional social-scientific study would require, which might mean that it would be hasty to take our impressions into account when creating our intervention. Here we found ourselves in the classic action research tension between rigor and relevance. We chose relevance. And so we took these unplanned and insufficiently sourced findings into account when shaping our intervention for the IDP communities. Time would tell if the gamble would pay off.

## Rigor, Relevance, and Method in Luke and Acts

My doctoral supervisor once wryly commented that graduate students often dedicate the first seventy pages of their theses to methodological throat-clearing before they get around to saying anything . . . the reader of this book might wish that I had taken his words to heart![35] But since Faith and Displacement was breaking so much new ground as a multidisciplinary, cross-cultural field-research project with a vulnerable population, we needed extensive methodological reflection to structure our work lest it collapse into a heap of arm-waving generalization. Nonetheless, however much we tried to peer into the future, eventually we reached the edges of our protocols and plans. At that point, we had to choose whether we would prioritize the scholarly guild's approbation of greater academic rigor, or the Colombian communities' pressing needs. We erred on the side of immanent relevance, but not without me feeling at times that I had left my methodological flank exposed.

I wonder if Luke the Evangelist felt similarly. Apropos of my previous comments about methodological throat clearing, New Testament scholars have written extensively on how Luke went about writing his works, and how he stacks up against other ancient biographers and historians. The passage most belabored in that inquiry is Luke 1:1–4:

> Since many have undertaken to set down an orderly account of the events that have been fulfilled among us, just as they were handed on to us by those who from the beginning were eyewitnesses and servants of the word, I too decided, after investigating everything carefully from the very first, to write an orderly account for you, most excellent Theophilus, so that you may know the truth concerning the things about which you have been instructed.

What an English translation cannot adequately communicate is that this single sentence is some of the best Greek in Luke's two volumes. You don't even get to the main verb of the sentence until the third verse, which bespeaks the stylistic refinement and complexity of this prologue! Luke's prose becomes more accessible in the subsequent verses (much to the relief of seminarian readers). Still, Luke isn't Thucydides, by any stretch.

35. A summary of the MAR method is available in chapter 8.

Luke does, however, here delineate the rudiments of the historiographic method he used to guide his research and compositional processes.

Luke's Gospel prologue reveals that he consulted testimonies that had been handed on by those who were "eyewitnesses and servants of the word" (see also 1:21–22). Likewise, 1:1 indicates that he used some written texts, and a couple hundred years of Synoptic scholarship has made it clear that Luke consulted Mark and probably either Matthew or Q.[36] Further, the portions of his Gospel that do not preserve material found in Matthew and Mark could derive from numerous other written texts (notice that 1:1 says "*many* have undertaken to set down an orderly account . . .") that have disappeared from the historical record.

Alongside his *many* written sources, Luke incorporated oral traditions. While some have argued that those oral traditions were simply floating around in the ether of Christian discourse, Richard Bauckham has made a strong case that some of the materials found in Luke derived from (or were verified by) firsthand eyewitnesses of the events.[37] Bauckham proposes that these figures were named in the Gospels as a way of "footnoting" whence Luke had sourced his unique information. This is especially probable in the case of Zacchaeus (Luke 19:1–10), Joanna, Susanna (8:3), and Cleopas (24:13–35),[38] relatively insignificant characters who, for the purposes of the story, need not have been named. Bauckham proposes that these persons are named because they functioned as guarantors of the veracity of events in which they personally took part.[39]

In addition to consulting written sources and eyewitnesses, Luke incorporated his own firsthand experiences in the composition of Acts.

36. Q is hypothetical text many Gospel scholars suppose was consulted by both Matthew and Luke. Q's existence is posited to account for the close parallels between those two Gospels at junctures where no equivalent text is present in Mark.

37. See especially Richard Bauckham, *Jesus and the Eyewitnesses: The Gospels as Eyewitness Testimony*, 2nd ed. (Grand Rapids: Eerdmans, 2017), 39–55, 129–32.

38. Keener proposes, plausibly, that Luke's oral sources for Acts included Philip, Paul himself, and any number of members of the Jerusalem church, since the we-sections indicate that Luke traveled with Paul, crossed paths with Philip in Caesarea (Acts 21:8–10), and would have had a couple of years during Paul's incarceration to consult people in and around Judea (Acts 21:15; 24:27; 27:1); and Craig S. Keener, *Acts: An Exegetical Commentary*, 4 vols. (Grand Rapids: Baker, 2012), 1:180.

39. Classical historians also took pains to consult eyewitnesses of events to which they were contemporary but in which they did not personally participate; see, e.g., Thucydides, *History of the Peloponnesian War* 1.22.2–3; and Lucian, *How to Write History* 47.

The attentive reader will notice that, although Acts trundles along as a third-person narrative for more than half the volume, in the middle of Paul's second missionary journey there is an unexpected shift. Observe how the descriptions of Paul's fruitless perambulations through the central and western portions of Asia Minor (16:6–8) all occur in the third-person plural: "*They went* through the region of Phrygia and Galatia, having been forbidden by the Holy Spirit to speak the word in Asia. When *they had come* opposite Mysia, *they attempted* to go into Bithynia, but the Spirit of Jesus did not allow *them*; so, passing by Mysia, *they* went down to Troas."

Nonetheless, in Troas Paul has a dream of a Macedonian man pleading for the apostle to cross the Aegean and preach to the people there. The next morning, Paul wakes up and out of the blue the narrative advances using first-person plural verbs: "When he had seen the vision, *we* immediately tried to cross over to Macedonia, being convinced that God had called *us* to proclaim the good news to them" (16:10). The text thus implies that, in Troas or perhaps shortly beforehand, Luke joined Paul's cadre.

The rest of the book alternates between first- and third-person narratives, but passages using the first-person plural—which scholars inelegantly call the "we-sections"—permeate the rest of the volume (16:10–17; 20:5–15; 21:1–18; 27:1–28:16). Although one could explain these sections in various fashions (e.g., literary fabrications to provide a veneer of historical verisimilitude; traces of an underlying written source, perhaps a travel log written by a companion of Paul's other than Luke), the simplest explanation is that Luke was personally present for the events described. Indeed, ancient historiographers extolled the importance of incorporating their firsthand experience of the events and locales that appear in their accounts (without thereby denigrating the importance of incorporating written sources).[40] In sum, then, Luke's historical research combined written sources, eyewitness testimony, and firsthand experience.

In spite of this diversity of sources, the works exhibit significant stylistic continuity across most materials, implying that Luke smoothed out much of what he found in his sources and expressed many things in his own language. This sort of observation is innocuous in relation to narrative descriptions, but has caused some consternation in relation to the speeches of Acts, where Peter the uneducated (Acts 4:13) Galilean

40. Polybius, *Histories* 3.4.3; Josephus, *Contra Apion* 1.47, 55; Keener, *Acts*, 1:170–73, 83–88; and Bauckham, *Jesus and the Eyewitnesses*, 118–19.

fisherman (Acts 2:14–36; 3:12–26; 4:8–11; 10:34–43; cf. Luke 5:1–3) sounds rather like Paul the (former) Pharisaic theologian (Acts 13:16–41; see especially 22:3; 26:4–5), not to mention Stephen the Hellenistic migrant who captained the Jerusalem Christian debate team (Acts 6:9–10; 7:2–53). Some have argued that the significant theological coherence (though not homogeneity) of the speeches renders dubious their historical reliability.

This skepticism has, nonetheless, been responded to by scholars like Gene Green,[41] who demonstrates that classical historians were expected to walk a line between slavish transcription of their sources (of that sort that prizes historical reliability over argumentative lucidity) and frivolously eloquent recounting of events (of the sort that showcases the author's rhetorical skills at the expense of accuracy).[42] Effective historical writings were composed with careful attention to the facts (as far as they could be ascertained), to be sure. But the premier ancient historians also wrote with the purpose of making a point, arguing a case, and they sought to shape their histories with sufficient stylistic prowess to engage the interest of their audiences. Green argues that Luke reveals this same balance of concerns in his historiography: he uses diverse sources of material conscientiously, but with stylistic attentiveness and in the service of a larger endeavor.[43] That endeavor is succinctly—if only partially—stated in Luke 1:4: that his audience(s) "may know the truth concerning the things about which you have been instructed."

In spite of approximating the approaches of leading ancient historians, Luke was still just a doctor. Even though twentieth- and twenty-first-century Western societies place physicians rather high on the intellectual scale, in the first century, medical doctors occupied more a middling position.[44] Luke was certainly not an elite intellectual, not a biographer of the stature of Plutarch, nor a historian in the ilk of Livy. While he clearly had access to some written materials, there is no evidence that he carried a library card from the library of Alexandria or that he could consult the extensive collections available to Polybius. The good doctor writes conscientiously, and at some points exhibits impressive precision (Luke's account of Paul's voyage to Rome in Acts 27 is one of the most

---

41. Gene L. Green, *Vox Petri: A Theology of Peter* (Eugene, OR: Cascade, 2019), 52–70.
42. See, e.g., Thucydides, *Histories* 1.21.1–1.22.4; and Polybius, *Hist.* 12.25.
43. Green, *Vox Petri*, 59–70.
44. Sometimes they were viewed as hacks and quacks; see Keener, *Acts*, 1:417–18.

detailed nautical texts surviving from that period). But he is probably best considered a diligent amateur among the writers of ancient biography and history. He was not worthy (on academic grounds) of being counted alongside Thucydides and Herodotus, and as far as we can tell had no pretenses of joining their ranks. He composed a biography and a history, yes, and did so in a scrupulous fashion given his limitations. But being a biographer or historiographer was not per se the end of Luke's writing. He aimed to serve the community of believers, to support the Way in a work that was at once historical and theological.[45] He seems to have valued historical rigor, yes, but his primary aim was toward relevance to the Christian community. It is in relation to this latter purpose that his work should be judged.

I have thought a lot about Luke, the medical doctor trying his hand at biography and history, perhaps well aware that his works would not have stacked up (in terms of research and rhetoric) with the elite authors of his day. Being a biblical scholar appropriating the social sciences for the purpose of MAR, working in foreign cultures and a foreign language, imposter syndrome loomed large in my mind (the same was true for a number of my theologian colleagues). So, we did our best to learn from the social scientists in our ranks. We plaited together insights from academic literature with new empirical research and our own firsthand experiences talking, eating, praying, and worshipping with IDPs. In this, we were not unlike Luke, who stitched his own lived experiences to interviews of eyewitnesses and previously written documents. Our primary goal was not to publish peer-reviewed, social-scientific research. It was to foster holistic IDP flourishing by creating an intervention founded on serious research. Precisely how we did that is the focus of our next chapter.

---

45. So, famously, I. Howard Marshall, *Luke: Historian & Theologian*, 3rd ed. (Guernsey, UK: Paternoster, 1988).

# Marco Tulio Cuspián and Ananías Cuetumbo

For a split second, Jhohan[46] and I considered leaping clear of the yawing truck bed in which we rode, as the pickup fishtailed through the mud. Heavy rains had saturated the region and we had counted ourselves lucky to find a driver who could get us to the little-known indigenous settlement of Nasa IDPs. But as we slid sideways through the muck, the end of the country lane approaching all too quickly, we questioned our prudence in selecting this rather foolhardy wheelman. Fortunately, just before running out of road, the truck rocked to a halt sideways. Relieved, we jumped down into the sludge and were soon met by the community's leaders, Marco Tulio Cuspián and Ananías Cuetumbo.

We had learned of this community of fifty displaced indigenous families from our coresearcher, Leonardo Rondón. Part of a denomination known as the Iglesia Cristiana Evangélica Nasa, in 2007 they had been expelled from their reservation by their own tribe because of cultural and economic tensions resulting from their conversion to Christianity. For six years they and hundreds of other Nasa believers lived in abject poverty, dwelling in dirt-floored, tarpaulin-roofed huts that they lashed together on the peripheries of country towns. They scratched out a meager existence while excluded from government aid, rejected by their tribe, and disdained by the townspeople among whom they begged. But in 2013, with a few thousand dollars supplied by a Scandinavian faith-based organization (FBO), they were able to purchase five hectares of virgin

46. Jhohan Centeno, researcher from the pedagogy team.

jungle several kilometers outside the town of Piendamó, in the south of Colombia. Under the leadership of Ananías and Marco Tulio,[47] this small community of displaced Nasa Christians began the most exceptional trajectory of recovery that we witnessed in all of our travels.

Ananías Cuetumbo and Marco Tulio Cuspián aren't brothers, but they have something of a Moses-and-Aaron schtick. Ananías is the community's governor. Marco Tulio is his number two in command, the community coordinator. Marco Tulio is Aaron to Ananías's Moses. Although Spanish is a second language to both men (the Nasa grow up speaking the Nasa Yuwe language), Marco Tulio holds forth with fluency and precision. He's also much more an Alpha personality. All five of the Cuspián brothers are handsome, broad-shouldered men, with prominent cheekbones, strong jawlines, and forearms heavily muscled by working the earth. Ananías, by contrast, is thin, gentle in his mannerisms and affect. Like most Nasa, Ananías is diminutive. Even though I'm short by North American standards, at five foot eight I am easily four or five inches taller than Ananías. But like Moses and Aaron, this soft-spoken governor and his more outgoing coordinator were inspiring in the way they were leading their community through their exodus from the Nasa reservation and into their own promised land, which they named La Grandeza de Dios (The Grandeur of God).

Community leadership did not come naturally to Ananías. "I'm a farmer more than anything else," he told me the first day we met, a rainy Friday in January 2017. "I didn't have the chance to study, because I was orphaned while I still young." Even the community dynamics typical to living on the reservation were foreign to him. "I didn't understand what a community was because I grew up on a mountain. My grandfather placed me on the mountain, caring for the flowers, a dog, and that's how I lived. I didn't speak Spanish or understand anything."

Still, when he grew up, Ananías became involved with the governance of the tribal council, serving in roles such as treasurer, secretary, and even interim governor. Although this governance experience did not protect him from displacement, it prepared him for the leadership he would eventually exercise in La Grandeza de Dios.

---

47. Under the influence of their tribal heritage, the Nasa believers remain strongly collectivist and patriarchal. As such, Marco Tulio and Ananías serve, together, as the linchpin of this community's recovery.

In the 1990s and early 2000s, tensions had been rising between the Christian and non-Christian Nasa. The tribal leadership became involved with an armed group which it used to push out the believers. They were threatened, beaten, and tortured. "I used to have to fight for my land with my [non-Christian] neighbors," Ananías explained. "Three times they nearly killed me, but it was by the grace of God, and nothing else that I was saved. God heard my prayer and saved me from that death, because if not, where would I be? Better said, I would already be rotting. But thanks be to God, God saved me from what those neighbors did to me. Still, I don't think badly of them. Rather, I forgive them."

Still in 2007, the eruption of the volcano El Nevado de Huila finished the job, driving Ananías and dozens of other families off the reservation for good.

The ensuing six years in squatters' camps were awful. The government refused to recognize these Nasa as IDPs, and because they had left the reservation, they were no longer eligible for the benefits indigenous people receive from the government. They were reduced to begging.

A year after our first meeting, Marco Tulio and Ananías came to the seminary. They shared more with me about that season of their lives. As we sat on a balcony, the two of them side by side, Marco Tulio disclosed that the shame of their desperate poverty left them with deep emotional scars.

"One thing that has marked me in life," he said, "was that, having the brain of a thinking man, having feet to walk, having hands to work, I had to beg for food. This is a terrible thing." Marco Tulio's eyes began to well up. Ananías covered his mouth and looked away. His throat constricting his words, Marco Tulio pushed on: "It caused me such sorrow . . . a man with a wife, carrying a child on her back. I went down to Santander. I went down to Piendamó. . . . They insulted us, they said to us, 'And you, what are you going to do?' I asked myself, 'How? How is it possible that I have to go about begging, instead of giving? Begging, being a healthy man with hands and feet?'"

After time, Marco Tulio resolved not to leave his community's fate in the hands of others. "When you are a *desplazado,* you go and you sit in the office of the government or the Red Cross," so that someone else saves you. "We're not going to do that," they decided. "We're going to settle here, we're going to organize ourselves, we're going to work this way, and then we'll see what happens."

Marco Tulio and Ananías began to make plans. They worked with NGOs and FBOs until they came up with seed money to purchase a plot of land. Ananías overcame his timidity and reached out to the local governance to authorize settlement on their land. "It was embarrassing for me to talk to those people directly, but I kept learning. I had to go visit the governor, to talk to the mayor. I was afraid. I didn't want to do it. Even entering the office of the *mushca*[48] frightened me, but thanks be to God I had that opportunity.

Permission to settle and develop their land was a turning point for the community. Under Marco Tulio and Ananías's leadership, they engaged in community planning. They set aside half the land to build a school, a church, and a plaza. They divvied up small parcels to the fifty families. With land, they could finally put generations of farming knowledge into action. Each family planted the small parcel behind their home. Collectively they cultivated the other half of the land as a communal farm for aloe, coffee, and vegetables. Using the land as collateral, they secured a few microloans, including one to build a community greenhouse (out of bamboo and thick white plastic) in which they cultivated gorgeous tomatoes that are protected from the torrential downpours that buffet the region.

One of the five Cuspián brothers, Ricardo, plays a key role in the agricultural development. Ricardo is built like a bull and always has a tool—an axe, a shovel—in his hand. The first year, we watched him digging a large hole behind his home as if he were preparing an in-ground pool. The next year, we came back to find that he had lined the hole with plastic, constructed bamboo gutters to capture the runoff of rain from the row of houses alongside his own, and had created a fish farm.

Since the size of their plot is limited—a mere five hectares (twelve acres)—the community is figuring out how to add value to what they already produce: implementing organic farming practices, transforming their aloe into yogurt and medicinal products. They are improving their school in hopes that their children can eventually secure technical and professional degrees.

Marco Tulio shared, "When I go out to Popayán [the department capital] and come back down the road to [La Grandeza de Dios], I arrive giving thanks. [I give] thanks, because the day I first arrived, it was wilderness

---

48. The Nasa Yuwe word for a nonindigenous person.

all around. But now, I look around and see my family and friends, and they are not in huts anymore, now they have another form of life."

The path forward for them has not been easy. Violence still haunts them. I mentioned above that, when we first came to La Grandeza de Dios, there were five Cuspián brothers. The third time we visited, there were only four. One of them had been murdered by armed actors. The precarity of their situation notwithstanding, Ananías and Marco Tulio are already seeking to help other Nasa believers. "We have received help and now we want to help the others, so that they can work. It's very clear to us. We have suffered. We have gone through this. We hope that no other community has to go through what we've gone through, so we are going to support them, for example, supporting education in the mountains [with the indigenous believers that remain isolated there]."

The only pilot community we worked with that collectively self-identified as Christian was La Grandeza de Dios. In contrast to the other pilot community populations, Christianity was the reason that these Nasa were displaced in the first place. Yet for these believers God was not to blame for their suffering. Rather, they pointed to God as the reason they have not only persevered but built a new life. The academic might feel a certain haughty skepticism at such pious attributions. But considering the contrast between the recovery trajectories of the Nasa believers and those of every other IDP population we studied, it is hard to deny that their flourishing has been vitally impacted by their collective faith. And by the faith of two men that have been Moses and Aaron to this wandering people.

# CHAPTER 5

# Building the Intervention

In most scenarios when I, as a theologian, pontificate about ecclesial practice (whether in class or in writing), I enjoy a cozy insulation from falsification. What pastor reads an academic journal, tries something the author proposes, and then writes to tell her or him that their advice was rubbish? Never happens. But if a practitioner did write to dispute my scholarly acumen, I could easily brush them off as a nerdy troll and return to my impenetrable tower of blithe non-falsifiability.

By contrast, when we turned the Faith and Displacement field research into a missional intervention, I felt exposed. If the conclusions drawn from our extensive study were wrong, that would become embarrassingly apparent for all to see. Nonetheless, action research always puts scholarly reflection to the test. In July 2017 it was already too late for me to rejigger our research methodology. So we dug in.

As detailed in the last chapter, our initial investigation revealed that Christian professionals in local churches were keen, *in principle*, to help foster IDP recovery. But their actual involvement paled in comparison to their notional interest. The primary reasons for that disparity were a lack of training and a scarcity of opportunities to work with the displaced. As such, we decided *to create an educational intervention to mobilize the human capital of local churches, along with that of the IDPs themselves, for the purpose of fostering holistic IDP flourishing within the scope of the integral mission of the church.* This chapter describes how we created that intervention.

## Conceiving an Educational Intervention
## (July 2017–June 2018)

Our educational intervention—the *Action* of our Missional Action Research project—was designed to unfold in three successive steps, each focused on a distinct audience.

- Step 1: convince local pastors that ministry to the IDPs should be part of their holistic mission, and that their congregations possess the human capital necessary for such an undertaking.
- Step 2: mobilize Christian professionals to foster the multidimensional flourishing of IDPs.
- Step 3: build the capacities of IDPs through curricula implemented by Christian professionals in the context of a long-term relationship with the displaced community.

Each step of the process in this educational intervention required the creation of innovative curricula that converted the findings of every project team's field work into ecclesial action. We agreed that each team would create at least one curriculum focused on Christian professionals in their respective fields, then a second curriculum for those same professionals to implement with the displaced. For example, the sociology team was tasked to create (a) a curriculum for training social workers, youth leaders, and sociologists to work with IDPs from within their professional skill set, and (b) a second curriculum for those same professional participants to implement with IDPs, based on what they learned in the first curriculum. Owing to the centrality of curricular creation at this stage of the project, in the summer of 2017 the pedagogy team became the queen of Faith and Displacement.

### Six Principles for Curriculum Development

On a humid August afternoon, after finishing the day's seminary lectures, we gathered in a stuffy classroom, where the pedagogy team laid out what they had concluded about IDP education on the basis of their field research.

The fundamental principles they had established for IDP teaching-learning processes numbered four:

1. *Teaching processes with IDPs should forge deep and restorative relationships between the church and the displaced communities.* A short-term training bereft of personal connection will almost certainly fizzle out. Having suffered so much social isolation, IDP recovery will likely transpire in the context of deep and lasting relationships.

2. *The work should take its point of departure from the needs and interests of the displaced and should utilize the resources (human and otherwise) already available in their communities.* Without a felt emotional connection to the topics being addressed, and without a sense of the availability of the resources needed to generate change, IDP interest will wane quickly and devolve into passivity as they wait for outside entities to take action on their behalf.

3. *The learning activities should be participatory and should not depend on literacy or numeracy.* Given the low levels of antecedent IDP education, we needed to avoid training dynamics that required participants to read, write, or use even simple arithmetic. Although the curricula for the pastors and Christian professionals could include written material, the content for IDPs would need to utilize practical, oral, dialogical, artistic, and recreational dynamics to ensure active IDP participation.

4. *Each curriculum created would need to combine cognitive, affective, and practical outcomes.* While growth in knowledge could not be excluded from the educational materials, the appropriation of that knowledge would depend on an emotional buy-in and would require transformation into concrete skills.

Two further considerations would give form to the project materials, beyond the pedagogical criteria.

5. *The project design required the thoroughgoing integration of social sciences and theology.* As such, each lesson of each curriculum was required to combine insights from nontheological fields with contributions from Christian Scripture, doctrine, or ethics.

6. Furthermore, given the participatory commitments of the MAR method, teams were encouraged *to incorporate the insights of coresearchers into the materials.* For example, one of the coresearchers of the missiology team was Pastor Olger González (see vignette 3). His personal project systematized his experience of the diverse ways in which IDPs suffer as a consequence of displacement as well as the ways in which he had learned to mobilize his local church to minister to IDPs. His report was hardly structured like an academic document; rather, it had the feel of a sermon. We decided, therefore, to turn his report into scripts

for two short videos, one on multidimensional IDP suffering and another on the mobilization of the congregation in the ministry to IDPs. These videos, in turn, featured prominently in the first two lessons of the inaugural curriculum of Faith and Displacement, entitled *The Integral Mission of the Church*.[1] The videos garnered enthusiastic feedback from users, who warmed to the opportunity of receiving advice from a pastor with decades of hands-on experience.

This was, plainly, not the way we normally designed university syllabi. In fact, we felt rather out of our depths. The theologians remained unsure what to do with the social scientific data. The social scientists were uncertain about how to integrate Christian theology into their proposals. Nobody had clarity about what exactly the coresearchers would contribute. We all felt daunted by the prospect of trying to train IDPs without recourse to reading assignments! But we understood that the impact of our intervention hung on its pedagogical efficacy. Accordingly, a member of the pedagogy team was assigned to consult with the other project teams about each material they would develop. In other words, the pedagogues took us back to school.

## Initial Samples and Feedback

Time, however, was not on our side. We had less than a year to draft, film, edit, print, and ship all our content. Two curricula per team, multiplied by six teams, amounted to a dozen educational materials. Moreover, the process was supposed to be participatory, meaning that materials needed to be developed in conversation with a wide variety of stakeholders.

To get the ball rolling, each team was allowed three months to create a sample lesson of their curricula. During this brief window, we worked through the written content with our coresearchers, had a graphic designer lay out the curricular manuals, and recorded our first videos. Later that November we convened the first Faith and Displacement conference, this in order to secure the insights of key stakeholders and scholars.

---

1. For links to the video, see Christopher M. Hays, Isaura Espitia Zúñiga, and Steban Andrés Villadiego Ramos, *La misión integral de la iglesia: cómo fortalecer o crear un ministerio a favor de personas en situación de desplazamiento: manual del facilitador* (Medellín: Publicaciones SBC, 2018), 28–30, 48–50.

The conference proved a rousing success, well beyond what we had predicted. Participants included political figures (like the director of religious affairs for the National Ministry of the Interior); scholars from various theological and social-scientific disciplines; denominational leaders; FBO and NGO workers; and even tribal leaders from the Nasa people.

At times, the event felt like a traditional academic conference, with plenary sessions, panel discussions, and break-out groups for hashing out academic ideas. But when our coresearchers shared about their own experiences, the register changed dramatically. I vividly recall Pastor Ramón González, the coresearcher of the economics team, nervously summarizing his own research project. Ramón had chronicled the economic aftershocks of the mass displacement from Batata to Tierralta (see vignette 2). But the task had proven difficult, since he had no post-secondary education. I had worked with him on various drafts, which he sent to me in WhatsApp pictures of the notes he had deliberately penned on a yellow notepad. While his presentation was far from Ciceronian, the pastor captivated the audience with his incisive firsthand insights. No doubt about the value of a participatory approach to research lingered in the minds of those in attendance at that session.

The conference afforded an opportunity to share samples of ecclesial curricula with attendees. Here, the religious leaders shone. They provided insights into logistical challenges we had not foreseen, commenting on how different dynamics could confuse rural participants, or letting us know where the verbal register of the text had crept out of the comfortable range for non-scholars. We gathered feedback on each session, to feed our revision processes.

When people pointed out deficiencies in our materials, we fought the urge to defend our approach and instead inquired how they would improve our drafts. One attendee—Pastor Fernando Valencia of the church El Encuentro con Dios in Bogotá—told me that the curriculum *The Integral Mission of the Church* should incorporate warnings against common mistakes (the sorts of things he had learned the hard way in his church's work with IDPs). I nodded enthusiastically . . . and asked if he would write it for me. Which he did.[2]

Time and again, however, we heard the refrain that this undertaking was long overdue, that Faith and Displacement responded to questions

---

2. Hays, Espitia Zúñiga, and Villadiego Ramos, *La misión integral: manual*, 82.

that had afflicted local ministries for years. "When can we have Faith and Displacement in our church?" people asked. "How can we participate?"

In sum, the participatory dynamics of the Faith and Displacement conference confirmed that we were on the right track. But stakeholders from diverse walks of life also helped us to identify shortcomings and to overcome them.

## Completing the Intervention

The euphoria of the generally warm feedback received at the conference lasted one night. Monday morning rolled in and the now familiar sense of panic enveloped me once again as I remembered that we had just a handful of months to complete all the curricular materials. We leapt into a flurry of activity that from the outside must have looked like a cartoon-ish cloud of dust and tumult, from which we emerged six months later, panting and grinning.

Although our goal had been to create a dozen curricula by mid-2018, we actually generated fifteen. By the end of the grant in 2019, a total of nineteen curricula had been finalized, proof of the great enthusiasm and buy-in of the project teams. Thanks to the guidance of the pedagogy team, the curricula incorporated a wide variety of educational strategies including videos, games, visual images, audio recordings, dialogues, art, spiritual reflections, activities applying practical skills, songs, puzzles, dramas, and sports.[3] To support the curricula, project researchers and even seminary students created original artistic productions: four original songs, music videos, poems, and paintings.[4]

Although nineteen curricula were created, the project design did not entail that individual communities would implement all or even most of these curricula. Rather, only one introductory curriculum is essential for all communities: *The Integral Mission of the Church*.[5] In the course of that curriculum, church leaders are guided through a process of identifying how the human capital of their congregations corresponds to the needs of the local IDP population. Based on those correspondences, the

---

3. The curricula and supporting materials (audio recordings, games, videos, images, etc.) are freely available on the project website, www.feydesplazamiento.org.

4. Since one of our pilot communities was from the Nasa indigenous tribe (see vignette 4), twenty-four of the videos were subtitled in the Nasa Yuwe language.

5. Hays, Espitia Zúñiga, and Villadiego Ramos, *La misión integral: manual.*

curriculum helps the leaders to decide which materials to use to train the professional members of their congregation, so that those professional persons might in turn implement the curricula designed for IDPs. Accordingly, communities can construct a bespoke ministerial program for IDPs, instead of being straitjacketed by an inflexible curriculum or a program designed for an incompatible social context.

### The Incorporation of Social-Scientific Insight in the Curricula

What most set the Faith and Displacement materials apart from other faith-based curricula was the thoroughgoing integration of insights from the social sciences. In every curriculum, ecclesial practices were infused with vital insights from "secular" fields.

To illustrate, the curriculum *Peacemakers Tournament*, from the sociology team, fused Christian ethics with the Harvard method of conflict resolution in order to train Christians to teach nonviolent conflict resolution through football tournaments.[6] The psychology team applied findings from trauma studies to help equip pastors to provide trauma-informed care to IDPs in *Church Leaders as Agents of Healing After Trauma*.[7] And the pedagogy team applied their findings about IDP andragogy in a curriculum to resource the teachers within congregations to use art-based (pictorial, oral, musical, dramatic, craft-based, and game-based) educational methods with IDPs.[8]

Providing a detailed account of how each of the nineteen project curricula synthesized Christian theology and the social sciences would abuse the reader's patience, so I will limit myself to providing one in-depth example. It flows from our experience with the curriculum called *The Integral Mission of the Church*. This material serves as the Faith and Displacement project's point of the spear. Directed to church leaders, this curricular package demonstrates not only that their church's mission should entail holistic care for victims of the violent conflict, but also explains *how to mobilize the human capital of their congregation for that task*.

6. Duberney Rojas Seguro, *Torneo conciliadores de paz: una propuesta de desarrollo de capacidades en entornos de conflicto* (Medellín: Publicaciones SBC, 2018).

7. Lisseth Rojas-Flores et al., *Líderes de las iglesias como agentes de sanidad después del trauma* (Medellín: Publicaciones SBC, 2018).

8. Saskia Alexandra Donner and Leonela Orozco Álvarez, *Las artes: una herramienta eficaz para la enseñanza de adultos en situación de desplazamiento* (Medellín: Publicaciones SBC, 2018).

The curriculum communicates this fundamentally Christian message through theological means, beginning with Scripture studies. For example, a discussion of 1 Corinthians 12 explores how the diverse members of the body of Christ equip the church to respond to the variegated needs of the displaced community.[9] This Bible study is paired with a video from our coresearcher Pastor Olger González and an audio recording of selections from our interviews with IDPs,[10] which generate empathy for the multifaceted sufferings of the displaced. Thus, audiovisual materials cooperate with biblical reflections to achieve the curriculum's *cognitive* and *affective* objectives. But in order to accomplish the *practical* objectives of beginning to constitute a team of workers to contribute to the church's ministry with IDPs, we incorporated strategies from the social sciences.

The particular branch of the social sciences we applied was development studies, specifically an approach called Asset-Based Community Development (ABCD),[11] which fosters community development by focusing attention on the abilities of community members, especially of those vulnerable community members who can too easily become objectified by development workers. By zeroing in on the strengths of community members, ABCD avoids the objectification of marginalized populations and helps reverse their learned sense of impotence.[12]

Asset-Based Community Development operates on the conviction that communities will participate more proactively in their own transformation if they begin with an attentiveness to their own strengths and resources, as opposed to focusing on their needs and besetting

9. Hays, Espitia Zúñiga, and Villadiego Ramos, *La misión integral: manual*, 50–53.

10. Hays, Espitia Zúñiga, and Villadiego Ramos, *La misión integral: manual*, 59–60.

11. Our project's adaption of that approach for Colombian IDPs benefitted greatly from the work of the two seminarians at Fundación Universitaria Seminario Bíblico de Colombia (FUSBC). Steban Andrés Villadiego Ramos was part of the missiology team and played a key role in adapting ABCD for Faith and Displacement. He and his identical twin brother, Andrés Steban (*sic*), provide a detailed account of how ABCD was incorporated into the project in their thesis: Steban Andrés Villadiego Ramos and Andrés Steban Villadiego Ramos, "Una apropiación misio-teológica de una estrategia de desarrollo comunitario para la movilización de laicos y PSD (personas en situación de desplazamiento) en ministerios a favor de las PSD" (Undergraduate thesis, Fundación Universitaria Seminario Bíblico de Colombia, 2018), from which the following discussion draws.

12. John P. Kretzmann and John McKnight, *Building Communities from the Inside Out: A Path toward Finding and Mobilizing a Community's Assets* (Evanston, IL: Asset-Based Community Development Institute, 1993), 6–7.

difficulties.[13] A primary focus on needs and external actors can reinforce the sense that only outsiders (government agencies, NGOs, etc.) can
solve a community's problems.[14] Therefore, ABCD raises the awareness
of community members about their own potency and helps them apply
their skills for their collective well-being.[15]

This focus on empowering the vulnerable applies not only to the IDPs,
but also to the non-IDP churches that seek to minister to IDPs. Most of
the evangelical churches that Faith and Displacement works with are
themselves poor and easily succumb to the notion that social change
can only be achieved by the government. ABCD helps awaken both poor
non-displaced and displaced people to their own power to be agents of
change.

What is more, ABCD enjoys substantial compatibility with two of the
key tenets of integral missiology (see chapter 2). First, ABCD emphasizes
the participation of those typically viewed as "non-leaders" or "nonprofessionals," just as integral missiology underscores the missional potency
of lay persons (as opposed to just focusing on clergy). Second, just as
integral missiology engages with concrete situations of injustice, so also
ABCD focuses its efforts in response to specific local community challenges, without allowing those challenges to cripple the self-perception
of local actors.

We adapted two tools of ABCD for incorporation in *The Integral Mission of the Church*: a game called *We Can* and a *Skills Inventory*. *We Can*
features in the first lesson of the curriculum.[16] It helps awaken the church,
at an affective level, to the abundance of human capital in their congregations, thereby stimulating congregations to dream big about what they
might collectively do to accompany IDP flourishing. The *Skills Inventory*
is then implemented following the second lesson of *The Integral Mission of*

---

13. Alison Mathie and Gord Cunningham, "From Clients to Citizens: Asset-Based
Community Development as a Strategy for Community-Driven Development," *Development in Practice* 13, no. 5 (2003): 475.

14. Kretzmann and McKnight, *Building Communities*, 4; and Hanna Nel, "A Comparison between the Asset-Oriented and Needs-Based Community Development Approaches
in Terms of Systems Changes," *Practice* 30, no. 1 (2016): 37.

15. Kretzmann and McKnight, *Building Communities*, 17–18, 27.

16. Hays, Espitia Zúñiga, and Villadiego Ramos, *La misión integral: manual*, 31–39.

*the Church*, helping the congregations systematically to tabulate the talents of their church and to map those talents over the needs of the IDPs.[17]

The game *We Can* consists of one hundred cards, each with a different skill (everything from baking and painting to large appliance repair). The players sort the cards into different piles, depending on whether they or someone in their community possesses each ability, or not. The game invariably generates delight in the participants as it brings to light hidden talents that had never surfaced in the context of the church community.

Nonetheless, insofar as *We Can* was developed in Chicagoland, the game required significant adaptation for the Colombian context. Most obviously, the game had to be translated into Spanish. Additionally, we worked a swath of agriculturally based skills into the cards (fertilization, beekeeping, transporting cattle, etc.).

We also realized that, despite the game's simplicity, the written instructions that sufficed for the US audience were inadequate for our purposes, since board and card games are less common in Colombia. Consequently, we created a comic strip representing game play in order to help facilitators understand how the dynamic would unfold.

But even the comic strip generated contextual challenges. When our graphic designer (a dark-skinned Colombian) brought us a first draft of the comic, the characters were all young, professionally dressed, and white-skinned . . . largely unlike most of the parishioners and IDPs who would participate in the game. So we revised the images: we darkened the characters' skin and hair to reflect the palette of Andean ethnicities; we removed a high-volume American hairstyle from one character; and we swapped out blazers and waistcoats for Colombian styles of shirts.

The adaptation of *We Can* went hand in hand with a similar procedure for the *Skills Inventory*, which surveys people's professional, personal, and community-organizing abilities. As with the game, the *Skills Inventory* needed to be translated from Spanish and agricultural abilities were incorporated into the survey.

The *Skills Inventory* was originally designed as a paper survey, and so we too created a hard-copy version of the inventory for our purposes. We also decided to take a stab at digitizing the survey, using a bit of freeware that allowed participants to apply the *Skills Inventory* directly from their

---

17. Hays, Espitia Zúñiga, and Villadiego Ramos, *La misión integral: manual*, 60–62, 100–102.

cellphones. We also created detailed written instructions, with accompanying images, on how to apply the *Skills Inventory* in hard copy and digital forms, in hopes of minimizing user confusion. (Eventually, we would discover that we were not *entirely* successful in that undertaking!)

The incorporation of tools from Asset-Based Community Development into the curriculum *The Integral Mission of the Church* illustrates how the Faith and Displacement teams integrated social-scientific insights into diverse aspects of their educational interventions. It moved beyond identifying abstract points of contact between Christian faith and the social sciences, and drilled down into concrete practices and tactics developed by social scientists. Those practices were then worked into a Christian educational intervention with a theological framework. Finally, the tools had to be adapted for a largely rural Colombian culture. Slippage at any one of the aforementioned junctures would hamper the impact of the fusion significantly. In other words, there were ample opportunities for this interdisciplinary experiment to break down.

## Falling Short

In comparison to writing academic articles and grading papers, creating this interdisciplinary education was a ridiculous amount of fun. We got to "star" in videos, create games and puzzles, and produce illustrations and comics. As a bonus, the critical feedback the pedagogy team doled out stung far less than the nasty comments on one's journal articles from the notorious Reviewer #2. Nonetheless, I would be remiss to omit how, at times, we failed to live up to our own plans and ambitions.

In the first place, even prior to piloting the intervention, it was evident that not *all* the scholars had fully heeded our (repeated) admonitions to write their materials at a nonacademic level appropriate to a lay readership. While most responded dutifully to the prodding of the pedagogy team, a couple curricula (I shan't name titles!) landed in our laps more like scholarly compositions than ecclesial resources. Eventually, however, time ran out. We were forced to go to print with a pair of curricula that we knew to be pitched too high for our audience.

So also, the experience of working with coresearchers was not always as idyllic as the PAR literature romantically portrayed it. While certain coresearchers (like Pastor Olger González) delighted us with their insights and contributions, not everyone performed at the same level. One coresearcher ghosted us after our November 2017 conference, leaving his wife in the awkward position of making excuses for him when we called! Others were dynamite in person but less than attentive to deadlines. Even the coresearchers who were exceedingly conscientious required sustained accompaniment in rudimentary tasks (as when Pastor Ramón González sent me handwritten notes with a very loose logical thread, which required me to coax him through numerous drafts before he eventually produced a downright fine contribution).

In brief, the biggest benefit of participatory methodology is also its greatest bane: namely, the fact that coresearchers are definitionally nonacademics. That makes them a source of unique insights, but it also means that they work with significant educational limitations, not to mention that they have other obligations and may not share professional suppositions about things like deadlines or follow-through. As sketched out in chapter 4, large participatory projects almost always fall short of the participatory ideal.

The journey across disciplinary, social, professional, and cultural boundaries is bound to be bumpy. Imperfect communication and misunderstandings are unavoidable. Consequently, one's definition of overarching success needs to accommodate a mixture of smaller failures and modest interim victories in the pursuit of a long-term goal. Luke illustrates something analogous to this in his narrative of Paul's experience preaching in Athens (Acts 17), where the apostle did his own interdisciplinary and cross-cultural theology, speaking before the Areopagus council.

## Creating Interdisciplinary Theology
## (Paul's Areopagus Speech in Acts 17)

Paul's Areopagus speech provides fascinating insight into how the apostle (or at least Luke) conceived of doing interdisciplinary, cross-cultural theology in the service of mission while remaining realistic about the challenges presented by such an ambitious endeavor.

Paul's encounter with the Athenian leaders occurred after he had passed perhaps a couple of weeks in Athens, debating with his countrymen in the synagogues on the sabbath and spending the rest of the week rattling around the city while he awaited the arrival of Timothy and Silas from Macedonia (Acts 17:14–17). The abundance of idols in the polytheistic city grated on Paul's monotheistic sensibilities, an offense that he voiced to the Athenians in the agora, the city marketplace which served as the venue for all manner of public interactions, including philosophical discourse. Luke specifies that Paul crossed verbal swords with exponents of two of the preeminent philosophical schools of the age: the Stoics and the Epicureans (v. 18).

Unfortunately, Paul's initial critiques of idolatry did not connect readily with his non-Jewish Athenian interlocutors. While Paul's discourses in the synagogues could draw on a shared Jewish religio-cultural framework and lexicon, the Athenian worldview differed dramatically from Paul's. These differences generated barriers to communication.

Luke narrates two ways the Athenians misunderstood Paul's message. First, because of their polytheistic outlook, when the Athenians heard Paul preaching about *Iēsous kai anastasis*, "Jesus and the Resurrection," they assumed that the grammatically feminine term *anastasis* was the proper name for Jesus's consort (v. 18)! The concept of resurrection from the dead—however well known to Jewish people in the first century— remained so outlandish to the Greek mind that they concluded that *anastasis* must be a person's name. In short, the Athenians surmised that the apostle was the herald of two foreign deities (notice the plural noun, "divinities," in v. 18): Jesus and his goddess girlfriend, named "Anastasia!"

The second challenge Paul had to overcome was the calumny that he was a *spermologos*; v. 18. The NRSV translation "babbler" does not adequately capture the nuance of the word *spermologos*.[18] The term was something of an elitist philosophical "burn" toward amateur, eclectic philosophers, who picked up philosophical commonplaces from *florilegia* (sayings collections in wide circulation in the ancient world) and strung them together with no regard for the compatibility of the diverse schools of thought from which they arose.[19] Basically, Paul's message did not possess philosophical pedigree recognizable to the Athenians, given that it derived fundamentally from the Jewish tradition and not gentile philosophy. But because his discourse included points of contact with contemporary philosophical discourse (as will be laid out below), his listeners lumped him in with the eclectic philosophical amateurs that

18. Literally "seed-word," this term evokes the image of birds indiscriminately pecking at a mixture of seeds in the dirt.

19. Plutarch, *Moralia* 516C; Demosthenes, *De corona* 127; Philostratus, *Vita Apollonii* 5.20; and Craig S. Keener, *Acts*, 3:2596n956.

flocked to the agora and diminished the quality of erudite discourse in the great city.

Paul is presented with the opportunity to counter these two misunderstandings when he is brought before the Areopagus council to provide a fuller account of his teachings. The rather polite English rendering of vv. 19–20 ("May we know what this new teaching is that you are presenting? It sounds rather strange to us, so we would like to know what it means") does not quite capture the tension behind this meeting. An ancient reader with even the most rudimentary understanding of Athenian history would recognize that, as Paul is brought before the council and charged with introducing new deities, Luke evokes the trial of Socrates, who was brought up on similar charges and in the end fared rather worse than Paul.[20] Thus, when Paul opened his mouth to address the council, his own well-being was at much at stake as were his philosophical reputation and the clarity of his monotheistic gospel.

Luke presents Paul as giving a speech that is thoroughly Judeo-Christian in its content: he affirms the existence of a single creator deity, the origin of all humans in a single progenitor, the coming day of judgment, and the resurrection of the dead, thereby dispelling the erroneous notion that Paul sought to introduce a pair of new foreign deities. The message in no way runs afoul of the numerous sermons preached by Peter, Stephen, and Paul. Nonetheless, the argumentative approach of this discourse differs wildly from the other speeches of Acts. In all the other sermons of the book, Scripture features prominently. Paul, however, appreciates that Jewish Scriptures would hold no sway for his audience of pagan philosophers. He instead proceeds by way of arguments that by and large would have been congenial to the Stoic (if not Epicurean) members of the council.

Paul begins by claiming that the God he preaches is not a foreign or novel deity per se but is in fact the divine entity to whose existence the Athenians stipulated by making an altar "to an unknown God" (v. 23). After identifying his God with that hitherto anonymous deity, Paul undertakes to demonstrate that it is unfitting for that deity to be worshipped via the medium of idols. The God Paul proclaims is the creator of all the earth and by dint of that potency has no need of the manual services

---

20. Xenophon, *Memorabilia* 1.1.1; Plato, *Apologia* 24B-C; *Euthyphro* 3B; and Beverly Roberts Gaventa, *Acts*, Abingdon New Testament Commentaries (Nashville: Abingdon, 2003), 249.

pagans were wont to perform for their gods in, for example, building them shrines.

Both of Paul's affirmations in vv. 24–25 (that God is not served by human hands nor lives in man-made temples) would have found ready assent among the Stoics.[21] The Stoics conceived of the Divine as an incorporeal rational principle called the *logos*: an animating force which pervaded the universe, giving order and life to all things. So when Paul disputes the adequacy of physically representing a deity in the form of an idol and building a shrine for that god, he is preaching to the Stoic choir.

Paul goes on to argue that idols are unnecessary for mediating the divine presence insofar as God is eternally present with humans, guiding the affairs of their history, and indeed sustaining their very existence (vv. 26–28). God "is not far from each of us," Paul asserts (v. 27), perhaps eliciting the nods of his Stoic listeners.[22]

To buttress that declaration, Paul cites a pair of pagan authors (v. 28). The first quotation, "In him we live and move and have our being," most likely derives from the sixth-century poet Epimenides.[23] Although Epimenides predates Stoicism proper by at least a century, the Stoics agreed that the Deity pervades all things.[24] The second citation ("For we too are his offspring") is from the third-century poet, Aratus (*Phaen.* 5).[25] The belief that humans are the offspring of the divine was widespread in ancient thought and was also embraced by Stoic thinkers.[26] Supported by these two citations, Paul contends that, insofar as God pervades all

21. Zeno, the founder of Stoicism, famously denied that deities needed to live in temples; Diogenes Laertius, *Lives of the Eminent Philosophers* 7.32–34; Plutarch, *Mor.* 1034B; Seneca, *Epistulae morales* 95.47; Keener, *Acts*, 3:2639n3383; and Joseph A. Fitzmyer, *The Acts of the Apostles: A New Translation with Introduction and Commentary*, Anchor Bible (New York: Doubleday, 1998), 608. Against the notion that God is served by human hands, see, e.g., Seneca, *Epistulae morales ad Lucilium* 95.48–50.

22. For similar affirmations, see Seneca *Ep.* 41.1; Dio Chrysostom, *Oratio* 12.27–28; C. Kavin Rowe, *World Upside Down: Reading Acts in the Graeco-Roman Age* (Oxford: Oxford University Press, 2009), 37; and Fitzmyer, *Acts of the Apostles*, 608.

23. On the complexity of adjudicating the source of the quotation, see Keener, *Acts*, 3:2657–59.

24. Aratus, *Phaenomena* 2–4; Epictetus, *Diatribai* 1.6.23–24; Diogenes Laertius, *Lives of the Eminent Philosophers* 7.2.38; and Keener, *Acts*, 3:2659.

25. Aratus had known Zeno (the founder of Stoicism), although he was properly a disciple of a Peripatetic (i.e., Aristotelian) philosopher.

26. Seneca *Ep.* 44.1; Dio Chrysostom *Or.* 30.26; Epictetus *Diatr.* 1.6.40; Diogenes

our existence and insofar as humans in their rational corporeality are the offspring of the divine, it is ludicrous to think that the Deity could be adequately represented by an inanimate idol (v. 29). That point too would have resonated with Stoic listeners.[27]

In brief, Paul's speech constructs a polemic against idolatry—the phenomenon that had grieved him since his arrival in the city (v. 16)—without making the slightest appeal to the Jewish Scriptures. He instead appeals to concepts and literary sources that would have carried weight with his pagan audience—at least with those of a Stoic inclination. This is not to say that Acts simply pitches nascent Christianity as Stoicism by another name. Although he assiduously seeks common ground and compatible language, he puts pagan philosophical ideas to the service of a Jewish and Christian message.[28]

Eventually, however, Paul runs out of common ground with the Stoics and is obliged to go off-piste. Having completed his argument against idolatry, he calls his audience to repentance therefrom, warning of the forthcoming eschatological judgment of humanity and resurrection of the dead (vv. 30–31). By returning to the topic of resurrection, Paul dispels the confused Athenian surmise that *anastasis* (resurrection) was the proper name of a goddess. In so doing, however, he runs clear off the pagan metaphysical map.

Greek philosophers had no concept of resurrection of the dead. Epicureans disputed the very notion of an afterlife. Others maintained diverse beliefs about postmortem spiritual existence, although the shape of that existence varied depending on whether one queried, for example, a Middle Platonist or an adherent of more traditional Greek religion. Stoics, whose views overlapped with some aspects of budding Christian metaphysics, believed that, upon death, the rational human soul would flow back into the principle divine *logos*. Still, no pagan Greek conception of the afterlife included resurrection of the dead. Indeed, as Apollos himself was reputed to have said before the Areopagus, "When the dust has drawn up the blood of a man, once he is dead, there is no ἀνάστασις

---

Laertius, *Lives of the Eminent Philosophers* 7.1.147; Marcus Aurelius 10.1; Rowe, *World Upside Down*, 38; and Keener, *Acts*, 3:2663.

27. Seneca, *Ep.* 31.11; Gaventa, *Acts*, 252; and Rowe, *World Upside Down*, 35.

28. Rowe, *World Upside Down*, 27.

(*anastasis*, resurrection)" (Aeschylus, *Eum.* 647–48).[29] Consequently, when the council realized that Paul really was preaching the physical resurrection of the dead, many of them scoffed (v. 32). That was a bridge too far for most of them, Stoic or not. Paul's erudite creativity notwithstanding, his basic fidelity to a Jewish-Christian eschatology blunted his message's impact on the pagan council members.

Nonetheless, limited acceptance ought not be confused with failure. It should not be overlooked that Paul did successfully counter the accusation that he proclaimed foreign deities—both by identifying his God with the Athenian "unknown god" and dispelling confusion over the personal nature of *anastasis*. In so doing, he skirted Socrates's condemnation and the unappetizing prospect of quaffing a Hemlock cocktail.

What's more, Paul's audacious rhetorical sally did eventually win over some of Athens's philosophical elite. Although much of the council lost interest when Paul departed the beaten paths of Greek philosophy, some stayed on the hook, saying, "We will hear you again about this" (v. 32). Eventually, a few of them came to believe his message, Jewish eschatology and all. While it would be excessive to claim that Paul philosophized them into Christianity, his tactically interdisciplinary approach—highlighting common ground between Christianity and Stoicism as well as building his case through quotations from classical poetry—not only vindicated his innocence, but also sustained his declamation of Athenian idolatry and led some pagan Athenians to contemplate and ultimately accept the Jewish messiah.

The account of Paul's discourse before the Areopagus, with its numerically modest conversions, might seem a tepid testimonial to the benefit of interdisciplinary theologizing. After all, Christian preaching in the East generated mass repentance and baptisms. Thousands responded to Peter's sermons in Jerusalem (2:41; 4:4; 6:1, 7) and the disciples multiplied rapidly in Judea, Samaria, and Galilee (8:5–8, 14; 9:31). But in those regions, Christianity enjoyed the greatest ideological and cultural compatibility with the dominant religion of Judaism. As the book of Acts progresses, conversions gradually slow, eventually transpiring primarily among God-fearers (Gentiles already participating in synagogue life; 10:2, 44–47) or

29. Ben Witherington, *The Acts of the Apostles: A Socio-Rhetorical Commentary* (Grand Rapids: Eerdmans, 1998), 532.

in the context of synagogue preaching.[30] Straight-up Gentile converts
with no previous Jewish sympathies were sparser, often just a person or
a household at a time (e.g., the Philippian jailer in 16:34). In Lystra, on
one of the few occasions in the first missionary journey when Paul did
speak to a Gentile audience with no prior Jewish sympathies, "success"
consisted of convincing the Lystrans that he and Barnabas were not Zeus
and Hermes on holiday, whereby he averted becoming the recipient of
a pagan idolatrous sacrifice. But there were no converts among those
enthusiastic throngs in Lystra and, just a short time later, those same
crowds would stone Paul and drag his limp body outside the city walls
to rot (14:8–19)! The point is that, in Lystra, Paul was communicating
across a much wider cultural divide, such that his success there needs to
be evaluated differently than in Jerusalem.

This is hardly a surprise to those of us who are missionaries. After
all, lumping the baptisms of the Jews in Jerusalem together with that of
the Philippian jailer and calling them all "conversions" obscures the fact
that it is a relatively small ideological step for a Jerusalem Jew to believe
that Jesus was the Messiah. Most Jews already believed in the concept of
a Messiah! By contrast, assent to such a notion by a Macedonian with no
previous contact with Jewish theology would have been nothing short of
a flying leap into the epistemic abyss.

Therefore, when comparing apples with apples and setting the Athens
speech alongside Paul's other discourses in front of strictly pagan audiences with no prior Jewish influence, one appreciates that Paul's brief
interlude in Athens was a real win. Before the Areopagus, he refuted
charges of introducing foreign divinities, succeeding where Socrates had
famously failed. He sustained his critique of idolatry, a big victory by any
Jewish standard. Paul even won over a few converts from the Athenian
intellectual elite. Finally, when he left Athens, he was not chased out of
town by an angry mob as he had been in all the other cities he had hitherto
evangelized on the west side of the Aegean Sea (Philippi, Thessalonica,

---

30. This seems to be the case in Pisidian Antioch (13:42–48), Iconium (14:1), and Berea
(17:10). Paul enjoyed more significant evangelistic success among the Gentiles when he
remained in their cities for extended periods of time, as during his eighteen months in
Corinth (18:8–11). But even there one searches in vain for accounts of mass conversions
like those in Jerusalem.

and Berea). Rather, he advanced peaceably to Corinth where he would enjoy one of the most fruitful seasons of ministry of his career.

Athens was a win. And it was a win precisely because Paul ventured to create interdisciplinary theology in order to communicate his gospel most effectively to an audience whose worldview differed vastly from his own.

In Faith and Displacement, we had to overcome a set of paradigmatic disjunctions different from those that Paul confronted. Our three audiences—pastors, professionals in their congregations, and IDPs—were already mostly Christians. But ideological chasms separated these audiences' extant faith from the achievement of the holistic flourishing that Faith and Displacement pursued. The pastors by and large saw no connection between the social sciences and Christian theology, let alone preaching. The professionals perceived little relationship between their nine-to-five jobs and their Sunday confessions. The IDPs did not anticipate that God might relieve their suffering by mobilizing their own talents through and in conjunction with the professional human capital of local churches. By and large they looked to the government and NGOs for rescue. Our interdisciplinary theology sought to bridge those conceptual rifts, joining hearts and beliefs to minds and actions. Stated that way, it sounds neat and tidy. But in order to determine whether our interdisciplinary theology would succeed, we would actually have to implement our curricula. This I'll describe in the next chapter.

# Deiner Espitia (Part 1)

Deiner José Espitia Díaz was born in Venezuela in 1982. His parents were Colombians who migrated across the border after the Middle Eastern oil crises of the 1970s caused the price of oil—and therefore the oil-based Venezuelan economy—to spike. As a child, Deiner's parents went through an ugly separation, and Deiner's father secreted him out of the country, without his mother's knowledge.

They moved to the department of Antioquia to live with Deiner's paternal grandparents. Back in Colombia, Deiner and his father began to construct new lives. "The hole that had been left in me by my family's separation was being filled by the love of my grandparents, relatives, and new friends," he shared with me during our first meeting, one December morning in 2016.

But a normal childhood was not in the cards for Deiner. On September 16, 1992, the town had gathered for a school play in which ten-year-old Deiner was participating. Suddenly, from the stage, "I saw that everybody was running to hide. I heard an explosion and bursts of gunfire and people yelling 'The guerrillas are here!' But in reality, it was the Autodefensas Unidas de Colombia.[31] We heard gunfire, we saw the houses burned. We fled the school and took refuge in the mountains. It was a terrifying night."

After the noise abated, when they descended from the hills, he found his neighbors. "We saw sad and terrified faces. 'What happened?' I asked. 'They killed your grandparents,' they told me." Indeed, that night, both his grandparents, two of his uncles, and two cousins were murdered, half of them burned alive in the family cantina. "My cousin Tomás and I said,

---

31. A notorious Colombian paramilitary group; see chapter 1.

'When we grow up, we will kill all these *paracos*[32] and *guerrilleros*. We'll go into the Army and we swear to God that we will kill them.'"

Deiner's father took charge of his parents' business and land, but armed groups continued to battle over the region. In their own town, "the paramilitary group started to commit atrocious murders: they smashed heads, impaled bodies, disappeared people. What's more, they wanted the farm and pastures my grandparents had owned, 287 hectares. They threatened us. We had to leave in secret and leave everything behind."

Forced to abandon their home and considerable real estate assets, Deiner's father moved to Planeta Rica, Córdoba, in 1996. An entrepreneurial man, he succeeded in establishing another business and recovered financial stability. But the trauma that Deiner had suffered was not so easily overcome. "I fell into drug and alcohol abuse. In my heart there was only hatred, and a thirst for vengeance that gnawed at me."

Deiner and his father had already suffered extortion, threats, and the loss of family, friends, and land, but they would soon come to know another face of the armed conflict: kidnapping.

"On July 5th, 1998, I was told, 'They kidnapped your father.' It was the guerrilla." For six months, he heard nothing and lived in agonizing uncertainty. Finally, word came from the guerrillas: a ransom demand that consumed everything that the family had. "They left us with nothing, sleeping on the ground."

This was their second forced displacement. Deiner and his father became homeless, wandering from place to place. "We almost became nomads. In 1999 we went to Majagual, [in the department of] Sucre." There Deiner's alcohol abuse accelerated. "I became even more addicted to alcohol and made some bad friendships." And just as his father was regaining some economic stability, history repeated itself. The guerrilla forces took control of their town. They were displaced a third time. "We went back to Planeta Rica. We started to work on my Uncle Juan's farm. They were hard years, but . . . on that farm I met my wife, Diana."

Diana owned a small *discoteca* in town (a fact that, in subsequent years, has become a source of scandalous amusement to her evangelical friends!). She is a tiny woman with a huge smile. Diana combines in her diminutive form great sweetness and extraordinary perseverance.

32. A *paraco* is a paramilitary fighter.

She and Deiner moved in together and started to build a life. They had three children.

In this season, Deiner began to suffer from intense abdominal pain. He underwent a surgery for acute pancreatitis, an ailment stemming from his years of alcohol abuse. Relatives of Diana—who were also students at FUSBC—heard about their difficulties. They reached out to the young couple and spoke to them about Christ. But Deiner still bore deep wounds and anger toward God such that he was hardly receptive to the invitation. "What Christ?!" he shot back at them. "Where was God when they killed my grandparents? Where was God when they kidnapped my father and left us with nothing?!"

Two months after Deiner's first operation, his abdominal pains returned. Scans revealed a six-centimeter cyst that required another operation. "My heart was torn open and the *reclamos*[33] began. 'Why me? Isn't there anyone else who can suffer?'"

When Deiner had to travel to Medellín for the operation, Diana's family members took him into their home on the seminary campus. A second diagnostic confirmed the size and location of the cyst. Deiner was suffering a profound depression, so his hosts spoke to him again about Christ, suggesting that God had a purpose for all this.

> I thought of a phrase I had once read: "Man's need becomes God's opportunity." I told them, "If God heals me, I am willing not only to give him my life, but to serve him for the rest of it." My wife said the same. We began a beautiful time of prayer, and I started to feel something strange inside, I felt that something was burning me. I wept and could only weep. I collapsed and could not contain my tears.
>
> The day of the surgery, they ordered a CAT scan to confirm the size of the cyst. The surgeon had a surprised face. It scared me a lot. He said, "Señor Espitia, we don't know what has happened. The cyst has disappeared. It is as if your pancreas has never suffered. Rather, you have a new pancreas!"

As you might imagine, this put an end to Deiner's atheism. Healthy once again, he moved back to Planeta Rica and made good on his end of the bargain with God. The family began to worship at an evangelical church. He was discipled and trained for local ministry. He and Diana

---

33. A *reclamo* is a demand for answers or for justice.

got married and were baptized. "We started to volunteer in the church as deacons, children's teachers, youth pastor, and co-pastors." But the armed conflict found Deiner yet again. "Criminal groups began to encroach upon the town. We saw friends and neighbors killed. We were threatened and extorted."

So, for the fourth time, Deiner was forcibly displaced. This time, in 2012, Deiner, like many other *desplazados*, made his way to Puerto Libertador. "We knew that it would be difficult to pick ourselves back up yet again, but things were different now, because we trusted in God." And he ended up in the church of Olger González (see vignette 3).

(For the rest of Deiner Espitia's story, see vignette 6.)

CHAPTER 6

# Implementation and
# Impact Analysis

The British aphorism "the proof of the pudding is in the eating" rattled around in my head for the better part of 2018 and 2019.[1] All our dreams about interdisciplinary theology and MAR sounded lovely on paper. But would they work? Missional Action Research required that we not only create the intervention, but that we also implement and evaluate it. So in 2018 and 2019 we returned twice to our pilot communities, first to launch the intervention we created on the basis of their input and again several months later to see how that intervention had fared.

### Launching the Intervention (April–July 2018)

As I narrated in chapter 5, the first step of our intervention consisted of organizing the leaders of the local churches so that they in turn would mobilize the professional people of their congregations into a concerted holistic ministry to IDPs. The curriculum designed to achieve this first step was *The Integral Mission of the Church*. We mailed this curriculum to our coresearchers in the pilot communities in April 2018 so that they could implement it with their local churches, thereby laying the groundwork for our ensuing visits. In the course of that four-lesson curriculum, they were to implement the *Skills Inventory* and decide which of the other five tracks of Faith and Displacement they would like to launch in their own communities, all on the basis of the human capital they identified in their congregations. If, for example, they found that the congregation included a number of counselors and businesspeople, they would be well placed

1. This saying means that the only way to evaluate a dessert is by tasting it (as opposed to making a judgment about a cake or a pie based on its recipe). It is the precursor of the American expression, "the proof is in the pudding," which is just nonsensical.

to implement the Mental Health and Economics tracks of the project. If they identified several teachers, the Teaching and Learning track would be a good fit. We mailed our coresearchers a couple of big boxes with curriculum manuals, print copies of the *Skills Inventory* and all the other supporting materials required for the curriculum, and carefully composed instructions. Since the coresearchers had all seen samples of the materials in our November conference, I figured that these instructions, in addition to regular phone calls from Faith and Displacement support staff, would be ample guidance to ensure the successful completion of that short curriculum.

I was not entirely correct. I will get to that later.

Between May 30 and July 15, we traveled in person to the pilot communities for a second time. On this second visit, each researcher would sit down with the professional congregants whose skills matched the focus of that researcher's track. Together, they would lay out how the curricular materials of their track should be implemented.

First they would explain that the professionals should study a curriculum designed for their skill set, teaching them how to use their training and talents to help IDPs. Once they had studied that first discipline-specific curriculum together, they would begin to work directly with IDPs, using the second curriculum of that track—the one designed for Christian professionals to implement directly with IDPs. One curriculum would serve to educate the professionals. Another would for the IDPs themselves. Simple, right?

We practiced some selections of the lessons, answered questions, and handed over the materials to them so that in the coming months they could train themselves and thereafter work with the IDPs. We also assigned a couple of project members to communicate weekly with each church and help them stay on track, answering any questions that might crop up.

By and large, the curriculum launch visits were delightful. We deepened our relationships with the pastors, congregations, and coresearchers. People enthused over the materials and expressed eagerness to begin their work. My fellow researchers lit up to see their curricula in the hands of the sisters and brothers whose own experiences had shaped those materials. Hugs and warm feeling abounded. It was all very "kumbaya."

Still, around the edges, I had a certain amount of unease. Because I had authored *The Integral Mission of the Church* and all the churches had received it, I figured I would get a jump start on our pending impact analysis, running some interviews and focus groups with participants to see how things went (see further below). In some instances, things had worked swimmingly. But in a couple of cases, we found that the *Skills Inventory* had never been implemented or that the pastor had decided which tracks of the project he wanted to launch without taking the findings of the *Skills Inventory* into account. (One church with more teachers than representatives of any other profession decided nonetheless *not* to launch the Teaching and Learning track in favor of implementing the Mental Health track for which they were woefully undermanned.) I winced during those interviews and focus groups, tried to reorient the pastors thereafter, and left hoping that we were back on track.

## Impact Analysis (November 2018–February 2019)

During the ensuing months, the churches beavered away, implementing the curricula while my merry band of nerds and I turned our attention to the creation of twenty new research protocols, designed to evaluate the impact of the curricula. Those protocols (interviews, focus groups, and surveys) complemented an array of short online surveys that participants were asked to fill out following every single lesson of each curriculum. These surveys sought to capture immediate participant reactions to the lesson content, knowing that such detailed recollection would have faded by the time we returned for our in-person research.

Between November 2018 and February 2019, we circled back to the pilot communities a third time. During those months, the department of Córdoba grew especially difficult to access. The withdrawal of the FARC from the region had left a power vacuum, setting off a new wildfire of paramilitary conflict between the Caparrapos and Clan de Golfo, which in turn drove new waves of IDPs to the very cities where we had been working. We consulted with our coresearchers to determine if and when we could travel. For the most part, they could read the local tea leaves and find safe windows for our visit. Still, we did have a close call or two. When we were working in the municipality of Tierralta, we made the forty-km day trip up to the village of Batata to visit the IDP settlement there; while we were in the mountains, an armed group came into Tierralta and attacked the locals, murdering one man in broad daylight. The event underscored the ongoing dangers in which our coresearchers and their communities lived on a daily basis.

A couple months later, when organizing a follow-up trip, things had become too hot in Puerto Libertador for the whole team to visit. We agreed that I would come alone, flying into an airport some hours away and then being secreted into the town by private car, the seat laid all the way back so that nobody would witness a gringo crossing the city limits. The ambience of Puerto Libertador was eerie. On a normal weekend, people would stay out on their front patios late into the night, laughing and drinking and listening to *vallenato*. But during that season, come nightfall all the doors were closed, the city quiet. I soon learned that the paramilitary groups had sent spies into Puerto Libertador, forcing locals to host them and to present them as out-of-town cousins, though the reality of their presence was far more sinister.

To be clear: the Colombian armed conflict and the attendant displacement crisis did not end when the government signed the peace accord with the FARC.

## Overarching Evaluations of Curricular Efficacy

Social unrest notwithstanding, thanks to some agile planning and the purchase of truckloads of soda and empanadas, we succeeded in implementing our research protocols. All told, we registered a total of 372 participants in our pilot test of the intervention. To our delight, the data all pointed in the same direction: the Faith and Displacement intervention worked.

Let me start by summarizing what we learned about overall perceptions of the efficacy of the curricula. In each of our curriculum-specific focus groups and interviews, we asked the participants individually whether the curriculum under evaluation was, in general terms, (1) deficient, (2) poor, (3) average, (4) good, or (5) excellent. Of the 289 responses tabulated across the board, seven people (2%) said that the curriculum in which they participated was average, 126 participants (44%) said it was good, and 156 participants (54%) said it was excellent. Not a single respondent characterized a curriculum as poor or deficient. The fact that a total of 98 percent of respondents characterized the materials as either good or excellent seemed decisive evidence of the quality of the curricula created.

These enthusiastic quantitative evaluations of the curricula were borne out by the comments made by interviewees and focus-group participants. Consider the following statements made by participants in the economics and missiology curricula.[2] Neudid Lara, a displaced woman in Tierralta, commented that the curriculum *Economic Hope after Forced Displacement* "is effective because it has all the elements that one needs to have stable finances. It is excellent." Ingrid Tatiana Ura, one of the facilitators of the economics curricula in Puerto Libertador, commented, "All the lessons—with their Bible studies, their questions—all their themes were very easy to understand and to implement, despite the fact that the [topics] were complex." Her colleague, Jorge Tapia (whose day job is as a teacher), added, "Something very important I observed in this curriculum is that these people [the IDP participants] have been so strongly empowered . . . that, within their own lexicon, they use key terms that they previously did not use . . . [words like] the 'vision of a microenterprise'. . . . These words were not in their lexicon and now they manage them with a precision that leaves us surprised. . . . Indeed, at the end, they told us, 'You are causing us to dream.'"

Nicolai Orjuela and Marcela Zambrano, facilitators of the economics material in the church El Encuentro in Bogotá, affirmed, "The audiovisual materials are irreplaceable . . . and refreshing." Deiner Espitia, pastor of an IDP church, said the following of *The Integral Mission of the Church*: "The people go home and keep studying the text and when they come to the next lesson, they arrive motivated. We could see in each meeting a different [level of] motivation, and it filled us with joy to know that the people wanted more, that they were keen, asking when the next lesson would be." In brief, facilitators and users enthused about the overall shape and efficacy of the materials.

## The Theological Features of the Intervention

One question that had niggled at me throughout the previous months was whether users would see value in the specifically *theological* shape of the project, or whether they would primarily connect with the practical skills taught, those undergirded by social-scientific scholarship. To my delight, users consistently highlighted their appreciation for the theological contours of the materials and the ways that Scripture helped communicate

2. Specifically, *The Integral Mission of the Church*, *The Christian Professional and the Economic Recuperation of IDPs*, and *Economic Hope after Forced Displacement*. These curricula were selected because (a) they were the most widely implemented, and (b) I authored them and evaluated their impact, and therefore am most intimately acquainted with them.

the social-scientific and practical lessons. As John Fredy Zea, facilitator of *The Integral Mission of the Church* among an IDP community in El Granizal (just outside Medellín), commented, "The motivation is very good because it comes from the Word. . . . That motivates me greatly because I believe that from there [the Bible], you can gather together all the realities of social work."

While North American professionals might not share an interest in the religious compatibility of social-scientific theories, the deeply religious epistemology of Colombians renders biblical argumentation a vital ally in motivating Colombian Protestant actors. Consider the comments of Stefanith Castro, a Bogotá lawyer who also facilitated curricula at the church El Redil: "The biblical topic . . . of integrality—be it emotional or spiritual or psychological—[was] lovely, because . . . it was not the theory of a psychologist who tells us such-and-such. Rather, [it shows how] the psychological theory exists but is also supported biblically."

Hayden Cardenas, a systems engineer and high-level director at a major international bank, emphasized the importance of the curricula's synthesis between the biblical teaching and the social reality. "The biblical studies contextualize the biblical text for [our] reality. The [discussion] questions are pertinent for bringing the biblical text to bear on what we are currently living. It does not simply remain a theological concept, but [results] in a socio-cultural application."

These comments reveal the degree to which religion is a fundamental motivational factor for Colombians, and thus corroborate the importance of the project's synthetic combination of theology and the social sciences.

## Mobilizing Christian Human Capital for the Churches' Integral Mission

Professional participants highlighted the importance of a theological vision for mobilizing their service to the IDPs. The comments of Iván Beltran, a participant in *The Integral Mission of the Church* in Bogotá, underscored the urgency of inculcating a vision of the church's integral mission in communities dominated by isolationist or overly spiritualizing worldviews:

> I have been a Christian for thirty years, and we have always emphasized the spiritual and emotional part of our lives . . . but we left social action to the side. . . . Something was needed to wake the church up, to make us think,

"You have a lot to give, and you cannot limit yourself just to spirituality. Rather, there is a need that God demands us to respond to: a physical one, an economic one, an accompaniment," and not to do it just to win converts to the church. . . . We learned that in this curriculum: Go and do the work, love the people . . . and let's do it without expecting anything in return. . . . Let's love! That's the answer.

This expansion of their understanding of the church's mission went hand in hand with the message that they themselves, the people sitting in the pews, are the key agents of fostering transformation in the lives of their IDP neighbors. Soraida Marcela Sicachá Díaz, a businesswoman from Bogotá, excitedly shared that the curriculum *The Christian Professional and the Economic Recovery of IDPs* "shattered the paradigm, by saying . . . if you are a businessperson, an entrepreneur, you can help God's work. That is, God's work is not just done inside the church, but outside it. . . . For me, that was liberating, because I have been a businesswoman for twenty-two years, . . . for me it was like, 'Wow!' Now I understand that everything that I have lived as a businessperson can be used today and woven together [with the work of the church]. . . . One thing can help the other."

Her fellow participant, Hayden Cardenas, described this insight as "devastating, devastating, because it responds to the great divorce that you sometimes have between the profession and the church, right? It totally breaks the paradigm according to which the church is over there, and my professional life is here."

The emotion in these comments reveals how Colombian professionals feel sidelined in the work of their faith communities. But Maribel Colina, facilitator of *The Integral Mission of the Church* in Cartagena, said that, upon playing the game *We Can*, the participants "felt discovered, like on *American Idol*, like, 'Hey, I've got this talent!'"

### Fostering Holistic Flourishing among Colombian IDPs

Upon being "discovered," these Christian laypersons were inspired to apply their skills as bankers, lawyers, and teachers to fostering the recuperation of the displaced. But did they have an impact? Much to my relief, participants expressed that the curricula achieved that goal.

For example, Deiner Espitia (see vignettes 5 and 6) spoke of the holistically transforming impact of helping people recover economically.

"Displacement is something my family has suffered since I was very young, and I had not seen things in the way that Faith and Displacement helped me to see them. . . . When you draw near to a [displaced] person to help them to exercise their work and you remunerate that work, then the displaced person does not feel forgotten as they continually did in the past, they do not feel alone."

Let's zero in further on the impact of the economics curricula. IDP participants manifested a high degree of enthusiasm about the materials of this track. Surveys following each lesson of the *Economic Hope after Forced Displacement* curriculum asked whether participants considered the lesson: (1) deficient, (2) poor, (3) average, (4) good, or (5) excellent. Converted numerically, the average response across all five lessons and in several communities was 4.79, which we took to be an extremely positive assessment.

Even in the pilot's early days, the economics curricula had real emotional and financial impact. Ana Cristina Hoyos, a displaced woman in Puerto Libertador, shared: "Something that I really liked was discovering that we often have abilities that we did not realize we had. . . . We can see that we *do* have abilities; we are not using them, but we do have abilities. So this study, *The Economic Hope*, seemed really good to me, because "hope" is what we have, if we give our abilities a chance."

Ubaldo Ramos, a victim of displacement living in the remote settlement of Batata, revealed candidly:

> The curriculum, well, it helped me a lot. After I was displaced, I had doubt, and I thought that when you are displaced you are left with nothing. Starting again . . . is really hard and I said, "It does not look like I am going to be able to overcome this difficulty." But through these studies that have come into my life, well, I have learned a lot, and I say "Forward is the way [*pa'lante es para allá*]." . . . I learned how to push forward, and nothing—no difficulties or trials that may come—will be able to defeat us so easily, because with God we can do anything.

Indeed, the process of recovery began quickly. A focus group on the *Small Business Development* curriculum was conducted just a few weeks after it had been implemented in Batata, but by the time I sat down with the participants, new businesses had already been founded. One woman said, "Since I began [*Small Business Development*], I started a business, [a small store,] and I started it with 7,000 pesos [2.20 USD]. . . . Now I am going on about 150,000 pesos. So, I would like to start another business!" Another participant, Mario José Blanco, celebrated via these words:

> Thanks to God and the help of the [*Small Business Development*] curriculum, we have the knowledge of how to generate or make a business. Also, thanks to the [*Church Leaders as Agents of Healing After Trauma*] curriculum, we have come through some traumas. Today, this year, on the basis of this curriculum . . . well, I have always liked fish farming and pig farming. So this year I also started to make a pond, thanks be to God, and I am working on a [fish-farming] business. I also am thinking, with the help the curriculum gave me, of making a pig farm. . . . Often, we have a closed mind, a mind unaware of the many things the curriculum teaches us, that have been so important for us.

Notice that, without prompting, Mario José connected the *Small Business Development* curriculum with the mental health curricula on trauma (even though this focus group only examined the economics curricula). This is not an insignificant free association. Rather, it is a vindication of the Faith and Displacement project design.

As mentioned in chapter 4, psychological trauma typically distorts the economic behaviors of IDPs, causing them to prefer low-risk, low-reward activity, which in turn stifles entrepreneurialism and fosters dependency on government aid. Knowing this to be the case, the project sought to provide diverse and complementary curricula so that communities could address both the superficial economic behavior and the underlying psychological and dynamics that impede economic productivity. Mario José's experience suggests that our approach was right headed.

Rachel Caraballo, who facilitated the missions and mental health materials in Cartagena, made a similar observation,

> I have a sister who is an IDP. . . . She commented that when she arrived in Cartagena as a displaced person she did not know what to do, logically, because [she was] traumatized. The State gave her relief aid, and then left her. What's more, Christopher, they are still giving them money as IDPs. . . . But they do not know what to do with the money . . . because they have not addressed emotional issues with them, much less spiritual ones. . . . [But now they are addressing] their own healing—they are working on the mental

health [curricula]—and I realized that I am preparing them so that they can help others. But at the same time, Christopher, I realized that they are healing their own wounds.

These comments show the potency of an approach that catalyzes IDP recovery through a combination of spiritual motivation and social-scientific insights. It is this blend of attention to diverse themes such as economics, psychology, and spirituality that makes this intervention unique as a strategy for fostering *holistic* human flourishing. Faith and Displacement helps IDPs overcome their seemingly intractable problems precisely because it dedicates simultaneous attention to the interconnected dynamics of poverty, spirituality, politics, social relationships, and mental health. It does so in ways that are unmatched by conventional developmental approaches and theological initiatives.

## Fumbles and Failures

In broad strokes, the impact analysis demonstrated that Faith and Displacement genuinely worked. But genuine success hardly implied that the curricula functioned exactly as hoped. The impact analysis also flagged numerous "opportunities for improvement" (i.e., screwups and letdowns). Most of the critical feedback related to minor issues (size of font, quality of binding, request for more visual images, time allocation). But participant feedback also identified a few problems that would require serious attention.

### Screwups with the Skills Inventory

As mentioned above, I had already noticed during the curriculum launch visits that some of the pastors had skated around a proper implementation of the *Skills Inventory* and then made decisions on which curricular tracks to implement on the basis of their presuppositions rather than on the basis of a careful analysis of the human capital of their congregations. When I gently inquired as to why they had cut these corners, a few causes surfaced.

First, some admitted to having felt confused about how to do the *Skills Inventory*. Although we had given them detailed written instructions, those who struggled with or avoided the *Skills Inventory* had not read those instructions well (or at all), feeling intimidated by the amount of text and the use of a digital app. Second, some felt that the inventory was too long, a point which I appreciated readily. While visually attractive with ample white space, the layout of the print version of the inventory brought it to over twenty pages in length! Third, some participants were confused about how to decide which tracks of Faith and Displacement to launch on the basis of the findings of the *Skills Inventory*. They asked for more explicit guidance on that process.

Despite the difficulties some had with the inventory, most users celebrated it enthusiastically, even identifying it as the most important feature of the curricula. David López, pastor of El Redil church in Bogotá, said, "For us, the *Skills Inventory* was a very, very powerful tool and exercise. . . . It allowed us to identify gifts, capacities, talents, and even callings [of new members of our community] and that also allowed us to motivate the involvement of these new people." Similarly, Ingrid Tatiana Lora Jiménez from Puerto Libertador enthused, "The *Skills Inventory* is . . . one of the most important tools. . . . I would dare to say that it upholds these [curricula], that it gives them weight, a foundation. . . . I do not know if anyone had [any idea] of the impact the *Skills Inventory* was going to have."

Given that users simultaneously expressed excitement about the *Skills Inventory* even as they struggled to implement it, we concluded that the *Skills Inventory* was worth keeping. But serious measures had to be taken to ensure that future users not freeze like a deer in headlights when confronted with the tool.

### Sequencing Misfires and Incomplete Implementation

Some of the biggest problems to emerge in the impact analysis had to do with curriculum sequencing and the completion of the materials. In Tierralta, the facilitators decided to re-sequence the economics curricula implemented with the IDP community. Instead of beginning with the introductory curriculum *Economic Hope after Forced Displacement*, as they were instructed, they started with *Small Business Development* and only later circled back to *Economic Hope after Forced Displacement*. When asked about this decision, they explained that they had been eager to get down to work and they felt that *Small Business Development* would be more immediately interesting for IDPs. Nonetheless, upon studying *Economic Hope after Forced Displacement*, they recognized that it would have been wiser to begin with that material, since (a) it uses a version of the *Skills Inventory* (modified expressly for IDPs in the Economics track) to help participants identify their marketable abilities and (b) it teaches moral principles that undergird the *Small Business Development* curricula. I resisted the urge to say "I told you so" as they narrated this "realization" to me.

In the same interview, the facilitators revealed they had omitted the curricular videos, explaining that playing videos was logistically difficult and that they did not think the participants would care whether the curricula had audiovisual content. Nonetheless, a few hours later the focus group with their participants revealed quite the opposite. Unprompted, various IDP women suggested that we create videos to complement the curricula, since that would further dynamize the lessons. I nodded dutifully as I took notes, feeling a small ulcer forming in my stomach.

These errors certainly hamstrung the impact of the Economics track in Tierralta. But at least the facilitators in Tierralta worked with IDPs! In Bogotá, one church launched all six tracks of Faith and Displacement, and the professional participants celebrated the quality of the curricula designed for their own training. Nonetheless, they did not go on to implement the curricula directly with the displaced population—even though more IDPs reside in Bogotá than anywhere else in the nation.

### Instructions Only Work If You Read Them

Something of a red thread ran through our findings about the lapses of the intervention: reading and following instructions. In the vast majority of cases, errors did not emerge because we had failed to provide proper information. Rather, people simply had not read the instructions or had not read them with sufficient care so as to assimilate the information.

Why did some pastors not select which tracks of Faith and Displacement to implement based on the procedure we laid out for them? They did not read the instructions we sent them. Why were people confused by the *Skills Inventory*? They did not read the instructions we included. Why did people not sequence the curricula as designed? They neither read the instructions carefully, nor assimilated the logic for the sequence delineated therein.

### Reacting to the Reality of Our Shortcomings

During the early trips of the impact analysis, I took the critical feedback in stride, expressing (mostly sincere) appreciation for their suggestions for improvement. But with time, I grew frustrated at the number of complaints that were rooted in the participants' lack of organization or follow-through. My emotional nadir occurred in Tierralta, following the economics interview described above.

After dusk in Córdoba, the humidity ebbs and the vicious temperatures relent. The team thus decided to go out for ice cream at a little shop just off the plaza described in vignette 2. Ever since my first high school job scooping ice cream, I've had zero interest in that dessert. But the ice cream parlor in Tierralta was run by Catholics, not evangelicals,[3] which means that they also served cheap rum. So, to take the edge off my surliness, I joined the team, hankering for liquor and an opaque glass.

I stewed while the rest of the team chattered (and Leonardo kept a lookout for church folk, warning me to cover my cup when our coresearcher Walberto sauntered up to chat). Eventually, I unloaded my frustrations on Josi Hwang, a psychology researcher who doubled as my informal therapist whenever we were on the road. First, she nodded empathetically. Then, she tactfully inquired what might be done to respond to the reality that—however much I might wish that our participants were more assiduous in following instructions—most Colombians are simply not going to operate like the anal-retentive, type-A gringo that designed Faith and Displacement.

As usual, Josi was right. In the end, the errors in implementation of the intervention were my shortcomings, my failings, because I had not sufficiently shaped the intervention for the personalities and culture of many of our audience members. It was my responsibility to figure out how to prevent these errors from happening. I needed to make it impossible to mess up the sequence of the curricula. I needed to ensure that pastors could never get to the point of selecting curricular tracks without having properly evaluated their congregation's human capital. I needed to take measures so that written instructions ceased to be the Achilles heel of the *Skills Inventory*.

That night, we began to brainstorm about how to improve the intervention. After all, notwithstanding some real deficiencies, the broad swath of testimony indicated that the intervention was a genuine success. It was an intervention worth improving. The intervention's failures were not fatal indictments. Rather, the ability to identify the failures and respond to them vindicated the project insofar as we developed the MAR method

---

3. Colombian evangelicalism tends toward teetotalism (at least in public). Colombian Catholicism, not so much.

precisely to generate, evaluate, and improve missional interventions. Because we could address our shortcomings, MAR was working.

When hard data showed us Faith and Displacement really did foster the holistic recuperation of victims of the violent conflict, we decided to implement it on a wider scale. But scalability would be a challenge. When working with only a handful of pilot communities, we could monitor and troubleshoot each church's progress. But if we were going to scale up the intervention, it would need to become more self-sufficient, less dependent on our manual fine-tuning. In brief, we needed to do another cycle of MAR, revising the materials and implementing them among new communities. So I typed up another stack of grant proposals and we prepared to launch a new cycle of MAR in 2020.

## Simon the Cyrenian, from Migrant to Missionary

As a seminary professor, when you help future pastors to understand their mission more clearly, that is success. If you help them to mobilize their congregations in missional service to the vulnerable, that is a huge win. But if you can help churches to transform the victim into an active agent of the kingdom of God on behalf of other victims, that is (in my experience) as good as it gets. It means that you helped churches to exist not just *for* the marginalized, but to a degree *as* the marginalized among whom God's reign is present. Then the kingdom of God really *is*—really subsists or has its existence—in our midst, among us (*entos humōn estin*; Luke 17:21).

That dynamic unfolded time and again in the early church, as sinners, lepers, the poor, and the crucified were used to bring and be Good News. The Faith and Displacement curricula explore dozens of these cases, which teem right on the surface of the Bible. But there is one example of a missional migrant that only peeks out from the edges of Luke and Acts: Simon the Cyrenian.

Simon the Cyrenian does not appear in any of our curricula. The evidence of his identity is too fragmentary for a simple Bible study. But depending on how you assemble puzzle pieces, you might discover a remarkable disciple.

*Scholarly disclaimer*: the reconstruction that follows is a speculative one in which I fill in various blanks and propose certain tenuous connections; the available evidence does not afford anything like historical certitude.[4] But I have decided to presume upon your indulgence in this imaginative historical reconstruction because, if I am right, it reveals a character from the first century who exemplifies our wildest dreams for participants in Faith and Displacement.

## Simon and Simeon

Everybody knows Simon as the man who bore Jesus's cross from Jerusalem to Calvary when the tortured and battered Messiah was too weak to haul the beam out of the Holy City. All three of the Synoptic Gospels mention him in a single verse (Luke 23:2 // Mark 15:21 // Matt. 27:32) and explain that he was from the Greek-speaking province of Cyrene, modern-day Libya. Luke informs us that Simon was conscripted into helping Jesus while he was "coming from the field/countryside" (*erchomenon ap' agrou*; Luke 23:26; translation mine). This suggests that he lived in a nearby village and worked in the fields (as a farmer or farmhand) and that he had trekked up the mountainside to celebrate the festival and to worship in the temple.

This Synoptic Gospels' testimony can be illuminated further by another Lukan text that may refer to the same person. Acts 13:1 mentions that "in the church at Antioch there were prophets and teachers: Barnabas, *Simeon who was called Niger*, Lucius the Cyrenian, Manaen a member of the court of Herod the ruler, and Saul" (translation mine). I would venture that the person Luke's Gospel called "Simon the Cyrenian" (under Markan influence; see Mark 15:21; translation mine) is referred to in Acts as "Simeon (*Sumeōn*) who was called Niger (*Niger*)."

As in the case of the apostle Simon Peter (who is typically referred to as *Simōn*, but is also called *Sumeōn* in Acts 15:14), Luke used the names "Simon" and "Simeon" interchangeably, as alternate spellings of the Hebrew/Aramaic name *Shim'on*. As to the term "Niger," it is likely a nickname bestowed because Simeon's skin had a darker color than most of his neighbors. Such a nickname would distinguish him from the other Simeons/Simons in the early church, such as Simon Peter and Simon the Tanner (Acts 9:43).[5] (This is analogous to the common

---

4. For the sake of clarity, in what follows I will use indicative constructions ("Simon was . . .") instead of the more cumbersome hypothetical phraseology ("Simon could have been . . ." "He might have . . ."). The reader should understand that the whole narrative is speculative rather than certain.

5. Not to mention Simeon the priest (Luke 2:25-35).

practice—one which makes foreigners feel intensely uncomfortable—of Spanish-speaking Latin Americans referring affectionately to darker-skinned friends as *negro* or *negrito*, even in reference to those who are mestizo rather than of African descent.) In Acts, Simon may be referred to as "Niger" rather than "Cyrenian" (as in the Gospels) in order to avoid repetition, given that the next person mentioned in the list—Lucius—is also called "Cyrenian." Craig Keener suggests that "Simeon may have been an African, or . . . a North African Jew, descended from African proselytes."[6]

## Simon the Campesino and Cross-Bearer

If Simeon called Niger of Acts 13:1 is the same person as Simon the Cyrenian in the Gospels, an intriguing picture emerges. Simon/Simeon[7] appears to have been a dark-skinned African proselyte (or descendant thereof) who moved to the Holy Land to build a life near the Jerusalem temple. Not being of Jewish lineage and therefore not qualified to inherit ancestral land, he likely worked as a farmhand in someone else's fields.

By this token, on the day of the crucifixion this dark-skinned, migrant campesino ascended Mount Zion with his two sons, Rufus and Alexander (Mark 15:21), to worship at the temple on the Passover. His path crossed with the procession of a condemned prisoner, stumbling under the weight of his cross. A Roman soldier, perhaps noticing the man's dark skin, rough clothes, and laborer's build, demanded that Simon interrupt his journey to the temple and swept him into the events of a public execution. Simon probably shrank at the summons, but like so many migrants living in the shadow of the empire, he was obliged to obey despite the humiliation of being treated like a pack animal in front of his sons on what should have been a celebratory day.

Despite the shame of that forced march to Golgotha, leaving Jerusalem for an execution instead of ascending Zion to celebrate deliverance, Simon's heart was captured by Jesus that day. Simeon is likely mentioned in all three of the Synoptic Gospels not because it was important to know that Jesus could not bear the weight of his own cross but because Simon

---

6. Keener, *Acts*, 3:1985.
7. In this chapter, I alternate intentionally between the spellings "Simon" and "Simeon," since the reconstruction developed here assumes that Luke did the same.

was an eyewitness of the crucifixion and thus a guarantor of the testimony of the Gospels.[8]

In the weeks after the resurrection, he and his family joined the community of believers in Jerusalem, making Simon one of the Hellenist members of the early church. Perhaps he was among the Hellenist believers who raised their voices when those in charge of the daily distribution neglected the Greek-speaking migrant widows (Acts 6:1; see chapter 3). But when the mob lynched Stephen, Simeon fled the city (7:54–8:1).

### Simon the Missionary

Nonetheless, leaving the city did not mean abandoning his faith. Simon and his family traveled north, along with a handful of other migrants from Cyrene and Cyprus, and made their way to Antioch. There, the Judean ("Hebrew") brothers and sisters began to share about the Messiah in the synagogues in the company of other Jews. But Simon, alongside others like Lucius, took the bold step (enabled by his native fluency in Greek) of sharing his testimony about the crucifixion of Jesus even with Gentiles. In response, many of the Gentiles turned to the Lord (Acts 11:19–21).

The growth of the community of believers in Antioch caught the attention of the apostles who remained in Jerusalem, both because of the volume of converts and because many of them were Gentiles. So, the apostles dispatched Barnabas to join the community in Antioch. Barnabas in turn recruited Saul from Tarsus (11:22–26). Saul and Barnabas worked side by side with dark-skinned Simeon in order to shepherd the vibrant community (13:1).

Simeon, despite being an uneducated campesino, distinguished himself as a man of great piety, serving either as a prophet or a teacher of that first community to be known as "Christians" (11:26; 13:1). He was one of the leaders who heard the Holy Spirit say to send Saul and Barnabas as missionaries, one of those who laid hands on the apostles and commissioned them. He then remained behind to lead the church in Antioch. Perhaps he stood among the leaders who resisted the Judaizers that attempted to force the circumcision of the Gentiles that *he* had helped convert, such that he eventually appointed Paul and Barnabas to return to Jerusalem to settle the matter (14:26–15:2, 22–35).

---

8. Bauckham, *Jesus and the Eyewitnesses: The Gospels as Eyewitness Testimony*, 2nd ed. (Grand Rapids: Eerdmans, 2017), 51–52.

## Simon's Family

Simeon's wife also appears to have played a part in the community, even though we do not know her name. She extended a maternal affection to Saul in particular, becoming a mother to him in a place where he had no biological family (see Rom. 16:13). She did so even though Saul was part of the very persecution that had forced her and her children to flee from Jerusalem not too many years beforehand. Perhaps she and her husband contributed from their own modest wages to send money back to Jerusalem in the time of famine (Acts 11:28–30).

My guess is that Simon died in the late 40s or early 50s. At that point, his son Rufus undertook his own journey. Loath to leave behind his widowed mother—perhaps under the influence of his memory of the events described in Acts 6:1, which showed that even Christians could neglect unprotected widows—Rufus the "Missionary Kid," the "Third Culture Kid," became a missionary in his own right and set out for Italy. As it happens, Rufus and his mother reached Rome before Paul himself did and the two of them helped establish the churches there, much to the delight of their old family friend. We catch a glimpse of the affection between these long-separated families who once ministered together in Antioch, when Paul addresses them in his epistle: "Greet Rufus, chosen in the Lord; and greet his mother—a mother to me also" (Rom. 16:13).[9]

The family of Simon the Cyrenian was a family of migrant missionaries, whose collective biographies trace half the circumference of the Mediterranean Sea. They were dark-skinned Africans, twice converts (first to Judaism, then to Christianity), displaced by violence in one generation and voluntarily migrating in a second, and breaking new ground for the gospel in each. Although not well educated, they became prophets, teachers, leaders. They gave of their limited income to help the needy in Jerusalem and yet they resisted false doctrine even when it emanated from that elite city. They worked alongside, loved, commissioned, and even parented the great Apostle to the Gentiles, even though they themselves probably preached the gospel to the Gentiles before Paul himself did.

Why engage in this imaginative historical reconstruction, which goes beyond what the evidence can establish, even if there is nothing particularly improbable about any of the connections ventured? Well, the fact

---

9. On the possibility that the Rufus of Rom. 16:13 is the same one mentioned in Mark 15:21, see Bauckham, *Jesus and the Eyewitnesses*, 51–52.

that Simon and his family have been nearly forgotten by history is part of what makes them especially worth celebrating in a book like this, which seeks to shine a spotlight on the overlooked, forgotten, and unsung heroes of the displaced church in Colombia.

Even though Simon and his family peek out at us timidly from the margins of the New Testament, they were a family of migrants, sufferers of forced displacement, who nonetheless exemplify how a victim of violence can become an agent of the kingdom. They were not simply put to flight by persecution. They were not merely scapegoats of the dominant ethnicity. They were not only victims of empire, cowed by Roman orders into collusion with the crucifixion of the Messiah. They were migrants who turned flight into a missionary opportunity. They preached to those whom their Jewish brethren could not or would not evangelize, and sent money back to Jerusalem in a time of famine. They loved the man whose persecution drove them from their home. Then they leapfrogged the Apostle to the Gentiles, establishing the church in the heart of the same empire that tried to make them complicit in the Messiah's death.

The family of Simon the Cyrene shows what the displaced can become. They exemplify our highest hopes for what Faith and Displacement could foster in IDP communities. And we have already witnessed a family like that: the family of Deiner Espitia.

VIGNETTE 6

# Deiner Espitia (Part 2)

*(This vignette continues the story of Deiner Espitia, begun in vignette 5.)*
Not long after Deiner and Diana settled into Puerto Libertador, a new wave of *desplazados* arrived and formed squatters' camps to the east of town. Pastor Olger (vignette 3) began to seek volunteers to reach out to the victimized population. But these encampments could be dangerous, often under the control of gangs or remnants of displaced armed groups who had been forced to cede territory to their enemies. Volunteers were not easy to come by.

The leadership of the church El Libertador "began to identify sites to start Bible studies. There was an *invasión* of *desplazados* called La Granja that nobody wanted to go to." But Deiner knew what it was like to be a *desplazado*: both the peril and the need. Despite his fear at the real danger such work entailed, Deiner volunteered to lead the ministry there.

"La Granja was a place of extreme poverty: houses made of plastic and cardboard, without water, without electricity, without sewers." But the community's need drew them toward Deiner and the church. "In less than a year, we were already [a group of] thirty adults and eighty children. We got to know the stories of their displacement. When they learned about my testimony, they took it as an example of overcoming. They saw me as someone who had lived the horror of the war, the loss of family and land. They felt heard, loved, and understood."

With Deiner running point, the community of El Libertador began to provide food, secondhand clothing, and medical assistance to the inhabitants of La Granja. When opposition arose, they persevered. "They took away our meeting place, so we had services in the streets. We didn't care about the mud or the rain or anything." El Libertador bought them a piece of land, so "we surrounded it with a plastic sheet, and we built a house with a zinc roof, and we started to meet there." They named the church Torre Fuerte: Strong Tower.

Together, Deiner and Olger created a partnership with Compassion International. The NGO financed the construction of the church's building and its social outreach to the displaced children. This in turn accelerated the growth of Torre Fuerte. During our first conversation in La Granja, in December 2016, Deiner shared proudly, "Today, we have a congregation of sixty-six active, baptized members. Two hundred fifteen people attend our Sunday service, and our Center for Holistic Development cares for 306 impoverished children.

◆  ◆  ◆

This was a story of great success, to be sure. Much progress had been made. But the scars of displacement did not simply disappear, neither in the congregation nor in Deiner's own family. In an interview at the end of January 2019, Deiner shared more candidly with me about how displacement's trauma had lingered with him, even as he had pastored in La Granja just a couple years earlier.

> Both in [the church members of La Granja] and in myself, I could see that, in addition to having lost everything, we existed under a sort of general anesthesia. This scourge often makes you forget all that you can do [for yourself] and it makes you an addict, dependent on the help that [others] can give you.
>
> There we were, having succumbed to lethargy, to forgetfulness, and to dependence on others. But this does not mean that these conditions cannot change. What you need is someone to understand what this calamity doesn't take away from us: abilities, skills, capacities, ingenuity. What you need is someone who gives you hope that you can flourish in the new place you are inhabiting. That is exactly what the Faith and Displacement project did.

Our first encounters with Torre Fuerte were for the purpose of field research. The people shared their stories and began to shape our understanding of how we might support their recuperation. But it took a while to overcome the expectations that we were yet another outside group there to offer a sack of groceries or some secondhand clothes. "At first, our expectations were few, and we thought like an IDP thinks: 'Maybe these brothers will give us an *ayudita*—material things or money." But as the project advanced, we realized that there existed a new hope, [a possibility] of moving forward."

Deiner then elated me with his narration of what transpired in Torre Fuerte when they implemented the Faith and Displacement intervention. "The turning point for us as a church happened while we studied the curriculum *The Integral Mission of the Church*. Within the framework of this curriculum, we played a game called *We Can*. The game made us remember all of our abilities and all that we could do with them." Deiner quickened his pace, growing excited and almost waxing poetic. "What riches we had in our hands! What human riches the church had! The change of focus was impressive. The opportunities that we perceived began to change everything. I remember that, at that time we felt simultaneously confronted and moved by the simple way that God reminded us of the different abilities he had given us. Their astonished faces are an indelible portrait in my mind. What began as a game for the purpose of discovering our abilities ended in a prayer of repentance that moved the church from passivity into a desire for community action."

The renewed belief in their own capacities moved the displaced members of Torre Fuerte to look beyond their present difficulty and to plan for the future. "Speaking with the brothers and sisters after that experience was gratifying. Now the conversations had a productive and constructive tone, and bore questions [like]: 'Pastor, what do we do? What business should we start? What should we aim for?' Many of them began to change their lifestyle. They started to build their houses out of [proper building] materials and even ventured to open small stores . . . Little by little [the church members] are growing in their economic independence and in their social aid [to others]."

Deiner's ministry in Torre Fuerte was powerful and the community loved him. But that did not exempt him from danger. Tragically, in 2020, new threats against Deiner and his family emerged and they were forced to leave Córdoba again. He returned to the place that he first found God: the Biblical Seminary of Colombia. The Espitias became our neighbors.

After making this move, Deiner decided to undertake seminary studies (having pastored for years with no formal training). But this seemed like a crazy idea: within a year, two of his other children also needed to start university. The prospect of father and two children entering university within the span of a year, and studying full-time, would be daunting to anyone. It seemed nearly impossible to the Espitias, who fled to FUSBC with little more than the clothes on their backs. But in spite of the massive obstacles they faced—to say nothing of the trauma caused by the events precipitating this fifth displacement—Deiner and his family are persevering and succeeding for reasons that he attributes in large part to Faith and Displacement. "I can say that many of those who participated in this project—and among them I count myself—are testimonies to the empowerment this project brought about in us. If you ask me, 'How did Faith and Displacement help you, as an IDP?' the answer would be: It helped change my perspective on displacement. I began to see that I can flourish no matter how much I had lost. It helped me to recognize all my abilities and what I can doing with them."

Indeed, the Espitias have found impressive ways to leverage their abilities. "A lot of people have asked how we provide for ourselves, being a large family and given that two of my children and I are in university. Apart from the provision that God gives us—which is great!—at FUSBC my wife, my children, and I have used abilities that we did not even realize we had. We formed a 'family work team' and started to sell lunch and refreshments. Thereafter, FUSBC contracted us for small events and now we serve in most of the events that take place in the seminary."

The five Espitias also clean houses on campus. Their daughter provides childcare to seminary kids (when she is not busy studying to be a medical doctor). Deiner's older son offers technical support to people in the neighborhood. All the while, Diana constantly gathers donations to take back to the people in La Granja, notwithstanding her family's own pressing needs.

The Espitias have no surplus (neither in money nor time nor sleep). The psychological trauma of their past still rears its head. But amid all this, Deiner is an exemplary seminarian; Diana is nearly superhuman in her stamina. Together with their children they love and invest in the rest of the seminary community, and the displaced community of La Granja. In a few years' time, three of them will have bachelor's degrees. They are an example of extraordinary resilience, rooted in their faith, persevering through one crisis after another, rebuilding themselves even as they build into the lives of others. They are what Faith and Displacement is all about.

# CHAPTER 7

# Scaling Up

"We should do a *diplomado*."

I blinked and stared blankly at Saskia. It was one of those moments when you are familiar with the words in a sentence and yet do not know what is being said. I knew *diplomado* can mean "someone who has a diploma." But what did it mean to "do a *diplomado*"?

The daughter of Theo and Sonja Donner—Dutch and Scottish missionaries to Colombia—Saskia Donner grew up on the Fundación Universitaria Seminario Bíblico de Colombia (FUSBC) campus. Her father is a towering figure both literally and figuratively: a six-foot-three Cambridge PhD who was the seminary's most awe-inspiring professor and a formidable rector. With a complexion like her European parents, Saskia is sometimes mistaken for an American, and then baffles people with her pristine bilingualism. In the mid-1990s, she married an affable seminarian with a wide smile, who would go on to become the dean and then president of FUSBC. While her husband was making his way through the seminary ranks, Saskia knocked out degrees in languages, spiritual formation, and Christian education before starting (and finishing) her PhD in education while she led the Faith and Displacement pedagogy team.

Thanks to her educational and cultural backgrounds, Saskia is quick to realize when foreigners are confused, while being polite enough to allow them to save face for being dense. These were qualities I appreciated when I did not know what a *diplomado* was. I closed one eye and cocked my head to signal my incomprehension.

Nodding patiently and closing her laptop, Saskia diplomatically explained to me that *diplomado*, in addition to meaning "someone with a diploma," can also mean a "diploma course." In this latter sense, a *diplomado* is a form of continuing education popular among Colombian evangelicals who lack the time or qualifications to undertake a proper course of seminary formation. As a training modality already attractive to the church members we hoped to enlist in Faith and Displacement, a diploma course could serve as a structure for training large numbers of people with the rigor required to implement our project curricula. Simply put, Saskia explained, a *diplomado* would be an apt mechanism for scaling up Faith and Displacement for implementation across the country.

Normally, my eyes glaze over when people talk about continuing education (whereas a scholarly paper analyzing adverbial uses of the dative case will set my hair on end and keep me awake at night).[1] But as Saskia built momentum, I leaned in.

Growing animated, she explained that this could not be a typical *diplomado* focused on mere knowledge transmission. And it wouldn't be the sort of course that an individual participant could knock out on their own in a couple of months. Instead, the *diplomado* would be offered to small teams from each local church that wanted to plant a ministry to IDPs. Every team would include a pastor and five professionals, each with skills relevant to one of our five project tracks (e.g., a teacher, a counselor, a businessperson, a lawyer, and a social worker). The face-to-face training sessions could be scheduled in modular intensives, spread out over the course of several months. The church teams would attend the modular intensives in person and then return to their communities to do their independent work, which would be nothing less than implementing our Faith and Displacement curricula with much larger groups in their churches and, thereafter, directly with the IDPs.

Effectively, instead of being a modality of traditional continuing education, we could convert the *diplomado* into a mechanism that directly launches Faith and Displacement ministries in churches and with IDPs. We would have to innovate dramatically on the modality—working with church teams rather than individuals, founding ministries rather than assigning papers, extending the course over several months rather than a few weeks—but if we transformed the *diplomado* the right way and then launched it in urban centers across the country, it would allow us to scale up the intervention on a national level.

---

1. The diploma course was shaped by the theories of Transformative Learning, Experiential Learning, and Communities of Practice. For a full account of the diploma's development, see chapter 9 of Christopher M. Hays, Milton Acosta, and Saskia Donner, eds., *Research Reports of the Six Teams That Comprise the Project Integral Missiology and the Human Flourishing of Internally Displaced Persons in Colombia*, https://feydesplazamiento .org/investigacion.

Suddenly, I understood Saskia's excitement. This could be precisely the tactic we needed to take Faith and Displacement to the next level. My office chair went spinning into my desk when I jumped up and hurried to my whiteboard, uncapping colored dry-erase markers as ideas started to churn. Saskia fired her laptop back up. We dug in. (That, dear readers, is what an academic action scene looks like.)

## *Diplomado* Design (January–November 2020)

What got me especially stoked was the realization that the *diplomado* would allow us to head off a number of the problems that had beset our pilot implementation of Faith and Displacement, including the infuriating way that some communities implemented curricula out of sequence.

### Sequencing

We decided to break the *diplomado* into four modules spread out over seven months:

1. The Integral Mission of the Church: God's Workmen Rebuilding Demolished Lives
2. Your Vocation and God's Call: Mobilizing Christian Professionals for the Flourishing of the Displaced
3. Training for Transformation: Working Directly with the Displaced
4. Reconstruction That Lasts: Evaluation and Planning for the Future

Each module is kicked off with an in-person weekend session in which we train the participants stage-by-stage to establish Faith and Displacement ministries, all the while limiting their access to the materials that they need only for that module—so that they *can't* do anything out of sequence.

This sequence fosters our progressive expansion to encompass the project's three audiences of church leaders, Christian laity, and IDPs. The first module focuses on planting the vision and values of Faith and Displacement in the churches' leadership teams. The second module (to be launched two months after the first) shifts attention to the training of Christian laity with the curricula of each of the other five project tracks designed to help them apply their professional skills to serving the IDP community. The third module (launched two months after the second) then sets the professionals to work directly with the displaced communities, structuring their first months of engagement through the project curricula designed for IDPs. Finally, three months later, the fourth module teaches participants to sustain the work for the long haul.

## Ensuring Engagement with the IDPs

The *diplomado* allowed us to correct other problems that emerged in our pilot. For example, in 2018–2019 a couple of churches, after training their professionals with the Faith and Displacement materials, simply failed to launch the curricula designed for IDPs. We worried that this problem would become more acute when we scaled up the intervention.

In response, we incorporated a tool to help participants establish contact with a local displaced community and learn about their needs. With the collaboration of Lady Serendipity (or Providence), we got connected with Opportunity International, which had created a research tool called the *Shalom Diagnostic*.[2] The *Shalom Diagnostic* includes an interview protocol that invites people to share five short stories of change (for better or worse) in different areas of their lives (economic, familial, environmental, personal, and spiritual). These stories are then aggregated and analyzed to identify where the community has (a) needs for change and (b) enthusiasm to create the required change.

I made a trip to Chicago to spend a couple of days with the tool's creator, Dr. Genzo Yamamoto, and his colleague Abigail Condie. Together we worked out a way to adapt the *Shalom Diagnostic* so that it would align with the various tracks of Faith and Displacement. Additionally, Mitzi Machado and Berta Sierra (researchers from Opportunity's Colombian sister organization, the Fundación AGAPE) ended up joining the Faith and Displacement team for every diploma course, training our participants and analyzing their findings.

The *Shalom Diagnostic* gave *diplomado* participants a way to connect with IDP communities immediately following module 1, listening to the communities' needs and dreams. Thereafter, module 2 helped participants plan one-off events with the displaced community, things like a soccer tournament, a cookout, a health clinic, or an afternoon of free haircuts

2. See Opportunity International, *Holistic Community Assessment: An Immersive Story-Capture Approach: User's Guide* (Chicago: Opportunity International, 2018).

and manicures.[3] The goal of these events was to build on the relational foundation created by the *Shalom Diagnostic* in preparation for launching the curricula with the IDPs after module 3.

### Skills Inventory

The *diplomado* also allowed us to rectify shortcomings of the *Skills Inventory*. As narrated in chapter 6, the Faith and Displacement pilot had revealed that many users struggled with the proper implementation of the *Skills Inventory*. Some complained that it was too long. Others had trouble analyzing its results. Certain leaders made decisions on which of the five project tracks to launch without considering what the inventory had revealed about the profile of their congregation.

In response, we overhauled the *Skills Inventory* in preparation for the *diplomado*, cutting the length of the hard-copy version from twenty pages to seven. Remembering that people got a deer-in-the-headlights look when they encountered our printed instructions, we created training videos to teach people how to use the *Skills Inventory*. Also, during the first module, we demoed the use of the inventory and had the participants practice interviewing one another.

Finally, during module 2 we included a dynamic to help participants select which of the five project tracks to prioritize based on the findings of the *Skills Inventory* and the *Shalom Diagnostic*. The *Skills Inventory* helped the churches identify which of the five project tracks they were *able to* launch, given the personnel in their congregations. The *Shalom Diagnostic* showed the churches which of the five project tracks the IDP community both *needed* and *wanted*. Wherever the *abilities* of the church and the *interests* of the IDPs coincided with a given Faith and Displacement project track, the churches were encouraged to prioritize that track's implementation. The hope was that this would eliminate the problems some participants had with the inventory during our pilot phase.

---

3. In Colombia, manicures are cheap, because having manicured nails is not a bourgeois luxury, but considered a sign of basic dignity (akin to the way a US American views wearing clean clothes). My wife's unmanicured nails left Colombians aghast more than once.

## Streamlining and Cost Cutting

The other major challenge the *diplomado* design needed to confront was the cost of travel. In the pilot phase, I had taken a representative of each of the six teams to each pilot community for each visit. Although necessary for project research, it was not scalable. Four modules per *diplomado* times six team members plus the project administrator meant twenty-eight round-trip plane tickets per *diplomado* . . . multiplying that over several cities became prohibitive.

We came up with a different approach. Instead of sending representatives from each project team to each module, each team developed small-group learning activities that could be conducted with the help of a video guide. (We would not repeat the mistake of making the groups depend exclusively on written instructions!) The videos provided oral instructions and time for the groups to do each activity (complete with countdown clocks to ensure that the groups stayed on track).[4] This approach reduced the personnel traveling to each module from seven to two people, radically cutting costs to make the *diplomado* locally sustainable when outside funding dried up.

## Micro-curricular Revisions

In addition to the aforementioned design of the *diplomado*, the adaptation of the *Shalom Diagnostic*, and the creation of the *diplomado* videos, participant handbooks, PowerPoints, and activities, each project team had a load of work to do. Our impact analyses had highlighted a slew of opportunities for improvement in each of the curricula beta tested in the pilot communities. So, we wrote second editions for a dozen of our curricula:

- shortening lessons
- swapping in new activities
- revising some videos for brevity and liveliness (bet you wish I had done that to this chapter, eh?)
- printing participant handbooks in larger fonts for the visually impaired
- making countless other adjustments suggested by users during the pilot phase

4. Since most venues for the diploma course were technologically limited, we ordered a half dozen battery-powered portable projectors that could play the videos from USB sticks and piled them into a single suitcase that could be easily schlepped around the country.

It was a huge amount of work. We did it all in one year. Along the way, disaster struck.

## Pandemics, Protests, and Perseverance

If you have been paying attention to the dates that I have parenthetically included along the way, you will have noticed that we did our diploma design and micro-curricular revisions in 2020. Yeah, *that* 2020. On March 6, the virus we had heard about in China—COVID-19—had made it to Colombia. Within a few weeks, the seminary was locked down and the students had been sent home . . . just until Easter, we thought. Then the quarantine was extended. Again. And again.

We had scheduled a major conference in May to promote the *diplomado*. Initially, we pushed the date of the event by a couple of months, but then realized that we would simply have to hold the conference virtually. We slashed the academic detail of our conference presentations, knowing that people's attention span on Zoom would be dramatically less than in person. We recorded a great deal of content in advance, editing together multiple camera angles and supporting slides. Some of those presentations were circulated in advance of the conference. Others were stitched together and streamed through Zoom, interspersed with live individual and small-group dynamics. By ensuring that we wore the same clothes and styled our hair in the same ways, the participants had the impression that they were seeing a completely live event, mostly in HD. The conference was, much to our surprise, a huge success.

This made us ask whether we should offer our *diplomado* virtually as well. After all, we had a moral responsibility not to put participants at risk. Some proposed deferring the *diplomado* until the pandemic was over. But moral responsibility cut both ways. Colombia was in an economic crisis that made the US's supply chain problems pale by comparison. By implementing severe lockdown procedures, the government left those living in or near poverty in peril. It was suggested that, if someone was in acute need of food, they should hang out a red flag from their home. In short order, the poor neighborhoods of Colombia had red rags and T-shirts hung from every window, and streets were lined with people waving scraps of red cloth. The poorer you were, the faster food scarcity crushed you. The IDPs, being among the most indigent of Colombia, were hit the hardest. While the professional class of Colombia could telecommute and ride out the pandemic in relative safety, the displaced could not.

Feeling the weight of this responsibility, we decided to press ahead offering the *diplomado* in person, knowing that (a) a virtual *diplomado* would utterly fail to achieve the mobilization outcomes at which we aimed, and that (b) if participants would not engage in the *diplomado* in person, they certainly would not work directly with the IDPs (who did not have the luxury of a Zoom account or an ample supply of surgical masks). So we created rigorous biosecurity protocols and slashed the number of church teams allowed to participate in each *diplomado*. We understood that this would undermine our ability to reach our numerical targets for participation, but it was better to do an event with social distancing and low numbers than to have no event and leave the displaced population to fend for themselves.

With trepidation, we launched the first module of the first *diplomado* in Medellín in December 2020, planning to move into Bogotá, Cartagena, and Montería early in 2021. Those latter events were bumped by several weeks as ICUs across the country were saturated and travel was prohibited. We pushed ahead, launching module 1 in those three cities in March and then offering module 2 in May.

As if things weren't already hard enough, in April violent protests began to rage in the major cities of Colombia, notionally in reaction to a tax reform perceived prejudicial to the lower and middle classes but fueled by anger over Colombia's bloody civil conflict and police brutality. Massive demonstrations shut down major arteries across the Colombian metropolises, sometimes turning violent. Fear of the virus combined with fear of the protests and plummeting attendance and tithes in churches caused high desertion rates from our *diplomado*. In fact, they were over 30 percent. During the summer of 2020, I recall carting our training materials across a pedestrian bridge that straddled an angry crowd of flag-burning demonstrators, only to find that a mere three church teams dared to brave the streets to show up for the training.

It was a hard season for Colombia and for our project team. But it was more difficult for the IDPs, so we pushed ahead. To compensate partially for the desertion rates and the fact that we had to cap our group numbers in each territory, we increased the number of cities in which we would launch the *diplomado*. Whereas we had initially aimed to offer the course in six cities (Bogotá, Medellín, Cartagena, Montería, Cali, and Villavicencio), we increased our offering by 50 percent (adding the cities of Ibagué, Santa Marta, and Bucaramanga to the roster).

Notwithstanding the hardships of the pandemic, the protests, the poverty, and the blow to team morale caused by desertion rates, we could quickly see that the *diplomado* was working. Churches pushed through major obstacles to enter and engage IDP communities. They trained professionals in every project track and made their ways to the edges of their cities and beyond to work with the victimized population. Teams in Cartagena and Villavicencio gained access to displaced indigenous settlements, which are often especially reticent about the incursions of outsiders (see vignette 7). Groups in Villavicencio (a team completely comprised of women) and Bucaramanga even committed themselves to focus on women who as a consequence of displacement had been obliged to take up sex work. Our groups were working with the poorest of the poor, outcasts, and prostitutes. They reminded me of Jesus.

## In Spite of Everything, It Worked
## (February 2021–October 2022)

In keeping with our MAR methodology—including the commitment to reevaluate our revised interventions—we built new data-gathering tools into the diploma course. Individual participants and church teams filled out short surveys in each module (the surveys were created on Google forms, which the participants accessed by scanning QR codes from their phones, thus avoiding viral transmission). In modules 2–4, church teams created audio recordings of their responses to discussion questions, and then submitted them to us for transcription. Effectively this afforded us an efficient way to conduct short group interviews with each church in each module. Finally, in module 4 we held in-person focus groups with the participants in each of the five project tracks. These tools allowed us empirical verification of the efficacy of the *diplomado*.

A systematic review of the data gathered has been conducted elsewhere,[5] but for the sake of demonstrating the efficacy of the MAR method, it is worth providing an inductive thematic analysis of a few key threads in participant responses to the *diplomado*.

---

5. Christopher M. Hays and Milton Acosta, eds., *Fe y Desplazamiento: la investigación-acción misional ante la crisis colombiana del desplazamiento forzoso* (Eugene, OR: Wipf & Stock, 2022).

## Overarching Responses to the Diploma Course

Across the country, in different denominations, and throughout the diploma course, participants affirmed the efficacy of this approach to church mobilization. In Ibagué, at the beginning of Module 2 in February 2021, participants from the Lluvias Assemblies of God church said, "The Faith and Displacement program is going to bring a more complete organization to the church.... Now there will be many people focused in different areas, responding to the needs. It won't just be a single person leading [the work], rather the whole community will be leading for the sake of the community."

The influence of the diploma grew over the course of the experience, as was underscored by the Fuente de Salvación church in Medellín in module 3. "Each and every one of the activities has content that was important for forming our perception. Every trip to the [displaced] community, every lesson, every class, every module that we've done here has progressively broadened [our] perspective."

At the end of the *diplomado*, the following affirmation of the Comunidad Renuevo in Cartagena was representative of most groups' sentiments. "Before being able to work with the internally displaced persons, the victims of displacement, I had no idea how to approach them, and how to work with them. Thanks to everything we've seen in the diploma course, ... we have acquired tools ... first to draw near and then to interact with them more effectively."

## Reactions to the Revised *Skills Inventory*

Drilling down into the specific components that were added to the diploma course or revised on the basis of our pilot intervention, it was gratifying to see the overwhelmingly positive response to, for example, the revisions to the *Skills Inventory*. Over 81 percent of *diplomado* teams completed the *Skills Inventory*, a dramatic improvement over the pilot phase. In Villavicencio, in July 2021, participants from the Casa de Misericordia commented that, because of the *Skills Inventory*, they realized "that we have an innumerable number of people with capacities, gifts, and talents that can ... contribute positively to the development of this mission to help internally displaced persons.... We didn't know how much potential we had within our community. The potential is immense. It's just that many of them are to be found sitting in a chair unless you activate the gift or the talent or the ability that they have."

A member of the Presbyterian church Torre Fuerte in Bucaramanga celebrated in April 2022, "When we did the *Skills Inventory*, it was exciting to see the participants discover that we had so many capacities. The amount that we had initially guessed didn't even end up being half the quantity of abilities and capacities the group had." The pastor of the Castilla Roblemar church in Medellín exulted, "When you do this inventory, the people are so happy! 'I know how to do this!' . . . You didn't know about it, you get so excited: 'Oh my God, all these gifts that we have, all these abilities!' We just need to activate these people with all these capacities and abilities."

Since our pilot test originally generated some complaints that the *Skills Inventory* was difficult to implement, I was encouraged that those comments disappeared in the course of the *diplomado*, even though we were implementing it on a larger scale. In fact, one church in Cali found the *Skills Inventory* to be so helpful that they included it in their intake process for membership!

### New Strategies for Preliminary Engagements with IDPs

Our analysis of the *diplomado* paid close attention to people's reactions to the new dynamics we had incorporated in the intervention, especially the *Shalom Diagnostic*.

The *Shalom Diagnostic* did weed out some of the groups that deserted the diploma course (being intimidated at the prospect of reaching out directly to flesh-and-blood victims of displacement), but those who implemented it (81 percent of the teams) commented repeatedly on the profound impact it had on them. Pastor Gregorio Restrepo, from the El Olivo church in Medellín, characterized the *Shalom Diagnostic* as "the activity that most defined my perception. . . . Looking them in the eyes, getting to know their problems firsthand, . . . seeing the person, with their children, with their feelings, with their dreams, with their worries, . . . being able to see myself in the eyes of that other person, a person just like me."

Others commented that the *Shalom Diagnostic* helped overcome their objectifying assumptions that the IDPs were simply passive victims in need of charity and rescue. A congregant from the Confraternidad Ciudad Salitre in Bogotá admitted, "I used to think that [the IDPs] were always, well, stretching at their hands, like, 'I need help,' and that's it. But when I was face-to-face with them, I realized that . . . they are very resilient, and not just looking for somebody to give to them, but rather [they are seeking] the trampoline, to get out [of the situation]."

## Mobilization of Professionals

The *diplomado* participants unequivocally affirmed the efficacy of the curricular materials designed for Christian professionals, underscoring how they provided the training and the inspiration to join in the ministry with the displaced. In September 2021, an all-woman team in Villavicencio enthused, "The changes that we encountered in the professionals of Familia Feliz church were very positive, because we really pushed ourselves; the energy given was practically a hundred percent. We realized that we have a functional capacity—of the brain and of [our] faith—to allow many people to get ahead. We motivated many people who were otherwise afraid of working with sex workers."

In Cali, we had two teams from an ecumenical association in which a range of church leaders worked together to implement Faith and Displacement in both Protestant and Catholic communities. In spite of their confessional breadth, they galvanized church volunteers in their common cause. "In teaching the curricula about Mental Health and Economics, I saw that the people were, like, euphoric! Everyone wanted to talk, everyone wanted to say, 'Look, this is what we've got to do!'"

Nataly, a business consultant in Medellín, expressed how the *diplomado* had renewed her personal faith:

> I'll confess something to you: when the pandemic had begun and we were in the virtual worship service at church, I was saying to the Lord, "Lord, I don't [just] want to go back to church . . . I want to do something more. I want to go out. . . ." I didn't feel that I could do in the church the things that make me feel that I am "in my sauce" (*en mi salsa*).
>
> When Faith and Displacement came out, . . . I felt, like, renewed. Yes, I feel renewed, because this is my day-to-day work, what I do from seven o'clock in the morning to ten o'clock at night, and I want to do it as service to the Lord. . . . I'd been saying to the Lord, "Lord, I want to serve you through what I do, because I love what I do, I love to do business consultation." And now, I feel like I'm "in my sauce" (*en mi salsa*). I feel happy.

That is not to say that professionals in every church jumped on board with the same level of enthusiasm. Some pastors expressed frustration with the lack of commitment of their congregations. In Bogotá, people pointed to their busy schedules or the pandemic as reasons why their buy-in to the project faltered. Indeed, throughout 2021, Colombia seemed to be suffering from a sort of national ennui, given the pandemic, protests, and financial depression the country was enduring. In that light, what is surprising is not that some churches struggled to secure buy-in from laity, but that so many were able to rouse the enthusiasm of their congregations.

## Curricular Revisions

Being the leader of the economics team, I was especially interested whether our curricular revisions had generated higher levels of satisfaction. The approval ratings of the economics materials in the pilot phase were already high: when people had been asked whether they rated the curricula in the economics track as deficient, poor, average, good, or excellent, 5 percent of respondents gave them an average rating, 47 percent of respondents gave them a good rating, and 48 percent stated that they were excellent. Nobody rated them as deficient or poor.

Nonetheless, when the same question was put to the participants at the conclusion of the *diplomado* course, those numbers shifted even further, with 19 percent categorizing the materials as good and 81 percent calling them excellent. This data indicated that the revisions had the desired effect, a finding corroborated by our focus groups.

### Intensified Enthusiasm

During the focus groups of module 4, I noticed an intensification in participant enthusiasm about the curricular quality. For example, in Medellín in August 2021, Shyrley commented, "This material submerged us, it brought us to see reality. It caused us to take personal ownership for the process of this project. . . . Personally, it changed my [mental] chip." Another woman piled on, enthusing about the curricular activities in the second edition of *Economic Hope after Forced Displacement*: "The acting, the notecards, the posters, the images, the soccer exercise with the narration of the match—they all yelled 'Goal!' there—we all plunged ourselves into the exercise. [The curriculum] is pertinent, because it doesn't just look at the biblical text and leave it at that, but it also submerges people in daily reality."

Ultimately, the curricula created intimacy between participants and facilitators, as Eliana Ríos from the Comunidad cristiana de fe in Cali shared, "The hope [that I saw] in the eyes of every person receiving the material generated great heartbreak in me personally. The people . . . opened their hearts [and] discussed their experiences. . . . They want to develop their businesses and to hand them this material based on the Word of God, very much moved my heart. There were moments in which I had to stop myself. I would see them there expectantly and I would take deep breaths so the tears wouldn't escape while I shared with them the stories from the Word of God."

### Change in Worldview

Even though the focus group protocol did not inquire into the effect of the curricula on the participants' paradigms, respondents repeatedly volunteered that the material had dramatically changed their worldview. In the words of a participant from Comunidad Renuevo in Cartagena in October 2021,

> Many of the topics that were addressed in the economics track had been unknown. Many people, if not everyone there, would [now] say that finances, viewed from a biblical perspective, are totally different from what is our typical practice. It's a totally distinct perspective. I think that there was . . . some shock about what [the materials] said about the social responsibility of the church, the social responsibility of businesses.
>
> You're left with a completely different worldview. . . . The concern becomes: "Okay, so what should I do? How can I correct my behavior? What do I do in order to improve this lack of concern for people in need?" Above all, because the church [typically] has the perspective that it is about "winning souls." These curricula brought that concept up short, they changed it completely, because what we are really aiming for is to reach people, people who are not merely souls.

With great energy, that August, Carolina in Medellín described how

> the material really . . . changes your worldview. For example, the people in the economics track always had thought that they were the ones who gave [money] so that the missionaries would go do the work with the poor—well, sorry, I'm going to say it, that's what we discovered—and as we advanced, we realized, first, that we couldn't just focus on charity (because that was our posture), and, second, that we could promote for [the IDPs] not only the

spiritual part, but also the holistic part, their economic sustainability. . . . For us, that was a change of worldview. . . . People always came to class saying, "*Uy, juemadre,*[6] how are they gonna' shake me today?"

Bibiana, a facilitator from another church, piled on that the transformation of worldview extended also to the IDP participants:

When *Economic Hope [after Forced Displacement]* comes along . . . with the Bible study that we read in the first lesson, that said that "Work isn't a curse, a punishment. What is it?" Everyone said, "Well, no, it is a punishment, because Adam and Eve sinned and what God ordained for us [as a result] was work." They all had, like, that chip, and when we started to read the Word and see that it wasn't a punishment but a gift, many of them were like, "Look, yes, a gift! What we have here is a gift!" It was impressive, because women who are already of advanced age were saying, "I always believed that it had been a punishment from God, always." Since that the first class erased . . . that concept of work, it made the people say, "If [work] is a gift that God is giving me, I'm going to do it with greater love, dedication." So I think that this does challenge [the participants], but then the hope arrives—the name [of the curriculum] says it well—and it generates this new awareness, such that when we finished the second lesson, there was so much hope.

### Deficiencies Corrected

To my further delight, the main criticisms of the pilot phase (see chapter 6) disappeared during the diploma course. People ceased to comment that some lessons took longer than expected, ostensibly because we had reduced the content and trained facilitators to manage time. One woman in Medellín volunteered, "I really like the material because it explains the timing to you. . . . You say, 'From this time to this time I can prepare this. At this time, this lesson follows.' We saw that this created a culture of order."

I was also relieved to find that the structure of the diploma course had eliminated the problematic mis-sequencing that emerged a couple

---

6. Literally, "Whoa, sonofamother," this euphemism for "sonofabitch" would not feel as impious to most Colombian evangelicals as it might to a conservative Christian in the United States.

times during our pilot phase. One particularly revealing comment came in August 2021 from a woman named Nataly, who admitted that she initially had been tempted to break from the prescribed sequence. She shared that initially she thought that *Economic Hope after Forced Displacement* was an excessively slow on-ramp to the Economics track and that she feared it would lose IDP interest:

> It doesn't once talk about [founding] the [new] business. It's very focused on sensitizing them [to different possibilities]. But once we had taught [the first lesson], we saw that this . . . was necessary, because you can't imagine the way that they left [that] Sunday, like, "How is this going to continue?!" They had a euphoria to be able to continue to learn. . . . We started with nine [participants], and we ended with thirteen, and they were super faithful. . . . And they felt, like, excited. So, I said, "Yes, it was necessary to take this step [of teaching *Economic Hope after Forced Displacement*] first." So, I think that [the track] is very well structured.

### Progress toward IDP Economic Flourishing

Notwithstanding the short interval between these focus groups and the beginning of the work with IDPs, respondents could identify numerous new income-generation activities that had been established because of the curricula. Participants in Medellín spoke of helping IDPs with small businesses raising pigs and chickens, or selling fast food, ice cream, or clothing. They described how they connected IDPs who possessed skills in baking and sewing with others interested in starting businesses in those areas.

In Montería in October 2021, one respondent shared, "We started to give them these courses on entrepreneurialism, where they should start to generate income so that they would cease to depend on other people. And now they're practically micro-entrepreneurs: some are making *bollos*[7] and selling them to other people in the town and with that are generating income and creating some jobs. . . . Others make *arepas*, others sell *empanadas*. In brief, because of the training that we have given in the church, some of these displaced women have begun to generate income."

Edwin, an impressive nineteen-year-old facilitator in Cartagena, shared, "The church in Santa Catalina where we're working with the group

---

7. Small savory cakes made from maize, yuca, or sweet potatoes.

of victims of displacement . . . the place they meet is like a small farm. . . . We prayed together with the pastor about starting a chicken business. This has helped him to maintain his family and it's also helping us with a group of displaced people. We have about two hundred chickens that we've been raising. We already had the first slaughter. . . . And now, this week, we're going to get another two hundred chickens. . . . This has been the effect of the Economics track."

Despite the pandemic and protests, by 2022 I could see that our revisions had improved our materials notably. Christian churches around the country were working with IDPs to establish income-generating projects that would free them from dependency and restore their awareness of their own dignity and power.

## Perfect Is the Enemy of Good

I have a bit of a perfectionist streak. That tendency doesn't necessarily manifest itself in a sterling success rate so much as in a propensity to focus on failings—mine and others'! In a similar way, MAR, with its commitment to the critical analysis of one's interventions, fosters awareness of a project's deficiencies. In the case of the Faith and Displacement diploma course, the desertion rate (approximately one-third) stands out among our shortcomings. Even though I recognize that the pandemic, protests, and riots contributed to that desertion rate, I still wish the *diplomado* had been sufficiently compelling to keep all participants engaged. The fact that 19 percent of teams did not complete the *Skills Inventory*, and that a similar number skipped the *Shalom Diagnostic*, reveals room for improvement on those tools in the future. However much it may sting to shed light on these deficiencies, seeing them clearly is prerequisite to improving them in the future.

In my lowest moments, these shortcomings would swell to disproportionate dimensions in my mind's eye, as if bespeaking a failure of the project in toto. At those junctions, I had to remind myself of the Italian proverb *Il meglio è l'inimico del bene*, "The best is the enemy of the good." After all, the imperfections in our intervention do not falsify its substantive benefit to the churches and displaced communities of Colombia. Through the Faith and Displacement diploma course, dozens of churches in nine cities across the nation established relationships with victims of the violent conflict who otherwise languished at the margins of Colombian society. For many displaced people, spiritual and emotional healing began. They established new businesses, re-grew social tissue, reaffirmed their spiritual hope, and recovered a sense of their agency and potency in their society at large.

For my own seminary, the project profoundly impacted the faculty and students' sense of what research could mean for the gravest wounds of the world. We fused social-scientific, empirical study with constructive theological reflection and then did the painstaking pedagogical work of transforming our academic findings into content to train the hearts, minds, and skills of local Christian churches. The project helped us to drive research all the way into practice, both in the local Christian communities and in some of the most disadvantaged *barrios* and *veredas* of Colombia. Not perfect work. But genuinely good work.

When I first arrived at the seminary in 2013, I was dismayed to hear members of the community intone that tired quip that a "seminary is like a cemetery" (a wordplay that works just as well in Spanish as it does in English). But in the ensuing years, that remark faded away. Our students stopped asking questions about whether theological scholarship mattered for real life. Faith and Displacement removed all doubt.

We have now done two cycles of MAR. Following the first cycle, we greatly improved our intervention and achieved excellent scalability. The second round of critical analysis showed us further opportunities for improvement. We certainly haven't arrived at anything like perfection. But the things that we did achieve were pretty good.

## Jesus Scaling Up His Intervention
## (The Sending of the Twelve and the Seventy-Two)

Luke 9–10 narrates an intriguing instance of Jesus "scaling up" his own evangelistic intervention. In these chapters, Jesus initially commissions the Twelve to preach around Galilee (9:1–10). A short while later, Jesus expands his preaching force sixfold and dispatches seventy-two disciples to precede him on his journey to Jerusalem (10:1–24), apparently to much better effect. The fascinating question is, What changed between the first and second sending?

### The Sending and Failings of the Twelve (Mark 6 and Luke 9)
All three of the Synoptic Gospels include the account of the sending of the Twelve (see Mark 6:6–13, 30; Matt. 10:5–11:1). In each of the three

narratives, Jesus equips his disciples with authority to cast out demons, cure diseases, and proclaim the kingdom of God. But none of these accounts portray the apostles' preaching tours as outstanding triumphs.

Consider Mark's version. Although Mark 6:30 indicates that the Twelve were competent in doing what Jesus instructed, the accounts of their sending (vv. 6–13) and their return (v. 30) bracket the narrative of John the Baptist's beheading by Herod. This structuring of the account implies that a similar demise awaits the disciples: irrespective of what accomplished preachers they were, they could expect eventual martyrdom.

As Mark's narrative advances beyond the sending of the Twelve, it's all downhill for the disciples. By the time you get to Mark 9:14–29, a group of *nine* disciples (the ones who didn't join Jesus for the Transfiguration; 9:2) reveal themselves to be incapable of casting out a single seizure-inducing demon. From that point on, they are never again depicted as successful exorcists (a point about which they appear to be rather sore in 9:38). In short order, the disciples also

- failed to understand Jesus's prophecy of his future resurrection (9:11),
- could not fathom Jesus's plain teaching about divorce (10:11),
- opposed other exorcists (9:38),
- impeded people of low status (children)[8] from drawing near to Jesus (10:13), and
- exhibited a persistent preoccupation with advancing their own social status (9:33–34; 10:35–41), contrary to Jesus's example of humility and self-sacrifice.

In other words, in Mark's Gospel the sending of the Twelve was not an especially positive or transformative event for the disciples. After the apparent preliminary success of their preaching tour, the disciples' character and insight decline steadily, reaching their nadir when they abandon Jesus to die alone.

These observations about Mark are salient for Luke, who adopts many features of this portion of Mark's narrative. Luke 9 replicates much of Mark's structure, sandwiching a reference to the beheading of

---

8. Notwithstanding today's Western tendency to center family life around children, in the ancient Mediterranean world children were at the bottom of the social hierarchy.

John between the sending and return of the disciples (9:1–10). Luke also includes many of the same boneheaded mistakes committed by the disciples in Mark:

- not being able to cast out a demon (9:37–43),
- not understanding Jesus's prediction of his passion (9:44–45),
- arguing about their social status (9:46–48, in which Jesus tells them to welcome little children), and
- impeding another exorcist (9:49–50).

On top of this, they even propose to torch a village full of Samaritans because they had offended Jesus (9:51–55), which is hardly a commendable evangelistic strategy.

In both Mark and Luke, the juxtaposition of the disciples' inability to cast out the seizure-inducing demon with their subsequent failure to understand Jesus's teaching about suffering and self-sacrifice suggests that *their exorcistic impotence is linked to their incomprehension of Jesus's message.*[9] Luke 10 will make that implication clearer.

## The Sending and Successes of the Seventy-Two (Luke 10)

Because of Luke's continuity with Mark's account of the sending of the Twelve, it comes as a surprise that Luke incorporates a second commissioning of itinerant preaching disciples—the sending of the seventy-two, whose mission takes place not in Galilee but en route to Jerusalem. This latter itinerancy proves a drastically superior experience.

Luke says that the seventy-two returned to Jesus "with joy" and excitedly reported the success of their exorcistic endeavors: "Lord, in your name even the demons submit to us!" (Luke 10:17). Whereas Mark's disciples, following their failure to exorcise the seizure-inducing demon, never again cast out a demon, Luke's disciples rally after the same event (9:37–43) and are here depicted as adept exorcists. What's more, Luke's Jesus interprets their success in cosmic terms, celebrating that in their actions he witnessed "Satan fall from heaven like a flash of lightning"

---

9. Note that Luke 9:37–43 excises Mark's original explanation of the disciples' failure: "This kind [of demon] can come out only through prayer" (Mark 9:29). Luke may have done this to redirect attention to the subsequent shortcomings in the disciples' understanding as an explanation for their sudden inability to cast out a demon.

(10:18). While Luke 9 may have been ambivalent about the success of the Twelve, Luke 10 exhibits no such reserve regarding the ministry of the seventy-two, to the point that Jesus even affirms that their names are now "written in heaven" (10:20).

Jesus's own jubilation confirms that the disciples' delight at their ministerial accomplishments was not misguided enthusiasm. In response to their report ("At that same hour . . ." 10:21), Jesus "rejoiced in the Holy Spirit," and thanked God for the *insight* that the disciples had come to possess and manifest:

> I thank you, Father . . . because you have hidden these things from the wise and intelligent and have revealed them to infants. . . . No one knows who the Son is except the Father, or who the Father is except the Son and anyone to whom the Son chooses to reveal him. . . . Blessed are the eyes that see what you see! For I tell you that many prophets and kings desired to see what you see, but did not see it, and to hear what you hear, but did not hear it. (10:21–24)

These comments on the insight the disciples now possess should tantalize the reader, given that the previous chapter was a litany of the disciples' *misunderstandings* and given that the disciples' report of their ministerial success consisted only of the celebration "Lord, in your name, even the demons submit to us!" What, then, accounts for Jesus's sudden delight in the disciples' theological perspicacity?

The text gives two bits of evidence that explain Jesus's perception of the disciples' increased spiritual insight. In the first place, the disciples' affirmation that they cast out demons *in Jesus's name* suggests a sudden leap forward in their Christological understanding. Whereas Jewish exorcists typically invoked the authority of Israel's God, the disciples here recurred to the name of Jesus, revealing a growing apprehension of the linkage between Jesus's own identity and that of his divine Father (cf. 9:35; 10:16).

Second, just as the sequence of Luke 9 suggests that the disciples' incapacity to cast out the seizure-inducing spirit owed something to their lack of understanding of Jesus's message of self-sacrificial downward mobility, the disciples' recuperation of exorcistic authority implies that they were overcoming their previous ignorance. In Luke 9, Jesus had told the status-obsessed disciples "whoever welcomes this child in my name welcomes me . . . for the least among all of you is the greatest" (9:48). But in chapter 10 the disciples seem to have learned something of their lesson, since Jesus celebrates the insight of his followers whom he nonetheless calls "infants" (10:21; cf. 1 Cor. 1:18–31; 2:6–13; 3:18–20).

In brief, the great shift that transpired in chapter 10 was this: the disciples had integrated their growing understanding of Jesus's divine-messianic identity—and the authority that they wielded as his envoys—*with* an apprehension that serving a suffering messiah entailed that they experience lack (9:58), vulnerability (10:3–4), and rejection (10:10–11). Therein lay their insight, their potency, and perhaps even their own salvation (10:19–20). In the words of Joel Green: "What has been lacking in their understanding thus far is the wherewithal for integrating the exercise of power and authority, the motif of glory, with the experience of suffering and rejection. . . . Luke's readers may well be reminded of Simeon, whose eyes beheld God's salvation in its universal proportions, and whose vision of God's redemptive purpose was not diminished by the knowledge that the coming of salvation would engender conflict and anguish (2:29–35)."[10]

Admittedly, Luke's characterization of the disciples does not develop in a straight-line trajectory. Chapter 10 is a high point for Jesus's followers during his earthly ministry. As the story unfolds further, they will falter. When following Jesus proves to entail not only vulnerability and rejection, but also suffering and death, the disciples abandon him (22:31–34, 47–62). But progress does not demand perfection. Advance is not falsified by faltering. And eventually, the disciples are restored, imbued once again with power from the Holy Spirit, and sent out a third time in a group, not of Twelve or seventy-two, but of hundreds and thousands (Luke 24:49; Acts 1:8; 2:41; 4:4; 8:1).

## Evaluating Faith and Displacement in Light of Luke 9–10

Read anachronistically from the perspective of MAR, these chapters of the Third Gospel could be construed as a story of Jesus scaling up his intervention through cyclical revisions. Jesus's first intervention, sending out the Twelve, was certainly not fruitless. But the disciples did suffer from a number of shortcomings in their understanding and practice. Jesus nonetheless persisted in teaching and correcting his disciples,

10. Joel B. Green, *The Gospel of Luke*, New International Commentary on the New Testament (Grand Rapids: Eerdmans, 1997), 423–24.

re-implementing the intervention on a larger scale when he sent out seventy-two. That second mission outshone the first, not only in scale but also in the understanding and impact of the practitioners.

The genuine progress made by the disciples was neither total nor permanent. They would go on to falter, to misunderstand, and to fail. Still, on a road between Samaria and Jerusalem Jesus rejoices in the Holy Spirit because names really are being written in heaven (10:20), because the kingdom really is present in the ministry of Christ and his envoys (Luke 17:20–21), because Satan really is falling like lightning (10:18), even if some do reject the message of the disciples, even if not all of the demons are gone, even if the Messiah ends up being crucified. Eventually, the dead Messiah would rise again and renew his salvific intervention in the world, sending his disciples to Jerusalem, Judea, Samaria, and the ends of the earth (Acts 1:8). As he does to this day.

It would be anachronistic and hermeneutically specious to suggest that Luke's Gospel provides a handbook for the MAR practices of the cyclical revision and scaling up of missional interventions. These chapters simply narrate, in more everyday Christian parlance, the realities of sin and failure, the virtues of patience and persistence, and the grace of the Holy Spirit, who works good despite the disciples' deficiencies. As a missionary and a Christian researcher, these parallels, however anachronistically adduced, are deeply comforting to me.

In Faith and Displacement as in most missional work, our efforts generated some success and some failure. But we did understand that being a disciple meant welcoming in Christ's name those whom society ignores, especially because we thereby welcome Christ and the Father who sent him (Luke 9:48). Consequently, we spent time with people who were desperately poor and wounded. It was not glamorous. Unbridled, trauma-induced grief is not pretty. Confronting deep poverty is discomfiting and guilt-inspiring. Those who have been wounded by society are not always grateful that you care about them and will sometimes vent their bitterness on the nearest live target. Churches do not always welcome hard truths about what it means to minister to this population. That's all part of the package.

We spent an enormous amount of time gathering data that by and large would be unpublishable and do little to advance our academic careers. For every focus group that yielded data that would prove useful for publication, there were three that would only serve our church curricula, and one that was largely a waste of time. Those curricula themselves required a massive investment of time and creativity. Furthermore, after we had created those educational materials, we requested critique of the materials by the users, some of whom issued criticisms that stung. But it was necessary. So we submitted to the criticism and made changes to the curricula because the IDPs really do deserve it. They deserve for somebody to love them enough to admit if they hadn't done a good enough job the first time, and to try to do better the second time.

We learned and we relaunched on a larger scale. And although the improvement was marked, progress remained comingled with failure and deficiency. But all that is okay. Because the kingdom of God really is present in the imperfect faithfulness of disciples. Progress and partial success are still reasons for rejoicing in the Holy Spirit, recognizing that the Father has revealed something to us who count ourselves wise and yet remain, in a great many senses, infants.

# Justo Arnedo Cabarcas

After a while, the faces start to blur together.

We piloted the Faith and Displacement intervention in six communities and then launched the *diplomado* in nine territorial hubs. Although certain people and moments are etched deeply enough in my memory to ensure that the passage of decades won't wear them away, most of my memories are melting together in a swirl of dirt roads, praise choruses, *plátano* dishes, and hugs with strangers. For every person I'll never forget, there are dozens I never knew beyond the exchange of a smile or a greeting over burnt coffee.

I find myself wondering what happened to the now faceless faces in the seats at the diploma courses, the ones I could never personally encourage or whose ministries I couldn't troubleshoot. Especially in my more melancholic moments, now a continent away from Colombia, I ask myself how much of our work evaporated when we were no longer there to attend to it. When I looked away, did it all disappear?

Leonardo Ramírez (whom I introduced in chapter 3) sent me a transcript of an interview he conducted some months after I had bought my one-way ticket back to the United States.[11] The interviewee had participated in the *diplomado* in Cartagena but when I looked at his picture, I didn't recognize him. Maybe that's not surprising. He would have been just another set of eyes peeking over a surgical mask. At least that's all I saw.

---

11. The full interview can be found in the artistic memoirs of the project. Isabel Orozco and H. Leonardo Ramírez, *Recorridos de Fe y Desplazamiento: memorias de una iniciativa de capacitación, movilización y reconstrucción* (Medellín: Publicaciones SBC, 2022), 140–42. I'm grateful for Leo's permission to translate and reproduce the interview here.

♦ ♦ ♦

"My name is Justo Arnedo Cabarcas. For eight years, I've pastored in [the town of] Arjona [in the department of] Bolívar, a population near the city of Cartagena la Heroica. The ministry is called Centro Cristiano Amor, Luz y Vida [Love, Light and Life Christian Center] and belongs to the AIEC Denomination."

Fistfuls of extraordinary history are stuffed into that apparently banal introduction. Let me draw out a couple pieces that are easy for a foreigner to miss.

Justo refers to Cartagena as La Heroica, a nickname the city garnered two hundred years ago. During the Spanish American wars of independence (1808–1833), Cartagena was the site of multiple military conflicts. It stood as a key port city, surrounded by a formidable stone wall and defended by an impressive fortress (the Castillo de San Felipe). Cartagena declared independence from Spain in 1810. But in 1815, the Spanish sent General Pablo Morillo to retake the port. For 115 days he blockaded and besieged the walled city and castle. An estimated third of the population starved to death before surrendering to Morillo. When Simón de Bolívar[12]—for whom the department of Bolívar is named—eventually liberated the city, he praised her resistance to Spain by bestowing on her the moniker "Cartagena the Heroic." And it stuck.

Contrast the history of colonialism that peeks out from behind the name Cartagena la Heroica with Justo's affiliation with the Denominación AIEC (Asociación de Iglesias Evangélicas del Cáribe). The AIEC is an evangelical Colombian denomination that was formed in the mid-twentieth century.[13] In 1958, independent of any external occidental influence, a sort of Pentecost broke out in the remote and tiny town of Corozalito. The moment was marked by tongues, prophecy, and healing. A quasi-Pentecostal revival spread throughout the region. Today the AIEC is one of the most vibrant evangelical denominations in Colombia, a striking counterpoint to so much of the colonialist Catholic and mainline Protestant heritage from Europe and North America. With 1,100 churches

---

12. Bolivar was the George Washington of the countries now known as Venezuela, Colombia, Ecuador, Panama, Peru, and his namesake, Bolivia.

13. For a history of the denomination, see Ubaldo Restan Padilla and Miguel Bedoya Cárdenas, *70 años de historia y misión AIEC* (Sincelejo, Colombia: AIEC, 2015).

spread throughout Colombia's Caribbean coastal departments, the AIEC is mostly rural, mostly poor, and utterly beautiful.

> Even though Arjona has become a center that receives many displaced people, before we started the Faith and Displacement diploma, the church did not focus any direct attention on displaced communities.
>
> We started to do the *diplomado*, and its theme struck us as most excellent and very timely. For me as a pastor and a minister of the Lord, it was a great task and challenge to see clearly what the mission of the church really is. Taking that into account, we see that the displaced population is part of the church and should be attended by the church.
>
> As part of the *diplomado*, we approached an indigenous community that had been a victim of displacement—a Zenú settlement. Its name is Sueños de libertad.

The Zenú are the second-largest indigenous tribe in Colombia. In the pre-colonial period, they were the dominant population of what is now the Colombian Caribbean coast. For over 1,700 years they constructed massive waterworks to irrigate the region and became exquisite gold workers. Alas, their gold poured gasoline on the fire of the Spanish conquest. And the Spaniards nearly wiped them out.

In more recent years, the Zenú have been victimized, time and again, by the guerrilla and paramilitary forces that crawl all over their ancestral lands. That history helps you understand the name of the settlement that Justo mentions: Sueños de libertad—"Dreams of Liberty."

> When we approached them, we were prejudiced, because it's a dangerous zone, where people live in truly extreme poverty. We were afraid and, because the Zenú community is rather closed off, we thought that we would be rejected, that we wouldn't be well received. Indeed, they themselves said, "We have been deceived many times. People come with the pretext of helping us, but they really have the intention of taking pictures, of simply having a publicity opportunity. They sow hope in us and then nothing happens."
>
> So, there was a certain reticence, on their part and on ours. But when we entered, we told them exactly what the desire of our work was. We identified ourselves as Christians, as people who have the Lord. We didn't just bring a social message, but we also had the desire to introduce them to Christ. So, from there they opened their doors to us, and we could undertake our work.

One of the important aspects of the *diplomado* was to inspire us to work with the IDPs and to give us a structure for that work. For example, it guided us to begin our engagement with them through some surveys. That wouldn't have occurred to us. It was key to discover the needs of the community through the survey, which was called the *Shalom Diagnostic*. And through the *Skills Inventory*, we discovered the people in the church who didn't contribute to preaching or serve on the praise team yet had a fervent desire to serve the Lord. These individuals had abilities that were ready to be put into practice in response to the needs of the victimized displaced community.

We've already begun to see fruit. For us, it is of great importance that the chief of the Zenú settlement (who at the beginning was hesitant) was impacted by seeing the work, by our commitment, and especially that we really were not expecting anything from them in exchange. We were simply serving, teaching some things, and using what God has given us for their benefit. That impacted her, to the point that she wanted to put us in touch with another indigenous settlement in the rural environs of Arjona called El Remanso.[14]

We approached the chief of El Remanso and he told us, "Pastor, yes, of course we will receive you. Count us in." That community has a farm of *caña flecha*,[15] they have other resources to which we want to [help them] add value, seizing the opportunity to teach them the curricula from the Economics track and to support them in that way.

The work that we have done has been like a bridge, opening spaces in other sectors. As I said, we already have started working with the other indigenous settlement, El Remanso, and next we are going to start a series of trainings following the curricula we received in the *diplomado*. In the community Sueños de libertad [where we already implemented the curricula], we are motivated to develop work with children, and in both communities, we will start work with single mothers. They are very open, and they want to keep working.

The displacement crisis is only the latest chapter of a multi-century saga of violence, colonialism, exploitation, and manipulation, perpetrated

---

14. Meaning "The Haven" or "The Refuge." The names of the settlements founded by displaced Zenú say a great deal about the longings of this repeatedly victimized population.

15. Known in English as "wild cane," *caña flecha* is a tall grass used for weaving, especially of the traditional Colombian hat, the *sombrero vueltiao*.

by foreigners and nationals alike. Money, warfare, religion, and race have generated and shaped intergenerational waves of abuse. But in the testimony of Pastor Justo Arnedo Cabarcas, I witnessed God healing the communities of Colombia.

A poor mestizo church in a small town opened its eyes to the greater poverty afflicting the Zenú population in the nearby countryside. This congregation committed itself to indigenous neighbors who had been victimized from one generation to the next. In a reciprocal gesture of openness, the woman chief of the Zenú community Sueños de libertad became a host to Christian mestizos who call themselves Amor, Luz, y Vida (Love, Light, and Life). Upon realizing that these Christians were true to their name, that chieftess also brought them into friendship with another Zenú settlement seeking a *remanso*, a safe haven. Now Pastor Justo's congregation is extending God's refuge to wives without husbands, to children without fathers, to tribes without a home.

And the words of Luke's Gospel came to me.

*I saw Satan fall from heaven like a flash of lightning. Behold, the kingdom of God is among us* (cf. Luke 10:18; 17:21).

# CHAPTER 8

# The Theological Productivity
# of Missional Action Research

Because downtown Cartagena has such a vigorous nightlife, it tends to be strangely silent in the early morning. So on my final day teaching the Faith and Displacement *diplomado* in that city, I took advantage of the tranquil dawn to walk from the colonial walled city to a decaying church in a rough barrio to which the *diplomado* participants would soon flock.

As I progressed, the sun's rays began to illuminate children asleep on the sidewalk and curled into the fetal position on the thresholds of abandoned buildings. One of those boys lay stretched out on his back, unbent and stiff beneath a filthy sheet that covered him from head to foot in a way that called to my mind the image of an Egyptian mummy. It almost seemed as though he died during the night, before he ever had a chance to live.

I crossed a stone bridge and looked across the surface of the San Lázaro lagoon, beyond which rose the shimmering white towers of Bocagrande, where many of Colombia's ultra-rich reside. In the middle of the lagoon, against the backdrop of harbors crowded with ostentatious yachts, was a weather-beaten old man with a sagging red T-shirt hanging cockeyed off one shoulder. He tottered to maintain his balance on a crude wooden canoe, from which he cast a net into the brackish water. Looking out at him, I recalled a conversation I had with a displaced Afro-Colombian woman in a slum a few miles away on my first research trip to this city. She had shared the anxiety she felt daily when her fisherman husband would catch a smoke-belching bus to the docks. She feared for him, trying to scrape together a living on the ocean, without knowing how to swim. I pondered the socioeconomic abyss that separated that indigent fisherman from the owners of the nearby yachts . . . and from me.

At a previous point in my life, my theological account of those homeless children would have included concepts like intergenerational sin and promises of future transformation. My counsel to the fisherman would have included rousing appeals to virtues like frugality and the inspirational example of the laborious ant (Prov. 6). Fortunately, that would not be the approach I would teach *diplomado* participants later that morning. Without categorically denying the merit of the aforementioned theological ideas, I now think differently about God, missions, and the situation of the impoverished. This is mainly because MAR—using social-scientific research to inform missional reflection on lived human experience—has shaped my theological evaluation of their realities and my understanding of how the church can love them most effectively.

The goal of this final chapter is to demonstrate how MAR deepens theological insight and fosters effective missional action, precisely because it attends earnestly to human experience. I begin with a concise account of the MAR method, synthesizing the steps detailed in the previous chapters in hopes of being a helpful reference to future researchers. I then compare MAR to a couple other theological methods that have engaged lessons from action research, thereby pressing an epistemic question flagged all the way back in chapter 1: How does human experience mediate divine revelation? I will argue that human experience is a *locus theologicus*—a source of insight that must be engaged seriously in the theological process. To support this point, I will examine Acts 15, unpacking how the apostles' lived experience shaped their exegesis and ethics. I conclude the book by offering snapshots of how Faith and Displacement vindicates the theological and missional fertility of MAR's use of social-scientific methodology to examine human experience as a *locus theologicus*.

## Missional Action Research in a Nutshell

The perennial epistemic concern with experience is its hermeneutical slipperiness: whose experience matters and how do you interpret one person's experience in relation to others with divergent perceptions? While MAR does not do away entirely with this problem, its methodological rigor and utilization of social-scientific empiricism differentiate it radically from a relativistic capitulation to theological impressionism. The following summary of the method will bear out that point and should also serve as a handy distillation of the MAR approach for others who may utilize it in the future.

As described in chapter 3, MAR is a cycle consisting of the following elements:

1. Initial research
2. Construction of an ecclesial-based intervention
3. Execution of the intervention
4. Impact analysis
5. Revision of the diagnosis or intervention
6. Re-implementation

### Initial Research

The research begins with an identification of the problem and its major components. This identification should ideally be done in cooperation with people close to the "wound," whether those who have lived it personally or those who have acquired extensive on-the-ground experience with the affected population. The process should attend to the multiple areas of life affected by the problem without allowing attention to gravitate to the research team's own professional bailiwick.

Once the basic dimensions of the problem have been mapped out, there follows a rigorous study of the problem's various facets and extant best practices for responding to it. This research should be conducted by interdisciplinary teams that reflect the commitments of integral missiology:

- concern for holistic realities
- attention to the Bible as one important source of revelation
- valuing laity

Teams put the holistic commitment into action by incorporating scholars from outside of the theological guild (in the case of Faith and Displacement, social scientists). Theologians, in particular biblical scholars, should also figure on each team in order to ensure that the Bible feeds the teams' intervention and that the intervention can eventually be communicated in biblically informed fashions that will connect optimally with ecclesial (especially Protestant) communities. Finally, nonacademics and non-clergy—that is, professionals and members of the affected population—should also form part of the project as coresearchers.

Research should be conducted in all the fields pertinent to the project. Obviously, one wants to avoid reinventing the wheel, which means attending to the relevant published literature. Nonetheless, the initial research cannot be confined to a library. Rather, it must engage directly with the suffering population. As such, fieldwork is of irreducible importance to this sort of scholarship.

Since few theologians have experience with empirical research, social scientists are vital in creating research protocols and ensuring ethical implementation. Those protocols should include approaches from the PAR toolkit[1] in order to ensure that respondents can shape the diagnosis of the problem, share the granular reality of their experiences, and identify strategies that they have already applied to positive effect.

Still, having social scientists take the lead in creating research protocols ought not skew the study in an unduly nontheological direction. The field research should also explore religious themes, engaging the community around their theology and spirituality. This will feed the ecclesial-based intervention developed in the next phase.

As discussed in chapter 4, coresearcher participation is a vital and delicate matter. Involving coresearchers from the victimized population in the creation, implementation, and analysis of field research protocols has numerous benefits. Chief among them are infusing the research with their intimate knowledge, heightening their buy-in, and contributing to their critical consciousness and awareness of personal agency. But research teams should be sensitive to the possibility that coresearchers may not desire that level of involvement in an investigative process that may feel like a distraction from more pressing responsibilities. Nevertheless, if the academics do run point on the research and analysis, it will be important to secure coresearcher engagement with the academics' findings and preliminary interpretations while the "concrete is still wet," that is, before they have firmed up their conclusions. Each team will have to weigh the trade-offs of greater or lesser degrees of participant involvement in the research. While a good deal is at stake in this process, there is no one-size-fits-all prescription for balancing the dynamics of coresearcher participation.

---

1. Such as the creation of community maps, like those utilized by the economics team; see chapter 4.

## Construction of an Ecclesial-Based Intervention

The social-scientific and theological research into problems and best practices will form the basis of the creation of an intervention, which constitutes the second phase of MAR. Because this brand of action research is *missional*, local churches must function as primary actors in the intervention. Academics are part of the community of faith, but the church collectively is the body of Christ. Therefore, MAR needs to equip the church.

In conformity with the holistic commitment of integral mission, the missional intervention should include attention to the concrete needs of the community being served. This requires the mobilization of congregants beyond the "usual suspects": people whose skills as engineers, lawyers, or entrepreneurs are not typically capitalized upon within local church ministries.

The mobilization of a range of congregants should go hand-in-hand with an activation of the insights, leadership, and talents of the vulnerable community that the MAR intervention seeks to serve. The engagement of coresearchers from the community is a start, not a substitute, to the process of engaging community members who might otherwise remain passive recipients of the church's good intentions.

In developing the intervention, the more input one can secure from coresearchers and community members, the better. Those who have lived amid the realities that the intervention confronts often serve as the intervention's best troubleshooters, anticipating how an intervention will falter without wasting valuable time and goodwill implementing a flawed procedure. In the same vein, the more that coresearchers and community members are involved in planning the intervention, the greater will be their sense of ownership and optimism about the pertinence of the intervention. This means they will give it a fair shake and keep at bay any creeping cynicism that might derail an otherwise promising intervention.

## Execution of the Intervention

Once developed, the intervention should be piloted in the very communities studied during the initial research phase. By so doing, the team will return the knowledge and the benefits of the research to the community, in contrast to the extractivist tendencies of most field-based scholarship. Furthermore, initially implementing the intervention in communities other than the ones originally researched could undermine the intervention to the degree that those communities differ from the ones in which the research was initially conducted. The intervention should be tested in conditions conducive to its success so that excuses cannot be blithely proffered for whatever shortcomings might emerge.

## Impact Analysis

Because MAR is a cyclical undertaking, the research continues subsequent to the execution of the intervention, for the intervention's impact must be analyzed. So, even as the researchers are designing the intervention, they should also consider how they will evaluate its efficacy.

The quality of the data compiled will be supported by the utilization of diverse tools designed to capture the immediate and longer-term reactions to and consequences of the intervention. Coresearchers are valuable interlocutors in developing the tools for the impact analysis, especially in relation to timelines and the quotidian constraints that could interfere with participant availability.

The impact analysis tools should not only measure the benefits of the intervention. They should also be designed to ferret out possible improvements to the intervention. Everything from the major premises of the intervention (values, modality, messaging) to its minutiae (timing, vocabulary, the physical quality of the materials) should be examined lest the researchers end up re-implementing a fundamentally flawed intervention or fumble a second implementation owing to easily fixable deficiencies.

## Revision of the Diagnosis and Intervention

The impact analysis is also an opportunity to revise the initial diagnosis that a team made of the situation and best practices in responding to it. Since the "proof of the pudding is in the eating," if the intervention does not have the desired impact, then something was wrong with the diagnosis or the cure.

Hopefully, the initial research will have been done well enough that the initial diagnosis or first-draft intervention need not be discarded as fundamentally flawed. But researchers should be willing to make alterations to their approach, and even abandon an intervention that proves an ineffective use of time and resources. Assuming, however, the basic competence of the researchers, it is more likely that the team will simply find that alterations and revisions are needed to improve the intervention. If funding, energy, and continued goodwill allow, those alterations should be given all due attention.

### Re-implementation

Once revised, the team should re-implement the intervention. They will need to assess whether it is most sensible to reapply the revised intervention in the initial locations—perhaps because the intervention was dramatically altered or because only a small portion of the population participated in the pilot—or if it should be implemented in other locations. Concomitantly, the team must decide whether they experienced sufficient success in the first stage of the intervention to justify scaling up the revised implementation.

Scaling up will likely feel attractive to researchers, operating on the assumption that their initial success could be repeated when applying the improved version of the intervention. This logic is nonetheless incomplete, insofar as it leaves out consideration of local community buy-in. Having involved the local community in the initial research would have secured a high level of buy-in to the intervention. But if one reapplies in a new context and on a larger scale, that same level of commitment is unlikely. Therefore, the success of re-implementation will require additional personal engagement with the newly engaged communities in order to assure their wholehearted participation. Fortunately, enthusiasm can be nourished in a new setting by sharing the results from the pilot.

### Continuing the Cycle

Like PAR, MAR can be an iterative, cyclical process. Accordingly, the re-implementation should include another round of impact analysis. While some of the protocols utilized to evaluate the first presentation might be reusable, this should not be taken for granted. On the upside, researchers may not need to reexamine the efficacy of strategies that were decisively confirmed during the pilot. But special attention should be given to the revisions made to the intervention, as well as to examining whether shifting the target population or scale of the intervention requires further alterations. Finally, new contextual dynamics may have arisen in the course of the re-implementation. These should receive careful attention.

In our re-implementation (2020–2022), we grappled with large-scale civic unrest and the COVID-19 pandemic.[2] We were also aware that the economies of scale that permitted us to run the *diplomado* in person required that multiple churches in one region implement the ministry at

---

2. Not to mention the influx of 2.5 million Venezuelan immigrants.

the same time. This obliged us to pass over individual churches that were interested in launching a ministry to IDPs simply because of the absence of similarly motivated congregations in their region. Consequently, our second round of revisions included the creation of a virtual version of the *diplomado*. While the virtual version loses some of the benefit of in-person gatherings, it allows us to reach a larger number of populations at a lower cost. We can also use the virtual course in a remedial fashion to support the in-person *diplomado* courses: if members of churches are unable to participate in one of the in-person weekend meetings, the virtual course allows them to catch up. In this sense, the virtual *diplomado* complements the in-person modality.

Before moving on from this summary of the MAR process, let me underscore that this method should be viewed as a resource rather than a straitjacket. Participatory Action Research scholarship is often so ideologically charged that the new researcher feels that deviation from the method is a scientific or even a moral failing. Although there are good reasons to apply MAR in the way described above, any number of constraints or asymmetrical circumstances will apply to other researchers' contexts. Accordingly, feel free to adapt this method in the way that most helpfully serves the mission of the church. I hope to have provided sufficient explanation of what is at stake in different aspects of the method to help other scholars evaluate the trade-offs they may need to make to modify it for their own contexts. But if minor alterations are not sufficient to contextualize MAR for a new project, there are other ways for theologians to draw on action research.

## Another Theological Approach to Action Research

Although we were unaware of other theological scholars utilizing aspects of action research when we initiated this project, in recent years I have been delighted to encounter fellow travelers who felt similarly inspired by the potential of action research to support Christian theology. Without taking a second pass at a history of research, I would like briefly to introduce one other approach: Theological Action Research (TAR). The purpose of introducing TAR is, first, to clarify its similarities and differences to MAR and, second, to tee up a conversation about the epistemic underpinnings of using action research for Christian theological purposes.

## Theological Action Research in a Nutshell

In the world of academic theology, the closest methodological analog to MAR is the similarly named method of TAR. This approach is most clearly laid out in the collaboratively authored volume *Talking about God in Practice: Theological Action Research and Practical Theology*. The book summarizes the work of the Action Research-Church & Society (ARCS) team, which was based at Heythrop College in London and Ripon College, Cuddesdon.

Pioneered by Catholic and Anglican systematicians and practical theologians, TAR is essentially an alternative approach to practical theology. The ARCS team emphasized, "practical theology names practice—with all its specificity and limitation—as *the* place of encounter with the infinite mystery of God, as *the* place of grace."[3] Accordingly, they seek to allow the experiences of practitioners to inform academic theology. "Theological Action Research is a partnership between an insider and an outsider team to undertake research and conversations answering theological questions about faithful practice in order to renew both theology and practice in the service of God's mission."[4] Indeed, one of the great virtues of TAR is how it ensures practitioner participation through structured partnerships between the "insider team" (members of the organization on whom the TAR project is focused) and the "outsider team" (the academic theological researchers).[5]

To foster the theological engagement between practice and scholarship, TAR utilizes a taxonomy of "four voices" of theology: normative theology (Scriptures, creeds, liturgies), formal theology (the work of academic theologians), espoused theology (how a community articulates its own beliefs), and operant theology (what is observed in the practice of

---

3. Helen Cameron et al., *Talking about God in Practice: Theological Action Research and Practical Theology* (London: SCM, 2010), 23.

4. Cameron et al., *Talking about God*, 63. In TAR, theologians and practitioners collaborate in exclusively theological research. Unlike MAR, TAR does not incorporate non-theologian academics in nontheological research.

5. Cameron et al., *Talking about God*, 64–65. Also unlike MAR, the TAR teams did not include victimized or marginalized populations.

the group).[6] TAR applies a conversational method to ensure that these voices critique and enrich one another.[7]

TAR aims for conversations between the four voices of theology in order to generate both the "transformation of practice" through "the learning and *changed attitudes* of the reflective practitioner"[8] and the "transformation of theology" through the incorporation of lived experience.[9] In other words, TAR aims to strengthen practitioner ministry through engagement with academic theology and also to critique and fortify academic theology with the lived experience of the local church.

## Differences between TAR and MAR

When I first stumbled across the work of the ARCS team (while drafting the proposal for this book), my pulse quickened: during my postdoctoral days in Oxford, when I was raising funds to move to Medellín, a team of theologians just down the road had been experimenting with action research! I could not believe it. I downloaded the Kindle book immediately and devoured *Talking about God in Practice* in two sittings. I found myself wishing I had met these fellow travelers eight years earlier.

Still, as I clicked through successive screens (instead of turning pages like God intended), it became clear how much TAR and MAR were constructed for differing contexts and how they foreground different academic subdisciplines.

In the first place, TAR is a subset of practical theology, whereas MAR flows out of integral missiology. This means, second, that they produce different products. While both are interested in a combination of theology and ecclesial practice, TAR's conversational methods conduce especially to theological reflection. For its part, MAR requires the generation, implementation, and analysis of a missional intervention. If one does not experiment with new missional practice, one is not doing MAR. This is doubtless the most important distinction between the two approaches.

---

6. Cameron et al., *Talking about God*, 53–56.

7. Cameron et al., *Talking about God*, 59–60; so also Clare Watkins, "Reflections on Particularity and Unity," in *Ecclesiology in the Trenches: Theory and Method under Construction*, ed. Sune Fahlgren and Jonas Ideström (Cambridge: James Clarke, 2015), 146.

8. Cameron et al., *Talking about God*, 58.

9. Cameron et al., *Talking about God*, 59.

Third, the theological knowledge generated by the two methods differs by subdiscipline. Since the creators of TAR are systematic and practical theologians from Roman Catholic and Anglican backgrounds, TAR seeks to provide contributions especially to systematic theology.[10] In slight contrast, since integral missiology focuses on Scripture, reflecting the biblicist orientation of Latin American evangelicalism, it is not surprising that the academic contributions of our MAR project more often emerged in the fields of biblical studies rather than dogmatics.

Finally, interdisciplinarity is far more central to MAR than to the work of the ARCS. Although ARCS authors mentioned interdisciplinarity on various occasions,[11] the only other academic discipline incorporated in the projects detailed in *Talking about God in Practice* was the sociology of religion,[12] which is a cognate field to theology. By contrast, Faith and Displacement is intensely interdisciplinary, engaging psychologists, economists, political scientists, sociologists, and pedagogues. The participation of scholars and practitioners from these fields resulted in the creation of concrete interventions that dramatically break the mold of traditional ecclesial ministry.

Nevertheless, however much MAR and TAR might differ in their theological orientations, their disciplinary foci, and their outputs, they share a basic conviction that Christian theology and ministry should be shaped by the lived practice of local churches. The remaining questions are: How far can that go? How much *should* ecclesial experience mold Christian theology? Does this not run the risk of placing the wisdom of man above the revelation of God?

## Praxis as a Locus of Revelation

A quick perusal of *Talking about God in Practice* will probably not set off epistemic alarm bells for conservative Christians. Theological Action Research's taxonomy of the four voices of theology—normative, formal, espoused, and operant—implies that normative theology (the theology of creeds, liturgy, and Scripture) enjoys pride of place over the voices of academic theologians and local practitioners. For a traditional Catholic or

10. Cameron et al., *Talking about God*, 150–51.
11. E.g., Cameron et al., *Talking about God*, 152.
12. Cameron et al., *Talking about God*, 80–81.

an evangelical Protestant, TAR's four voices of theology protect the unique authority of Scripture and the teaching of the church, while encouraging attention to the insights of academics and practitioners.

Still, this category of "normative" theology has generated criticism of the ARCS team. Scandinavian scholars Tone Stangeland Kaufman and Jonas Ideström have suggested that TAR is hamstrung by an epistemology that is "rooted in God's revelation, privileges revelation over human experience. This limits the capacity of practice and human experience to revise or reshape the received tradition."[13] The Scandinavians are not alone in their discontent. English theologian Elaine Graham puts a finer point on the matter: "Despite their commitment to research on and into practice, it appears that, as a human artifact, [practice] does not count as revelation. . . . This allows no possibility for those who experienced violence at the hands of another reaching a new apprehension of Christ's Passion; for those who have accompanied someone in the final stages of their lives discovering new insights into death and dying. . . . This falls some way short of the radical epistemology of action research, in which 'practice' is not simply a matter of technique but a source of meaning and disclosure."[14]

Graham contends that reflection on Christian practice enables the discernment of more profound theological knowledge, for the God who acted in the sacred and inscripturated history continues to act to this day. "The one who is actively engaged in mindful action in the world will encounter a transcendent dimension to experience by coming to know the God who continues to act in and reveal Godself in the world—including human culture and experience—and who is to be known in the processes of creation's unfolding towards its ultimate fulfillment. Reflection is a means of ensuring the authenticity and discernment by which we come to know ourselves but also . . . to know the reality of a God who continues to be revealed and encountered in the empirical world."[15]

13. Tone Stangeland Kaufman and Jonas Ideström, "Why Matter Matters in Theological Action Research: Attending to the Voices of Tradition," *International Journal of Practical Theology* 22, no. 1 (2018): 90.

14. Elaine Graham, "Is Practical Theology a Form of 'Action Research'?," *International Journal of Practical Theology* 17, no. 1 (2013):160–61.

15. Graham, "Practical Theology," 175–76.

For this reason, Graham argues that practice should be "understood as a *locus theologicus*; as a source of encounter with an apprehension of God. Reflection on practice is thus primary material for greater knowledge and understanding of God and source of insight into the nature of faithful living."[16]

More recently, a Colombian feminist Catholic theologian, Olga Consuelo Vélez Caro, has come to a similar epistemic conclusion by combining insights from PAR and liberation theology. She affirms that "all human reality is a theological *locus*, that is, a place where we can discover the occurrence of God."[17] Under this theological conviction, she highlights the overlap between PAR and the *See-Judge-Act*[18] method: both approaches reflect critically on reality in order to transform it.[19] In this sense, Vélez Caro's appropriation of PAR differs from TAR (and is closer to MAR), centering praxis as *the* goal of the theological reflection.

With an incisive liberationist edge, Vélez Caro draws out the ramifications of recognizing that divine revelation always occurs in particular cultural contexts. "Historical mediations such as Sacred Scripture and the Tradition, the Magisterium and the life of faith, and the life of the church, are the hermeneutical text for interpreting the context of situations and animating the pretext of liberation. It should not be forgotten that these very mediations are historically mediated, and for that reason, the criterion of fidelity to the central core of the faith must always liberate [those mediations] from interpretations accommodated to the interests of the few which do not correspond to interests of God."[20]

A red thread runs through the comments of Stangeland Kaufman, Ideström, Graham, and Vélez Caro. However varied their national, linguistic, and confessional backgrounds, each of them expresses a concern that established dogmatic traditions not suffocate the new theological insights that attention to ecclesial praxis might generate. The "scandal of particularity" of Christian history (expressed in the history of Israel,

16. Graham, "Practical Theology," 170.

17. Olga Consuelo Vélez Caro, "El quehacer teológico y el método de investigación acción participativa: una reflexión metodológica," *Theologica Xaveriana* 67, no. 183 (2017): 195.

18. Created by Cardinal Joseph Cardijn and developed by Consejo Episcopal Latinoamericano y Caribeño (CELAM) and liberation theologians.

19. Vélez Caro, "El quehacer teológico," 206.

20. Vélez Caro, "El quehacer teológico," 199–200.

the church, and the incarnate Christ) compels us to inquire how God might be speaking, not just again, but anew, in the praxis of the church and churches today.[21]

Of course, none of the figures addressed in this chapter are evangelicals. Or biblical scholars. As European mainline or Colombian Catholic intellectuals, these theologians think in terms more doctrinal than Scriptural. For the evangelical, this prompts the question: Can such a strong affirmation of the potential of Christian experience be squared with the Scriptural witness? Luke the migrant missionary theologian indicates that it can.

## The Experience of the Church as a Locus of Revelation

To my mind, no other biblical book is so instructive for contemporary Christians attempting to discern the divine will as the Acts of the Apostles. Acts provides fascinating insight into how to advance the mission of God in the world *after* the ascension: when the church has access to the revelatory deposits of the Scriptures, the teaching of Christ, the guidance of the Holy Spirit . . . and a bunch of new problems regarding which neither Jesus nor the Old Testament provided unambiguous instructions.

Among the unexpected challenges the apostles confronted, none was so practically and theologically complex as the question of what to do with Gentiles who decided to follow Jesus. That vexing matter lies squarely behind Galatians, Romans, and Ephesians, and also significantly shapes Matthew and John. The passage of Acts that most directly confronts this question is 15:1–35.

Acts 15 is pertinent to the subject of the present chapter because of what it discloses about the role of *experience* in the apostle's epistemic cocktail. It reveals that early Christian experience gave determinative shape to interpretations of Scriptures and of pneumatic manifestations that were otherwise ambiguous, thereby moving the apostles to unprecedented ethical conclusions.

---

21. Claire Watkins rightly emphasizes, "the central 'scandal' of God becoming a particular person, in a particular context affirms the significance of the detailed particularity of practical studies of church." Watkins, "Particularity and Unity," 149.

## The Logic of Circumcising Gentile Converts

After Paul and Barnabas's first missionary journey, in which they made significant evangelistic inroads among the Gentiles, the problems associated with non-Jewish converts came to a head. It is not that Gentiles had never converted to Judaism prior to the ministry of the apostles; such converts were known as proselytes (Acts 2:10; 6:5). But when Gentiles converted to Judaism, they basically became Jewish: fulfilling all the expectations of the law incumbent upon Jews, including Sabbath observation, dietary restrictions, and circumcision. The problem was that Paul and Barnabas did not require Gentile converts to the Way to act like proselytes.

In response, "some believers who belonged to the sect of the Pharisees" asserted that Paul and Barnabas's omission should be rectified: the Gentile converts should be circumcised and keep the Mosaic law (Acts 15:5).[22] These Pharisaic Christians had strong biblical reasons to make such a claim. They could, for example, point to Exodus 12:48, which explains that, for a Gentile sojourner in the land to participate in Passover—the apical celebration of Israelite religious life—he must adhere to one key condition: circumcision. "If an alien who resides with you wants to celebrate the Passover to the LORD, all his males shall be circumcised; then he may draw near to celebrate it; he shall be regarded as a native of the land" (Exod. 12:48). This was arguably the most direct Torah precedent for the systematic incorporation of Gentiles into the people of God. The Pharisaic Christians had made a sensible, traditional, and biblical proposal.

To evaluate this proposal, the authorities of the Jerusalem church—apostles and the elders—held an all-hands-on-deck theological discussion (15:6), engaging the collective wisdom of all their leaders. In the ensuing narrative, Luke foregrounds the views of Peter, Paul and Barnabas, and James. Their testimonies prove epistemically illuminating.

---

22. Acts reveals that some Pharisees (like Paul; Acts 23:6; 26:5) were convinced by the apostolic preaching. As Jews, following the Messiah did not entail a change of religion, let alone the abandonment of their Pharisaic hermeneutics (or at least that was not initially self-evident). So, for quite some time these members of the apostolic community continued to view the world like Pharisees.

## The Apostles and the Subjective Interpretation of Experience

Luke begins by adducing the witness of Peter. Peter had been the pivotal figure in extending the gospel to the Gentiles when he preached the good news to a Gentile centurion and his household and then witnessed the descent of the Spirit upon them (Acts 10–11). Peter presents the filling of the Gentiles with the Holy Spirit—manifested in tongues—as theologically decisive (15:8). On the basis of his experience, Peter *infers* that Gentile circumcision must be soteriologically and ethically unnecessary. If God did not require those Gentiles to be circumcised prior to granting them the gift of the Spirit, God must not be fussed about whether they ever be circumcised.

To modern Christian readers, Peter's inference sounds obvious. But this is not the only conclusion Peter could have drawn on the basis of what he witnessed. Biblical precedent could well have guided him to argue that God's initial miraculous work in Cornelius's household should have generated the response of circumcision. Is that not what the life of Moses teaches?

Consider Exodus 3:1–4:17. Moses's calling began with a passel of miraculous events: a theophany at a burning bush that was not consumed by the flames; the transformation of his staff into a snake; the making of a healthy hand leprous; and the reversing of both states. These miracles notwithstanding, when Moses thereafter set out from Midian to Egypt, God confronted Moses on the road and tried to kill him (4:24)! Why? Because *Moses was either himself uncircumcised or had not circumcised his son.*[23] It seems that God's wrath was only averted when Moses's wife Zipporah performed a hasty DIY circumcision on the boy and applied it vicariously to Moses (4:25).

An examination of Exodus 3–4 would have blown a rather large biblical hole in Peter's logic. If the example of Moses were any indication,

---

23. At first glance, it appears that the problem was the uncircumcision of Moses's son; after all, it is the boy's circumcision that backs God off. But when one is aware that Egyptian circumcision was a practice (a) applied to adults and (b) performed in a less complete fashion than Israelite circumcision (applying a vertical slit to the foreskin rather than removing it entirely), one becomes aware that Moses himself probably would not have been circumcised, at least not from an Israelite point of view. Moreover, the comment that Zipporah touched the bloody foreskin to Moses's "feet" (likely a euphemism for his genitals), indicates that the circumcision is being applied from the boy to Moses. For detail, see John I. Durham, *Exodus*, Word Biblical Commentary (Dallas: Word, 1987), 56–59.

the fact that the Spirit fell miraculously on Cornelius would not have implied that he was exempt from circumcision. But Luke and the Apostolic Council did not see things that way.

Doubling down on Peter's logic, Paul and Barnabas take the floor and narrate "all the signs and wonders that God had done through them among the Gentiles" (Acts 15:12). The relevance of this narrative to the subject at hand is implied to be the same as was Peter's account of the miraculous conversion of Cornelius's household: if God multiplied miracles among the Gentiles, their lack of Torah observance notwithstanding, why conclude that God was concerned that the Gentiles ought to be circumcised?

The historical facts of Peter's, Paul's, and Barnabas's ministries are vital for Luke's argument: they had experiences of divine power that dramatically shaped their theological conclusions. But those historical experiences were not self-interpreting. And at no point in Acts 1–14 did God *ever* tell Peter and Paul not to circumcise the Gentile converts.

## The Audacity of Interpreting Scripture

Finally, James weighs in. He offers the only explicitly biblical argumentation in this account (15:13–21), providing an Old Testament framework for Peter's experience with Cornelius. As we will see, James contends that Amos presaged the incorporation of the Gentiles qua Gentiles into the people of God. On the basis of that reading, he proposes Torah-compatible guidelines to facilitate that incorporation without requiring the Gentiles to be circumcised.

### So That All Other Peoples May Seek the Lord?

James begins his argument with a citation of Amos 9:11–12:

After this I will return,
and I will rebuild the dwelling of David, which has fallen;
    from its ruins I will rebuild it,
        and I will set it up,
so that all other peoples may seek the Lord—
    even all the Gentiles over whom my name has been called
    (*hopōs an ekzētēsōsin hoi kataloipoi tōn anthrōpōn ton kyrion kai panta ta ethnē eph' hous epikeklētai to onoma mou ep' autous*). (Acts 15:16–17)

The citation here largely aligns with the Septuagint (*hopōs ekzētēsōsin hoi kataloipoi tōn anthrōpōn kai panta ta ethnē, eph hous epikeklētai to onoma mou ep autous*; Amos 9:12 LXX).[24] By James's reading of the prophetic text, Amos believed that the restoration of the regal line of David had the purpose of drawing the nations into the worship of YHWH, and Amos gives no indication that they would need to cease to be Gentiles to do so.

Intriguingly, however, the Masoretic Text (MT) of Amos 9:12 differs dramatically from the Septuagint and James's citation thereof. It does so precisely at the point that is most crucial for James's argument! In fact, the message of the MT is nearly opposed to that of the LXX and Acts 15. Whereas James reads Amos 9:12 as a prophecy of the incorporation of the *non-Israelite humanity* into the cult of YHWH, the MT says that the line of David would be restored "in order that they [the Israelites] *may possess* the remnant of *Edom* (*yirshu et-she'rit 'edom*)."[25] "Edom" at this point in history functions largely as a cipher for "pagan bad guys." As such, the MT of Amos 9:12 proclaims the Israelites' future *domination* of their pagan enemies in the Messianic Kingdom.[26] Ruling your pagan enemies is a far cry from worshipping side by side with your gentile brethren!

I do not mean to imply that Luke (or James) nefariously altered the message of Amos 9:12. One can explain the divergence between the MT and LXX texts of Amos 9:12. It appears that the LXX had a *Vorlage* that said *'adam* (humanity) instead of *'edom* (Edom), or that the LXX translator thought this was what his *Vorlage* said. This would have given rise to Greek *anthrōpōn* (humans). Similarly, where the MT has *yirshu* (they will inherit), the LXX translator seems to have read *yidreshu* (they will seek), which accounts for the translation *ekzētēsōsin* (they might seek out). In sum, Luke's version of Amos 9:12 allowed him to make a case for the inclusion of the Gentiles in the cult of YHWH, as opposed to believing

24. The New English Translation of the Septuagint renders the operative phrase in Amos 9:12 thus: "In order that those remaining of humans and all the nations upon whom my name has been called might seek out me."

25. The Targum of Amos 9:12 reveals the same perspective as the MT: "That the house of Israel, upon whom my name is called, might take possession of the remnant of Edom and all the nations . . ." (*bet yisra'el de'itqeri shemi 'alehon bedil deyahsenun yat she'ara' da'edom wekol 'ammaya'*).

26. Cf. Beverly Roberts Gaventa, *Acts*, Abingdon New Testament Commentaries (Nashville: Abingdon, 2003), 219.

that the restoration of the Davidic Messiah entailed the submission of the Gentiles to Israel—a reading which might well have suggested that Gentile converts be circumcised, rather than incorporated in the people of God *as* Gentiles.[27]

### Torah Parameters for Gentile Believers

Having interpreted Peter's experience with Cornelius within the framework of the LXX version of Amos 9 (as opposed to Exodus 4!), James concludes, "We should not trouble those Gentiles who are turning to God, but we should write to them to abstain only from things polluted by idols and from fornication and from whatever has been strangled and from blood" (Acts 15:19–20). James's prohibitions (of fornication and the consumption of any animal sacrificed to an idol or not properly bled) may strike modern readers as idiosyncratic. But they would not have seemed terribly odd to a first-century Jewish audience.

Admittedly, there is some debate as to which biblical antecedent stands behind James's prohibition. One plausible option is that James takes inspiration from the Holiness Code of Leviticus 17–18, specifically, the prohibitions that apply to sojourners living in Israel. While the Torah did not expect all resident aliens to convert, Leviticus does include various least-common-denominator regulations that apply to all residents in the land, irrespective of nationality. Those laws include prohibitions of eating blood (Lev. 17:12–13), of making sacrifices outside of the tabernacle (17:8–9, plausibly suggestive of idolatry), and of what was considered sexually deviant behavior (18:6–23).[28] By this token, James's argument is merely that Gentile believers be asked to do no more than the Torah always required of resident aliens.

Other scholars have suggested that James's four prohibitions bespeak the influence of the so-called Noahide commandments, that is, the commandments that applied to all peoples in the pre-Abrahamic period.[29]

---

27. Cf. Eric D. Barreto, *Ethnic Negotiations: The Function of Race and Ethnicity in Acts 16*, Wissenschaftliche Untersuchungen zum Neuen Testament: Zweite Reihe, vol. 294 (Tübingen: Mohr Siebeck, 2010), 94–95.

28. Joseph A. Fitzmyer, *First Corinthians: A New Translation with Introduction and Commentary*, Anchor Yale Bible, vol. 32 (New Haven: Yale University Press, 2008), 557.

29. Markus Bockmuehl, "The Noachide Commandments and New Testament Ethics," in *Jewish Law in Gentile Churches: Halakhah and the Beginning of Christian Public Ethics*, ed. Markus Bockmuehl (Grand Rapids: Baker Academic, 2000), 164–67.

While the Noahide commandments were not standardized in the New Testament period, prohibitions of sexual immorality, idolatry, and consumption of blood were common features.[30] By this reasoning, James's prohibitions were rooted in his view of what were universal moral imperatives, based on the understanding that any mandates emitted prior to the Abrahamic covenant were binding on all of humanity.

The present chapter does not require hairsplitting over which antecedent is more likely. As Craig Keener points out, "The Noahide laws themselves probably depend on and develop these themes in Lev 17–18, and by the period of Luke, interpreters could use the latter in explaining the former."[31] In the end, the substance of James's argument is the same:

- The Torah includes moral norms that apply to both Jew and Gentile.
- Gentile followers of Jesus should live according to the norms applicable to Gentile and Jew alike and are not bound by laws directed exclusively to the Israelites.
- This is because the act of joining the Way is disanalogous to the act of converting to Judaism: one can become a Christian without becoming Jewish, per Amos's vision of the nations being called by God's name *as diverse nations*.

### Thinking with the Holy Spirit

The church leaders agreed with the wisdom of James's proposal and in consequence dispatched a letter to the converts in Antioch, Syria, and Cilicia in order to inform them of their decision. Notice how the four prohibitions are framed.

It has seemed good to the Holy Spirit and to us to impose on you no further burden than these essentials: that you abstain from what has been sacrificed to idols and from blood and from what is strangled and from fornication. (15:28–29)

---

30. For examples, see Jub. 7:20; t. 'Abodah Zarah 8:4; b. Sanhedrin 56a; *Genesis Rabbah* 34:8; Bockmuehl, "The Noachide Commandments and New Testament Ethics," 158–62; and Keener, *Acts*, 3:2263–67.
31. Keener, *Acts*, 3:2268.

The opening clause candidly reflects the two agents that contributed to the Council's decision: the Holy Spirit and the human council members themselves. The letter identifies the role of the Spirit in bringing them to this new salvation-historical moment and in accepting the Gentiles, despite their lack of Torah observance. Nonetheless, the missive also affirms that the apostles and elders played an active role in coming to this conclusion. They interpreted their own experience of the Holy Spirit's action in connection with the Scriptures and took responsibility for the ethical and theological determinations made on the basis of their interpretation.

### Interpretation as an Act of Quilting

Consider the epistemic assumptions that undergird the Apostolic Council's argument: Acts 15 sews together the apostles' miraculous experiences with a version of Amos 9:11–12 and with biblical traditions about how Gentiles should live alongside Jews. Willie Jennings aptly describes this way of interpreting the Spirit's action in the church as "quilting work."

> James, in a beautiful moment of pure theological interpretation, performs this quilting work. James pulls fragments from the prophets and weaves their words to this word of God revealed in the Spirit's workings on flesh. *This will be the way forward—interpreters of biblical texts that yield to the Spirit recognizing the grace of working with the fragments*. . . . Such interpretive work takes seriously a living God who lives in and with the human creature and who invites us to weave together word of God spoken (in the past) with word of God being spoken *into lives (in the present)* by the Spirit.[32]

Jennings's words draw me up short every time I read them. He makes the interpretive approach reflected in Acts 15 a model for subsequent theological activity. By this token, the interpreter pays attention to her own experience in the church community ("the Spirit's workings on flesh"), precisely because that experience can also be revelatory, the "word of God being spoken into lives (in the present) by the Spirit."

Attention to that experience does not displace what the ARCS calls the "normative voices" of theology but recognizes that the biblical texts

---

32. Willie James Jennings, *Acts*, Belief: A Theological Commentary on the Bible (Louisville, KY: Westminster John Knox, 2017), 143, emphasis mine.

have always been drawn together with contemporary experiences in piece-meal fashion. This is no deficiency, but the way that Spirit-yielded people operate under continuing divine grace, the "grace of working with the fragments." Doing this should not be dismissed as an act of high-handed human hubris. It is rather an expression of taking "seriously a living God who lives in and with the human creature and who invites us" to partic-ipate in the process of hearing and speaking and incarnating the living word of the Spirit.

Here in Acts 15, I see the answer to the question that emerges for me as an evangelical scholar reading Graham, Watkins, and Vélez Caro. The question that is prompted by incorporating action research into the theological endeavor: Does the on-the-ground experience of Christian communities count in our theological task? Or does studying local com-munities send us headlong into the teeth of the epistemic quandary fore-grounded in chapter 1—that experience is insuperably subjective and is therefore raw material of dubious quality for the theological endeavor?

Acts 15 reveals that Christian theology has from the beginning been a synthetic act, heavily shaped by experience. The apostles' experience with ministry among the Gentiles formed their selective reading of Scripture, shaped their rational inferences, and thus guided them to establish new traditions and practices that could very well have been different. Experi-ence has always exercised a formative, sometimes even dominant, role in Christian theology. However much that might rankle the evangelical bib-lical scholar, it should not be discarded as a blithe capitulation to human subjectivity. Why? Because the apostolic confidence in the normativity of their past experiences was rooted in their certitude that it was the *Spirit* that had brought about their experiences.

If one believes that the Spirit of God continues to act, then one should continue to examine the experience and praxis of the church as a locus of the Spirit's continued revelation.[33] That perception of how the Spirit continues to speak should shape and be shaped by our engagement with Scripture. Furthermore, we should recognize that our own reason and tradition (and traditioned-ness) will be operative in that shaping. It is

33. Similarly, the ARCS team argued, "Fundamentally TAR is built on the conviction that the Holy Spirit is moving Christ's people to an ever deeper understanding of faith, in faith; and that this 'theology' is before us, waiting to be 'seen' or recognized." Cameron et al., *Talking about God*, 148.

quilting work. "This will be the way forward—interpreters . . . that yield to the Spirit recognizing the grace of working with the fragments."[34]

## The Productivity of MAR Quilting Work

This chapter has made a biblical case for the use of extrabiblical consider-ations in the Christian theological and missional task. Missional Action Research, by dint of its extensive attention to local church praxis and social-scientific scholarship, stakes its credibility on the belief that our missional efficacy will be enhanced by insights from beyond the canon of "normative theological voices." But the inverse is also true: the social sciences and local community action can be enriched and strengthened by the contributions of Christian theology and biblical scholarship. The Faith and Displacement team made a seven-year-long bet that the whole of our work (theology operating in conjunction with the social sciences and community experience) would be greater than the sum of its parts.

Retrospect has vindicated that hypothesis: We generated better theol-ogy thanks to our social-scientific work in IDP communities. We created new ways to put social-scientific theory into action by interweaving it with Scripture and religious practices. We developed new ecclesial resources based on interdisciplinary research. The ensuing pages will illustrate each of these points with a smattering of additional components of the Faith and Displacement research, each of which deserves more attention than this short book can allot them. That notwithstanding, the point to bear in mind throughout this survey is that, in traditional disciplinary silos, all of this work would have been impossible.

### New Scriptural Insights

When we waded into Faith and Displacement, we expected that the Bible would be a resource for ministry to IDPs. But we were surprised by how much the work changed our reading of the Bible.

Sometimes, new interpretive insights came from studying the Bible with IDPs. Both the public sector interaction and sociology teams used *lectura popular de la Biblia* (the people's reading of Scripture) as a method to learn about IDP understandings of their experience of displacement. Milton Acosta sat with Colombian IDPs from the slums of Bogotá to

34. Jennings, *Acts*, 143.

the jungles of the Cauca and facilitated group reflections on the book of Ruth—since Ruth and Naomi were both women displaced by environmental factors and bereaved of their husbands and communities. Robert Heimburger and Guillermo Mejía explored the Parable of the Unforgiving Servant (Matt. 18:25–35) with victims of the violent conflict as a way of plumbing their thoughts about forgiveness. Fascinatingly, the IDPs revealed aspects of the text that we (and the larger biblical guild) had not yet glimpsed.

For example, when the IDPs read the Parable of the Unforgiving Servant, they interpreted it with a primary focus on violence and economic extortion. By contrast, critical scholars treat the parabolic details as incidental to a spiritualized message about the forgiveness of sins, pushing the matters of violence and debt forgiveness to the side as a narrative husk. Nevertheless, the story is transparently about economic desperation due to indebtedness and slavery, cycles of violent intimidation, imprisonment, and torture, and the way that forgiveness can transform fear, poverty, and brutality into freedom. While one need not *limit* the referent of the parable to matters of debt and violence, the fact that Western interpreters fail to see those as the *first and most obvious* points of relevance of the parable reveals our distance from the social world of the earliest Christians.[35] Communities of victims changed the way we read Scripture. We now see things more clearly, the glass a shade less dark than it was.[36]

So also the extended engagement with social-scientific theories, infused with the knowledge of real suffering communities, provided new ways to interpret the Scriptures. For instance, our early research revealed that the social polarization of Colombia is rooted in experiences of trauma, which have in turn been incorporated into religio-political narratives that drive wedges further between factions of Colombian society. Consequently, Milton Acosta and I delved into the social-scientific work on trauma, especially on *collective* trauma and the elaboration of *trauma narratives*. Sociologists like Jeffrey Alexander helped us see how traumatic

35. See Robert W. Heimburger, Christopher M. Hays, and Guillermo Mejía Castillo, "Forgiveness and Politics: Reading Matthew 18:21–35 with Survivors of the Armed Conflict in Colombia," *HTS Teologiese Studies / Theological Studies* 75, no. 4 (2019): 1–9.

36. See also Milton Acosta and Laura Milena Cadavid Valencia, "El Dios de las personas en situación de desplazamiento," in *Fe y Desplazamiento: la investigación-acción misional ante la crisis colombiana del desplazamiento forzoso*, ed. Christopher M. Hays and Milton Acosta (Eugene, OR: Wipf & Stock, 2023), 328–46.

experiences are publicly explained through stories (trauma narratives) that either perpetuate polarization or foster reconciliation.[37] We came to realize that the Scriptures themselves were rife with ancient trauma narratives and that Colombian Christian leaders were (for better and for worse) already involved in the generation of new trauma narratives, attempting to make sense of the conflict. So, we dug into biblical trauma narratives to show how the people of God made sense of traumatizing events. In turn, we offered these stories and this approach to the pastors of Colombia in order to nourish their preaching as they cast vision for a way out of the conflict.[38]

### New Theological and Pastoral Concepts for IDPs

I would not want to imply that as academic theologians we only learned from local communities and the social sciences without making reciprocal contributions. Rigorous theological study, drawing on the insights of the North Atlantic guild, also provided new resources to the Colombian church. For example, Guillermo Mejía, the leader of the public sector interaction team, recognized that the triumphalist tendencies of Colombian evangelicalism were perpetuating unresolved grief and undermining the resiliency of believers. He therefore mined the biblical witness about the practice of lamentation, buttressed with insights from Christian ethicist Luke Bretherton in order to affirm the place of grief and lament in the life of faith and the public Christian witness for peace.[39]

Or consider the topic of theodicy. The problem of evil stalks in the shadows of many victims' minds as they struggle to reconcile their suffering with their beliefs in a loving God. Facile theodicies make the rounds in Colombian churches, often doing more harm than good. So Milton Acosta and I scoured the resources of Western philosophical theology for nuanced theodicies that responded to the wounds of Colombian believers. We demonstrated the compatibility of these theodicies with the biblical

37. So Jeffery C. Alexander, *Trauma: A Social Theory* (Cambridge: Polity, 2012).

38. Christopher M. Hays and Milton Acosta, "A Concubine's Rape, an Apostle's Flight, and a Nation's Reconciliation: Biblical Interpretation, Collective Trauma Narratives, and the Armed Conflict in Colombia," *Biblical Interpretation* 28 (2020): 56–83.

39. Guillermo Mejía Castillo, "El lamento: terreno fértil de resiliencia política de las personas en situación de desplazamiento," in *Fe y Desplazamiento: la investigación-acción misional ante la crisis colombiana del desplazamiento forzoso*, ed. Christopher M. Hays and Milton Acosta (Eugene, OR: Wipf & Stock, 2023), 310–27.

224 • CHAPTER 8

witness, even in specific relation to the evils of forced migration.[40] While we would be the first to warn against the dangers of imposing occidental theology on Majority World communities, we also confirmed the pastoral value of well-contextualized insights deriving from the North Atlantic.

## Presenting Social-Scientific Strategies through Scripture and Religion

Christian theology and churches also proved powerful means for putting social-scientific insight into action in IDP communities. For instance, our psychology team created a curriculum to train church leaders to offer trauma-informed pastoral care.[41] They also resourced local communities to help victims process their trauma, using a range of Christian resources—recitation of Psalms, Scripture studies, hymnody, meditation—as mechanisms for teaching about traumatic stress, self-regulation, relapses, forgiveness, and healing.[42]

Analogous results were achieved in all the other project disciplines. Our economics team took recent research on small business development and alignment with national agendas and community paradigms, and used biblical expositions and ecclesial case studies to help Christian businesspeople create faith-based corporations to employ IDPs.[43] The sociology team trained Christian youth in participatory "Do-no-harm" (*Acción sin daño*) approaches to social work.[44] By engaging the resources of the Christian faith, we helped churches serve the displaced with some of the best practices from the social sciences.

40. Christopher M. Hays and Milton Acosta, "A Colombian Theology and Theodicy of Forced Migration: Interpreting the Bible from and for the Colombian Displacement Crisis," in *Theologies of Migration*, ed. K. K. Yeo and Gene L. Green (Eugene, OR: Cascade, 2023), forthcoming.

41. Lisseth Rojas-Flores et al., *Líderes de las iglesias como agentes de sanidad después del trauma*, 2nd ed. (Medellín: Publicaciones SBC, 2020).

42. Josephine Hwang Koo et al., *La iglesia y el trauma: una guía de recursos para profesionales de la salud mental cristianos que trabajan con personas en situación de desplazamiento en sus congregaciones*, 2nd ed. (Medellín: Publicaciones SBC, 2020).

43. Alexander Fajardo Sánchez and Christopher M. Hays, *Corporaciones para el Reino* (Medellín: Publicaciones SBC, 2018).

44. Laura Milena Cadavid Valencia and Ivón Natalia Cuervo, *Enfoque y metodologías participativas, dar voz a las comunidades*, 2nd ed. (Medellín: Publicaciones SBC, 2020).

## New Ecclesial Resources Based on Interdisciplinary Research

It was especially exciting to witness the generation of pedagogically astute ecclesial resources deriving from the fusion of social-scientific insight and Christian theology. As an academic, I was fascinated to see David López delve into irenology (peace studies) while Guillermo Mejía studied lament and Duberney Rojas Seguro examined the political agency of IDP campesinos. But as a missionary, I thrilled at how they interwove their scholarship in the curricula *Church, Politics, and Displacement*,[45] combining poetry, dramas, handicrafts, and *lectura popular de la Biblia*, all to mobilize churches for political action.

This pattern of parlaying academic research into missional resources repeated itself time and again across teams. Thus, South African sexual-violence researcher Elisabet LeRoux worked with Colombian sociologist Laura Cadavid to publish on sexual trauma among Colombian conflict victims.[46] That research was then combined with a biblical theology of mutual sexuality, allowing them to broach the nearly unspeakable issue of rape in the psychology team's curriculum for pastors.[47] So also, Duberney Rojas Seguro—a brilliant sociologist and political scientist who died tragically during the second stage of Faith and Displacement—demonstrated extraordinary creativity in creating the *Peacemakers Tournament* curriculum, which used football tournaments and Christian ethics to teach the Harvard method of nonviolent conflict resolution to IDP children,[48] thus helping break the cycles of intergenerational vengeance.

---

45. Robert W. Heimburger et al., *Iglesia, política y desplazamiento: cartilla para profesionales*, 2nd ed. (Medellín: Publicaciones SBC, 2020); and Robert W. Heimburger et al., *Iglesia, política y desplazamiento: currículo para personas en situación de desplazamiento*, 2nd ed. (Medellín: Publicaciones SBC, 2020).

46. Elisabet Le Roux and Laura Milena Cadavid Valencia, "'There's No-One You Can Trust to Talk to Here': Churches and Internally Displaced Survivors of Sexual Violence," *HTS Teologiese Studies* 75, no. 4 (2019): 1–10; Elisabet Le Roux and Laura Milena Cadavid Valencia, "Partnering with Local Faith Communities: Learning from the Response to Internal Displacement and Sexual Violence in Colombia," in *International Development and Local Faith Actors: Ideological and Cultural Encounters*, ed. Katherine Kraft and Olivia J. Wilkinson, Routledge Research in Religion and Development (Oxon: Routledge, 2020), 236–50; and Elisabet Le Roux and Laura Milena Cadavid Valencia, "'Las iglesias no pueden permanecer en silencio': debates y acciones frente a la violencia sexual en comunidades evangélicas en Colombia," *Revista colombiana de sociología* 45, no. 1 (2022): 243–65.

47. Rojas-Flores et al., *Líderes de iglesias*, 99–112.

48. Rojas Seguro, *Torneo conciliadores de paz*.

Speaking personally, much of my scholarly research had previously focused on wealth ethics. But Faith and Displacement required me to traverse a wide range of Scriptural material pertinent to IDP economic recovery[49] and to work with a team of professionals in order to braid Christian insight together with learnings from field research and development studies. As a result, we created a suite of materials on small-business development,[50] formal employment,[51] and even the formation of church-based productive associations to provide income-generating opportunities in rural environments.[52]

Mission Action Research enabled a level of productivity that would have been impossible for either theology or the social sciences operating alone. Faith and Displacement's combination of interdisciplinary scholarship, fieldwork in displaced communities and local churches, and implementation and revision of an intervention, allowed us to integrate social-scientific strategies in ecclesial ministries and to generate original Scriptural insight, new theological knowledge, and fresh ecclesial resources. The whole was greater than the sum of its parts. The fact that this was achieved by a little evangelical seminary in Colombia bespeaks the efficacy of the MAR method. More fundamentally, it testifies to the potency of theologians doing interdisciplinary scholarship that stays close to the wound.

## Conclusion

None of us at the Fundación Universitaria Seminario Bíblico de Colombia (FUSBC) ever hoped to "fix" the problem of displacement in Colombia.

---

49. Christopher M. Hays, "La teología cristiana y el avance económico de las personas en situación de desplazamiento: aportes bíblico-teológicos a la superación financiera de las víctimas," in *Fe y Desplazamiento: la investigación-acción misional ante la crisis colombiana del desplazamiento forzoso*, ed. Christopher M. Hays and Milton Acosta (Eugene, OR: Wipf & Stock, 2023).

50. Global Disciples et al., *Desarrollo de la microempresa: manual del facilitador*, 2nd ed. (Medellín: Publicaciones SBC, 2020).

51. Jobs for Life, Alexander Fajardo Sánchez, and Christopher M. Hays, *Trabajos para la vida* (Medellín: Publicaciones SBC, 2018).

52. H. Leonardo Ramírez and Isabel Orozco, *Asociados para el desarrollo: construcción de asociaciones de base eclesial para el desarrollo económico* (Medellín: Publicaciones SBC, 2019).

However much messiah complexes are real temptations to missionaries and theologians, we remained acutely aware that we were a crew of second-string scholars sitting around a plywood table in a razor-wire-enclosed seminary campus on the wrong side of Medellín. Originally, we were just trying to cobble together a little edited volume to boost our shot at graduate accreditation. But then an apprehension of the darkness of displacement settled upon us. We realized that a theology that could publish about the wounds of eight million exiles, shelve the volume, and walk away would be a theology that had little to do with the kingdom of God.

In this volume's opening chapter, I evoked Juan Mackay's notion of *teología del camino*, of doing theology not as a spectator seated on a balcony but rather as a fellow traveler on the road. "The Road . . . a place where life is tensely lived, where thought has its birth in conflict. . . . It is the place of action, of pilgrimage. . . . On the Road a goal is sought, dangers are faced, life is poured out. . ."[53]

Faith and Displacement got us off the balcony and onto the road. Through MAR, we came to a deep (if secondhand) understanding of the gutting realities of violent displacement. Engaging the experience of Christian communities as a *locus theologicus* generated superior missional praxis. We didn't rescue the IDPs or the Colombian church. But I think we prepared the way of the Lord (Luke 3:4; Isa 40:3) a little more.

As theologians, we were able to speak more truly about the will of God in the midst of pain. As seminary professors, we were able to resource pastors more effectively to be salt and light amid social darkness and missional insipidity. And as Christians and fellow pilgrims, we were able to tread a few steps on the *camino* of the Messiah who had nowhere to lay his head, who makes himself present among the hungry, the naked, and the displaced. "There can be no true knowledge of ultimate things, that is to say of God and man, of duty and destiny, that is not born in a concern and perfected in a commitment; which is the same as saying that religious truth is obtained only on the Road."[54]

---

53. John A. Mackay, *A Preface to Christian Theology* (New York: Macmillan, 1941), 30.
54. Mackay, *Preface*, 44–45.

# The Multidimensional Consequences of Displacement

The holistic efficacy of the Faith and Displacement intervention required a nuanced apprehension of the multidimensional experience of displacement. The most poignant features of that experience include family dismemberment, poverty, psychological trauma, government inefficacy, and social exclusion.

## Family Dismemberment

The vast majority of IDPs flee from the *campo* to a big city or at least a semi-urban municipality, trying to get out of the way and out of reach of the group that terrorized them. In that new location, the loss they most immediately feel is that of their family. Bear in mind that there have already been over one million victims of homicide in the armed conflict (meaning that the proportion of homicide victims to IDPs is 1:8). Thirty-nine percent of displaced families have only one parent, almost always a woman,[1] and 39 percent of those women personally witnessed the murder of a husband or a male child.[2] In other instances, victims are separated from their loved ones in the struggle that set them running, and live for years without being able to find a spouse or a child, insofar as many campesinos lack cell phones or email accounts with which to reestablish contact, once separated. A thirty-eight-year-old man who fled

1. Angela Consuelo Carillo, "Internal Displacement in Colombia: Humanitarian, Economic and Social Consequences in Urban Settings and Current Challenges," *International Review of the Red Cross* 91, no. 875 (2009): 531.

2. Jairo Arboleda and Elena Correa, "Forced Internal Displacement," in *Colombia: The Economic Foundation of Peace*, ed. Marcelo M. Guigale, Olivier Lafourcade, and Connie Luff (Washington, DC: World Bank, 2003), 834.

from the Huila department to Colombia's capital narrated: "When I got to Bogotá, I did not know where my wife was. We went for a year before finding each other. . . . The thing is that, when they came to the farm, I left running. I had to leave that way, I fled . . . and my wife stayed there, but they made her leave with the children."[3]

Thousands of women have lost children to recruitment by armed groups. Ana, from Chocó, saw her brother shot in the head and then was forced to flee with her kids, her brother's twenty-year-old widow, and his three small children.

> I am 39 years old and I have eight children. One . . . went with an armed group—the same one that threatened me and killed my brother. This [my eldest] daughter went with the other group. Imagine the day when these two meet face to face! What sorrow, this war!
>
> Without time even to get any clothing, I went with my six younger children, my sister-in-law, and my nephews. . . . Today I found a shelter in Quibdó [the capital of Chocó]. What am I going to live on? I don't know, but what options do I have? I am worried about the kids. There is no space for them in the schools. What will they do all day?[4]

Education is not only a problem for the children of IDPs. On average, an adult Colombian IDP has only five years of formal education, and 11 percent have not even completed a year of schooling.[5] Illiteracy and innumeracy are rampant among displaced adults, which presents a massive obstacle to navigating the tortuous bureaucratic process involved in registering as a victim of the conflict and eventually receiving the aid to which they notionally have a legal entitlement.

---

3. Interview conducted by Laura Milena Cadavid Valencia, "Elementos para comprender el desplazamiento forzado en Colombia: un recorrido por normas, conceptos y experiencias," in *Conversaciones teológicas del sur global americano: violencia, desplazamiento y fe*, ed. Oscar Garcia-Johnson and Milton Acosta (Eugene, OR: Wipf & Stock, 2016), 22.

4. Comité Internacional de la Cruz Roja, "Los desplazados de Chocó: testimonio," https://www.icrc.org/es/doc/resources/documents/misc/5tecx6.htm.

5. Carillo, "Internal Displacement in Colombia," 531.

## Poverty and Psychological Damage

The loss of family members, in conjunction with dramatic educational disadvantages,[6] exacerbates the long-term impoverishment suffered by IDPs following their displacement. People displaced from rural to urban environments experience an *extreme* poverty rate of 85 percent.[7] This acute indigence owes to a variety of mutually conspiring factors.[8] For example, upon leaving behind their homes, IDPs lose over 50 percent of their assets, even *without* including the value of their land.[9] In an attempt to grapple with these major financial disadvantages, IDPs often recur to strategies that damage their long-term prospects, such as taking usurious loans, eliminating meals, and removing their children from school so that they too can work.[10] Since their agricultural skills are largely incompatible with the urban labor markets, IDPs also struggle to find decent jobs. While women can frequently secure low-wage domestic employment, men (who are accustomed to being breadwinners for their families) struggle to generate income.[11] The combined effect of these factors is an endemic of chronic, intergenerational poverty.[12]

6. On which, see further Saskia Alexandra Donner, "Using Art in Adult Christian Education: An Option for Reflecting on Scripture and Building Relationships amongst Internally Displaced Adults in Colombia," *Christian Education Journal* 17, no. 1 (2020): 40–41.

7. Carillo, "Internal Displacement in Colombia," 534.

8. For an extended version of this argument, see Christopher M. Hays, "Justicia económica y la crisis del desplazamiento interno en Colombia," in *Conversaciones teológicas del sur global americano: violencia, desplazamiento y fe*, ed. Milton Acosta and Oscar Garcia-Johnson (Eugene, OR: Wipf & Stock, 2016), 44–52.

9. Bear in mind that 55 percent of displaced households have either informal or formal access to land (on average, a parcel of 13.2 hectares). Ana María Ibáñez and Andrés Moya, "Do Conflicts Create Poverty Traps? Asset Losses and Recovery for Displaced Households in Colombia," in *The Economics of Crime: Lessons for and from Latin America*, ed. Rafael Di Tella, Sebastian Edwards, and Ernesto Schargrodsky (Chicago: University of Chicago Press, 2010), 155.

10. Ana María Ibáñez and Carlos Eduardo Vélez, "Civil Conflict and Forced Migration: The Micro Determinants and Welfare Losses of Displacement and Colombia," *World Development* 36, no. 4 (2008): 658; and Carillo, "Internal Displacement in Colombia," 540.

11. The unemployment rate for IDP households in the first three months following displacement is 53 percent; Ibáñez and Moya, "Do Conflicts Create Poverty Traps?," 157.

12. Michael R. Carter and Christopher B. Barrett, "The Economics of Poverty Traps and Persistent Poverty: An Asset-Based Approach," *The Journal of Development Studies* 42,

As we saw in chapter 1 (p. 11), psychological trauma contributes to victims' chronic poverty, because trauma undermines the sorts of economic behaviors congenial to financial recovery. Those afflicted by psychological disturbances manifest a striking preference for low-risk/low-reward economic behavior,[13] such that they gravitate toward the saturated informal sector of the economy (selling candy on buses, washing windshields in intersections) and avoid the sorts of entrepreneurial activities that development economists often commend for nonmigrant, non-traumatized, low-income populations.

Of course, economic impacts are only side effects of IDP psychological suffering, which is itself nearly as widespread as IDP poverty and at least as devastating. Sixty-seven percent of displaced households report psychosocial suffering; 24 percent report having sought help; staggeringly, only 2 percent report receiving any professional support for emotional or mental health[14] Indeed, IDPs exhibit high levels of PTSD, anxiety, depression, nightmares, paranoia, survivor's guilt, and suicidal ideation.[15] These conditions in turn increase the likelihood of domestic abuse.

Furthermore, a failure to process loss and trauma contributes to the desire for vengeance among IDPs. As a thirty-eight-year-old woman from Guaviare (a department in southern Colombia) narrated: "In the second displacement, we were in the valley. We had to leave because they killed

no. 2 (2006): 189–95; Ibáñez and Moya, "Do Conflicts Create Poverty Traps?," 138–39; and Ana María Ibáñez and Andrés Moya, "Vulnerability of Victims of Civil Conflicts: Empirical Evidence for the Displaced Population of Colombia," *World Development* 38, no. 4 (2009): 649.

13. Andrés Moya, "Violence, Emotional Distress and Induced Changes in Risk Aversion," Working Paper No. 105, Programas dinámicas territoriales rurales (Rimisp - Centro Latinoamericano para el Desarrollo Rural, 2013), 11–12.

14. Carillo, "Internal Displacement in Colombia," 541.

15. Gloria Amparo Camilo, "Impacto psicológico del desplazamiento forzoso: estrategia de intervención," in *Efectos psicosociales y culturales del desplazamiento*, ed. Martha Nubia Bello, Elena Martín Cardinal, and Fernando Jiovani Arias (Bogotá: Universidad Nacional de Colombia, 2000), 31–35; Liliana Álvarez Woo, "Lectura de las implicaciones psicosociales derivadas del desplazamiento en las familias pertenecientes a la organización ADESCOP en el marco del proceso de restitución del derecho a la vivienda," in *Mesa de trabajo de Bogotá sobre desplazamiento interno* (Bogotá: Fundación Menonita Colombiana para el Desarrollo, 2006), 7–9; and cf. Lisseth Rojas-Flores, "Desplazamiento de centroamericanos y colombianos: violencia, trauma y el ministerio de la iglesia," in *Conversaciones teológicas del sur global americano: violencia, desplazamiento y fe*, ed. Oscar Garcia-Johnson and Milton Acosta (Eugene, OR: Wipf & Stock, 2016), 27–43.

my brother. My nephew saw everything, he was there watching. . . . He talks all the time about how he wants to take vengeance, even though he is only nine years old. My sister-in-law and I do not know what to do."[16]

Such a hunger for revenge, combined with a widespread Colombian pessimism about the efficacy of judiciary processes and state-administered justice,[17] has sustained successive waves of violence and recrimination across generations in Colombia and promise to continue to do the same in coming decades if matters of justice and mental health remain so pervasively unresolved. As Angélica Pinillo Mususú, a social worker who does community development with IDPs on the peripheries of Bogotá, explained to me in 2016: "If I was expelled by a paramilitary group, I become an enemy of the paramilitaries. . . . Or, conversely, if the guerrillas expelled me, . . . I generate so much hatred and so much thirst for vengeance that I end up joining the paramilitary groups in search of a justice the State has not been able to give."

## Governmental Inefficacy

As alluded to above, government corruption and bureaucracy both contribute to displacement and impede recuperation thereafter. This is not to say that the Colombian government as a whole is callous to the crisis, but that, even when well-meaning legislation is passed, it does not translate into anything like a sweeping solution.[18]

In 2011, the government ratified the Ley 1448 (a.k.a. the Law of Victims and Land Restitution), committing the state to provide reparations to victims of the conflict within a period of ten years. They failed miserably. So, in 2021, they passed the Ley 2078, extending the period for restitution another ten years. As of July 31, 2021, the Unit for Land Restitution had restored land to a total of 40,421 victims,[19] approximately one-half of

16. Cadavid Valencia, "Elementos para comprender," 23.

17. On pessimism and corruption, see Milton A. Acosta, *El mensaje del profeta Oseas: una teología práctica para combatir la corrupción* (Lima: Puma, 2018), 98.

18. This paragraph reproduces insights from Guillermo Mejía Castillo, "El equipo de Interacción con el sector público," in *Fe y Desplazamiento: la investigación-acción misional ante la crisis colombiana del desplazamiento forzoso*, ed. Christopher M. Hays and Milton Acosta (Eugene, OR: Wipf & Stock, 2022), 185–202.

19. Unidad de Restitución de Tierras, "Avances de restitución," https://www.restituciondetierras.gov.co/estadisticas-de-restitucion-de-tierras.

one percent of the total IDP population. In June of 2021, the government boasted of having made 1,235,018 financial payments, which amounted to the indemnification of 1,163,650 victims . . . that is, less than 15 percent of the total number of victims currently registered and recognized by the government. At that rate, it would take the government sixty-one years to indemnify all the victims financially, assuming that no other victims were added to the registry.[20] But over one million victims have been added to the registry just since 2016.

None of this is to deny the State has a role in helping heal the nation after this crisis. That notwithstanding, only the naive would expect the Colombian government to generate comprehensive change for the majority of the victimized population. Further, the government response focuses primarily on the restitution of land and money; it does not attempt to grapple seriously with the destruction of the social capital of displaced people.

## Social Exclusion

In all cultures, traumatizing events are processed in community, as the larger collective helps cradle the victims in their midst, providing emotional and material support.[21] This pertains especially to collectivist cultures, like Colombia and most Latin American nations. As the seminal trauma theorist Kai Erikson put matters, "It is the community that cushions pain, the community that provides a context for intimacy."[22] Indeed, in collectivist cultures, local community is heavily constitutive of people's sense of personal identity.[23]

Consequently, when violence expels Colombians from their communities, the victims are uprooted from that which sustained their very sense of self. As I was told by Pedro González Yanes, a pastor who lived and ministered in an IDP settlement in the department of Córdoba: "When they are displaced, a person suffers a disintegration. All the social tissue

20. "¿Ha cumplido el país en la reparación de las víctimas?," *El Tiempo*, 2021.
21. See further Hays and Acosta, "A Concubine's Rape," 56–83.
22. Kai T. Erikson, *Everything in Its Path: Destruction of Community in the Buffalo Creek Flood* (New York: Simon & Schuster, 1976), 193–94.
23. Erikson, *Everything in Its Path*, 214–15.

they had in their village is broken. . . . They feel diminished, they feel less than other people, they are not valued as people."

A number of factors compound IDPs' social disconnection in their arrival sites. In the first place, the intense regionalism of Colombia[24]— according to which people's sense of identity as being *costeño* or *paisa* outweighs their sense of being Colombian—means that an IDP from a different part of the country is perceived as "other" in a way that would be difficult for someone from the United States to understand, insofar as few Americans would consider their identity as a Midwesterner or a New Englander to be more primary than their identity as an American.[25] In other words, IDPs are obligated to confront a new culture and they do so having lost almost all of their social network and perhaps much of their family. Second, IDPs represent competition in the already saturated informal sector of the labor market of their arrival sites, taking jobs from locals and driving down wages. Third, victims of displacement often arouse the suspicion of their neighbors, who assume that the displaced must have done something sinister to deserve their misfortune (*Por algo será* is the speculation: "It must have been for something").[26]

This all means that displaced persons cannot simply put down new roots and generate new community upon arriving at their destination sites. It is a common mistake of people in individualist cultures to assume that collectivism is identical with sociability or extroversion, such that members of collectivist cultures can easily extricate themselves from one social context and re-embed themselves in a new location. That is not correct. "The difficulty is that when you invest so much of yourself in that kind of social arrangement, you become absorbed by it . . . and the larger collectivity around you becomes an extension of your own personality. . . . To 'be neighborly' is not a quality you can carry with you into a new situation like negotiable emotional currency; the old community was

24. German Puyana García, *¿Cómo somos? Los colombianos: reflexiones sobre nuestra idiosincrasia y cultura*, 2nd ed. (Bogotá: Bhandar, 2002), 83–86.

25. Texans might be the exception to prove the rule!

26. Fernando Jiovani Arias and Sandra Ruiz Ceballos, "Construyendo caminos con familias y comunidades afectadas por la situación del desplazamiento en Colombia: una experiencia de trabajo psicosocial," in *Efectos psicosociales y culturales del desplazamiento*, ed. Martha Nubia Bello, Elena Martín Cardinal, and Fernando Jiovani Arías (Bogotá: Universidad Nacional de Colombia, 2000), 52.

your niche in the classic ecological sense, and your ability to relate to that niche is not a skill easily transferred to another setting."[27]

Thus, the fact that Colombian culture is collectivist does not mean that displaced Colombians will regenerate strong social bonds in their new communities. On the contrary, the strength and integrality of the social bonds those Colombians previously enjoyed entail that displaced people experience a higher level of emotional suffering and possess a diminished capacity to recover following displacement.

27. Erikson, Everything in Its Path, 191.

# Summary Findings of the Field Research of the Public Sector Interaction, Psychology, and Sociology Teams

Chapter 4 of this volume laid out some of the key findings of the field research conducted by the missiology, pedagogy, and economics teams. This appendix complements that overview with summaries of the most important discoveries of the other three Faith and Displacement teams: public sector interaction, psychology, and sociology.

## Public Sector Interaction

The public sector interaction team combined focused groups, semi-structured interviews, the collection of life-stories, and groups of *lectura popular de la Biblia*[28] to explore how the church and Christian theology could re-enfranchise IDPs as political agents. They observed that numerous obstacles (excessive bureaucracy, unawareness of governmental processes, cooptation of IDPs by religious or political groups, etc.)

---

28. *People's Reading of the Bible* engages in the reading of Scripture with victims of the conflict and the exploration together of their understanding of the sociopolitical and spiritual ramifications of the text. For more information on the findings of the public sector interaction team, see Guillermo Mejía Castillo, "El equipo de Interacción con el sector público," in *Fe y Desplazamiento: la investigación-acción missional ante la crisis colombiana del desplazamiento forzoso*, ed. Christopher M. Hays and Milton Acosta (Eugene, OR: Wipf & Stock, 2022), 188–93; and cf. Robert W. Heimburger, Christopher M. Hays, and Guillermo Mejía Castillo, "Forgiveness and Politics: Reading Matthew 18:21–35 with Survivors of the Armed Conflict in Colombia," *HTS Teologiese Studies / Theological Studies* 75, no. 4 (2019): 1–9.

impede IDP political activity, but that IDPs can nonetheless prove to be important political agents if properly accompanied. Local churches can provide networks and support, both bureaucratic and emotional. They identified further that the Christian practice of lament can help generate emotional resiliency and catalyze political action, and they showed that Christian conceptions of forgiveness can similarly foster community engagement without sliding into the cycles of vengeance that have sustained the Colombian conflict for centuries.

The team concluded that a constructive intervention with IDPs would need to foster strong relationships with local churches, as well as a robust sense of the possibility and legitimacy of political agency. They also emphasized the importance of fostering an earnest process of spiritual reflection and formation—one including attention to lament and forgiveness—to help ensure healthy and enduring political action by IDPs.

## Psychology

The psychology team held focus groups with IDPs and in-depth interviews with faith leaders on a range of issues relating to mental health. They also conducted interviews, focus groups (in conjunction with the sociology team), a survey, and a workshop (directed to faith leaders) to explore the issue of sexual violence among IDPs.[29]

Time and again, the psychology team found that the IDPs displayed symptoms of PTSD that included pathological grief, depression, and despair about the future. While churches were typically viewed as positive entities and pastors were recognized as key leaders and potential allies, those same pastors made it clear that they felt a strong need for training to be able to respond responsibly to the emotional burdens born by IDP community members.

Similarly, the team discovered that sexual violence was a besetting problem prior to, during, and following displacement. They found

29. For a more detailed account of the psychology team's field research, see Lisseth Rojas-Flores, Josephine Hwang Koo, and Doribeth Tardillo, "El equipo de Psicología," in *Fe y Desplazamiento: la investigación-acción misional ante la crisis colombiana del desplazamiento forzoso*, ed. Christopher M. Hays and Milton Acosta (Eugene, OR: Wipf & Stock, 2022), 169–76; and cf. Joseph M. Currier et al., "Spiritual Struggles and Ministry-Related Quality of Life among Faith Leaders in Colombia," *Psychology of Religion and Spirituality* 11, no. 2 (2019): 148–56.

furthermore that survivors of sexual violence are often rejected by their families, such that they often turn to the church for support. The church leaders with whom they engaged affirmed that they were in principle open to addressing issues of sexual violence, but simultaneously expressed a need for training on how best to care for survivors. Accordingly, the psychology team concluded that their interventions would need to provide significant guidance to religious leaders (even more so than to mental health specialists) on how to offer trauma-informed care to victims of the violent conflict, including victims of sexual violence.

## Sociology

The sociology team (working in some instances in conjunction with the psychology team) implemented protocols for two different interviews with local leaders, a focus group for IDPs, a *lectura popular de la Biblia* on the book of Ruth (also conducted with IDPs), and an interview protocol for exploring the life stories of select IDPs.[30] Their research revealed that IDPs had far warmer estimations of the support provided by religious communities than of that provided by the government, ranking churches in the second place (after family networks) as a source of support following displacement. Similarly, in their *lectura popular* of the book of Ruth, they highlighted their trust in God and their obligations to care for other vulnerable people (like Naomi). They struggled, nonetheless, with the idea that Naomi would blame God for her suffering (Ruth 1:20–21), revealing that they understood strong piety to be incompatible with expressing doubts or anger toward God.

Additionally, in their joint work with the psychology group, the sociology team found that pastors were widely aware of the problems of sexual violence that existed in the IDP community, and that victims expected that the church leaders should be able to serve as allies in confronting sexual violence. Nonetheless, people expressed that there did not exist adequate spaces within the church community for addressing sexual

---

30. For a more detailed account of the sociology team's field research, see Laura Milena Cadavid Valencia, "El equipo de Sociología," in *Fe y Desplazamiento: la investigación-acción misional ante la crisis colombiana del desplazamiento forzoso*, ed. Christopher M. Hays and Milton Acosta (Eugene, OR: Wipf & Stock, 2022), 117–24.

violence, and church leaders typically felt ill-equipped to respond to such a volatile and delicate issue.[31]

In sum, the sociology team concluded that faith communities are poised to act as trusted agents and allies on behalf of IDPs, confirming the aptness of Faith and Displacement's decision to work through churches. They also identified that current ecclesial structures and teachings tend not to be well-resourced for dealing with some of the negative feelings and doubts that can be generated by displacement, and in particular with the aftermath of sexual violence.

31. See further Le Roux and Cadavid Valencia, "There's No-One You Can Trust," 1–10; and Le Roux and Cadavid Valencia, "Partnering with Local Faith Communities," 236–50.

# Bibliography

Acosta, Milton A. *El mensaje del profeta Oseas: una teología práctica para combatir la corrupción*. Lima: Puma, 2018.

Acosta, Milton, and Laura Milena Cadavid Valencia. "El Dios de las personas en situación de desplazamiento." In *Fe y Desplazamiento: la investigación-acción misional ante la crisis colombiana del desplazamiento forzoso*, edited by Christopher M. Hays and Milton Acosta, 328–46. Eugene, OR: Wipf & Stock, 2023.

Alexander, Jeffery C. *Trauma: A Social Theory*. Cambridge: Polity, 2012.

Álvarez Woo, Liliana. "Lectura de las implicaciones psicosociales derivadas del desplazamiento en las familias pertenecientes a la organización ADESCOP en el marco del proceso de restitución del derecho a la vivienda." In *Mesa de trabajo de Bogotá sobre desplazamiento interno*, 7–15. Bogotá: Fundación Menonita Colombiana para el Desarrollo, 2006.

Amparo Camilo, Gloria. "Impacto psicológico del desplazamiento forzoso: estrategia de intervención." In *Efectos psicosociales y culturales del desplazamiento*, edited by Martha Nubia Bello, Elena Martín Cardinal, and Fernando Jiovani Arias, 27–40. Bogotá: Universidad Nacional de Colombia, 2000.

Arboleda, Jairo, and Elena Correa. "Forced Internal Displacement." In *Colombia: The Economic Foundation of Peace*, edited by Marcelo M. Guigale, Olivier Lafourcade, and Connie Luff, 825–48. Washington, DC: World Bank, 2003.

Argyris, Chris, and Donald Schön. "Participatory Action Research and Action Science Compared: A Commentary." In *Participatory Action Research*, edited by William Foote Whyte, 85–96. London: Sage, 1991.

Arias, Fernando Jiovani, and Sandra Ruiz Ceballos. "Construyendo caminos con familias y comunidades afectadas por la situación del desplazamiento en Colombia: una experiencia de trabajo psicosocial." In *Efectos psicosociales y culturales del desplazamiento*, edited by Martha Nubia Bello, Elena Martín Cardinal, and Fernando Jiovani Arias, 41–62. Bogotá: Universidad Nacional de Colombia, 2000.

Arias Trujillo, Ricardo. *Historia de Colombia contemporánea (1920-2010)*. Bogotá: Universidad de los Andes, 2011.

Balcazar, Fabricio E. "Investigación acción participativa (iap): aspectos conceptuales y dificultades de implementación." *Fundamentos en humanidades* 4, no. 1/2 (2003): 59–77.

Barreto, Eric D. *Ethnic Negotiations: The Function of Race and Ethnicity in Acts 16*. Wissenschaftliche Untersuchungen zum Neuen Testament: Zweite Reihe. Vol. 294. Tübingen: Mohr Siebeck, 2010.

Bauckham, Richard. *Jesus and the Eyewitnesses: The Gospels as Eyewitness Testimony.* 2nd ed. Grand Rapids: Eerdmans, 2017.

BBC. "Peace Court: Colombia Army 'Behind 6,400 Extrajudicial Killings.'" BBC News, https://www.bbc.com/news/world-latin-america-56112386.

Bedford, Nancy Elizabeth. "La misión en el sufrimiento y ante el sufrimiento." In *Bases bíblicas de la misión: perspectivas latinoamericanas,* edited by C. René Padilla, 383–403. Buenos Aires: Kairós, 1998.

Bergold, Jarg, and Stefan Thomas. "Participatory Research Methods: A Methodological Approach in Motion." *Forum Qualitative Sozialforschung* 13, no. 1 (2012): §§1–110.

Bevans, Stephen B., and Roger P. Schroeder. *Constants in Context: A Theology of Mission for Today.* Maryknoll, NY: Orbis, 2004.

Bockmuehl, Markus. "The Noachide Commandments and New Testament Ethics." In *Jewish Law in Gentile Churches: Halakhah and the Beginning of Christian Public Ethics,* edited by Markus Bockmuehl, 145–73. Grand Rapids: Baker Academic, 2000.

Boff, Leonardo. *Jesus Christ Liberator: A Critical Christology for Our Time.* Translated by Patrick Hughes. Maryknoll, NY: Orbis, 1978.

Bolt, Peter G. "Mission and Witness." In *Witness to the Gospel: The Theology of Acts,* edited by I. Howard Marshall and David Peterson, 169–90. Grand Rapids: Eerdmans, 1998.

Cadavid Valencia, Laura Milena. "Elementos para comprender el desplazamiento forzado en Colombia: un recorrido por normas, conceptos y experiencias." In *Conversaciones teológicas del sur global americano: violencia, desplazamiento y fe,* edited by Oscar García-Johnson and Milton Acosta, 3–26. Eugene, OR: Wipf & Stock, 2016.

———. "El equipo de Sociología." In *Fe y Desplazamiento: la investigación-acción misional ante la crisis colombiana del desplazamiento forzoso,* edited by Christopher M. Hays and Milton Acosta, 113–28. Eugene, OR: Wipf & Stock, 2022.

Cadavid Valencia, Laura Milena, and Ivón Natalia Cuervo. *Enfoque y metodologías participativas, dar voz a las comunidades.* 2nd ed. Medellín: Publicaciones SBC, 2020.

Cameron, Helen, Deborah Bhatti, Catherine Duce, James Sweeney, and Clare Watkins. *Talking about God in Practice: Theological Action Research and Practical Theology.* London: SCM, 2010.

Carillo, Angela Consuelo. "Internal Displacement in Colombia: Humanitarian, Economic and Social Consequences in Urban Settings and Current Challenges." *International Review of the Red Cross* 91, no. 875 (2009): 527–46.

Carter, Michael R., and Christopher B. Barrett. "The Economics of Poverty Traps and Persistent Poverty: An Asset-Based Approach." *The Journal of Development Studies* 42, no. 2 (2006): 178–99.

Centro Nacional de Memoria Histórica. *La guerra inscrita en el cuerpo: informe nacional de violencia sexual en el conflicto armado.* Bogotá: Centro Nacional de Memoria Histórica, 2017.

———. *Una guerra sin edad: informe nacional de reclutamiento y utilización de niños, niñas y adolescentes en el conflicto armado colombiano.* Bogotá: Centro Nacional de Memoria Histórica, 2017.

Chambers, Robert. "Poverty and Livelihoods: Whose Reality Counts?" *Environment and Urbanization* 7, 1 (1995): 173-204.

Collier, Elizabeth W., and Charles R. Strain. *Global Migration: What's Happening, Why, and a Just Response*. Winona, MN: Anselm Academic, 2017.

Colmenares E., Ana Mercedes. "Investigación-acción participativa: una metodología integradora del conocimiento y la acción." *Voces y silencios: revista latinoamericana de educación* 3, no. 1 (2012): 102–15.

Comisión Intereclesial de Justicia y Paz. "Operación 'Génesis', tortura y ejecución extrajudicial de Marino Lopez Mena." https://www.justiciaypazcolombia.com/operacion -genesis-tortura-y-ejecucion-extrajudicial-de-marino-lopez-mena/.

Comité Internacional de la Cruz Roja. "Los desplazados de Chocó: testimonio." https:// www.icrc.org/es/doc/resources/documents/misc/5tecx6.htm.

Contreras Lara, Nancy Milena, and José Daniel Gutiérrez Rodríguez. "La parte religiosa e ignorada de Orlando Fals Borda." Corporación Universitaria Minuto de Dios, 2012.

Contreras O., Rodrigo. "La investigación acción participativa (IAP): revisandos sus metodologías y potencialidades." In *Experiencias y metodología de la investigación participativa*, edited by John Durston and Francisca Miranda. Políticas sociales, 9–17. Santiago, Chile: Naciones Unidas, 2002.

Cornwall, Andrea, and Rachel Jewkes. "What Is Participatory Research?" *Social Science & Medicine* 41, no. 12 (1995): 1666–76.

Currier, Joseph M., Lisseth Rojas-Flores, Wesley H. McCormick, Josephine Hwang Koo, Laura Milena Cadavid Valencia, Francis Alexis Pineda, Elisabet Le Roux, and Tommy Givens. "Spiritual Struggles and Ministry-Related Quality of Life among Faith Leaders in Colombia." *Psychology of Religion and Spirituality* 11, no. 2 (2019): 148–56.

Degenhardt, Hans-Joachim. *Lukas, Evangelist der Armen: Besitz und Besitzverzicht in den lukanischen Schriften: eine traditions- und redaktionsgeschichtliche Untersuchung*. Stuttgart: Katholisches Bibelwerk, 1965.

Deutsche Welle. "Más de 900 líderes sociales asesinados en Colombia desde 2016." *Deutsche Welle*, April 19, 2021.

Donner, Saskia Alexandra. "El equipo de Pedagogía." In *Fe y Desplazamiento: la investigación-acción misional ante la crisis colombiana del desplazamiento forzoso*, edited by Christopher M. Hays and Milton Acosta, 83–112. Eugene, OR: Wipf & Stock, 2022.

———. "Using Art in Adult Christian Education: An Option for Reflecting on Scripture and Building Relationships amongst Internally Displaced Adults in Colombia." *Christian Education Journal* 17, no. 1 (2020): 38–51.

Donner, Saskia Alexandra, and Leonela Orozco Álvarez. *Las artes: una herramienta eficaz para la enseñanza de adultos en situación de desplazamiento*. Medellín: Publicaciones SBC, 2018.

Durham, John I. *Exodus*. Word Biblical Commentary. Dallas: Word, 1987.

Erikson, Kai T. *Everything in Its Path: Destruction of Community in the Buffalo Creek Flood*. New York: Simon & Schuster, 1976.

Escobar, Samuel. "Doing Theology on Christ's Road." In *Global Theology in Evangelical Perspective: Exploring the Contextual Nature of Theology and Mission*, edited by Jeffrey P. Greenman and Gene L. Green, 67–85. Downer's Grove, IL: Intervarsity, 2012.

Fajardo Sánchez, Alexander, and Christopher M. Hays. *Corporaciones para el Reino*. Medellín: Publicaciones SBC, 2018.

Fals Borda, Orlando. *El problema de como investigar la realidad para transformala por la praxis*. 7th ed. Bogotá: Tercer mundo, 1997.

———. "Orígenes universales y retos actuales de la IAP." *Análisis político* 38 (1999): 71–88.

———. "Remaking Knowledge." In *Action and Knowledge: Breaking the Monopoly with Participatory Action Research*, edited by Orlando Fals Borda and Muhammad Anisur Rahman, 146–66. New York: Apex, 1991.

———. "Some Basic Ingredients." In *Action and Knowledge: Breaking the Monopoly with Participatory Action Research*, edited by Orlando Fals Borda and Muhammad Anisur Rahman, 3–12. New York: Apex, 1991.

Fitzmyer, Joseph A. *The Acts of the Apostles: A New Translation with Introduction and Commentary*. Anchor Bible. New York: Doubleday, 1998.

———. *First Corinthians: A New Translation with Introduction and Commentary*. Anchor Yale Bible. Vol. 32. New Haven: Yale University Press, 2008.

Freire, Paulo. *Pedagogy of the Oppressed*. Translated by Myra Bergman Ramos. 30th Anniversary ed. New York: Continuum International, 2000.

García-Johnson, Oscar, and Milton Acosta, eds. *Conversaciones teológicas del sur global americano: violencia, desplazamiento y fe*. Eugene, OR: Puertas Abiertas, 2016.

Gaventa, Beverly Roberts. *Acts*. Abingdon New Testament Commentaries. Nashville: Abingdon, 2003.

———. "'You Will Be My Witnesses': Aspects of Mission in the Acts of the Apostles." *Missiology* 10, no. 4 (1982): 413–25.

Global Disciples, Steve Rehner, Christopher M. Hays, Isaura Espitia Zúñiga, July Paola Fernández Rojas, Ever Enrique Maestre Alvarado, and Steban Andrés Villadiego Ramos. *Desarrollo de la microempresa: manual del facilitador*. 2nd ed. Medellín: Publicaciones SBC, 2020.

Gómez, Ricardo. *The Mission of God in Latin America*. Lexington, KY: Emeth, 2010.

Graham, Elaine. "Is Practical Theology a Form of 'Action Research'?" *International Journal of Practical Theology* 17, no. 1 (2013): 148–78.

Green, Gene L. *Vox Petri: A Theology of Peter*. Eugene, OR: Cascade, 2019.

Green, Joel B. *The Gospel of Luke*. New International Commentary on the New Testament. Grand Rapids: Eerdmans, 1997.

Grupo de Memoria Histórica. *¡Basta Ya! Colombia: Memorias de guerra y dignidad*. Bogotá: Centro Nacional de Memoria Histórica, 2013.

Gutiérrez, Gustavo. *A Theology of Liberation: History, Politics, and Salvation*. Translated by Sister Caridad Inda and John Eagleson. Rev. ed. Maryknoll, NY: Orbis, 1973.

"¿Ha cumplido el país en la reparación de las víctimas?" *El Tiempo*, 2021.

Haenchen, Ernst. *Die Apostelgeschichte*. Kritisch-exegetischer Kommentar über das Neue Testament. 7th ed. Vol. 3. Göttingen: Vandenhoeck & Ruprecht, 1977.

Hays, Christopher M. "Collaboration with Criminal Organisations in Colombia: An Obstacle to Economic Recovery." *Forced Migration Review* 58 (2018): 26–28.

———. "El equipo de Economía." In *Fe y Desplazamiento: la investigación-acción misional ante la crisis colombiana del desplazamiento forzoso*, edited by Christopher M. Hays and Milton Acosta, 129–66. Eugene, OR: Wipf & Stock, 2022.

———. "El equipo de Misiología." In *Fe y Desplazamiento: la investigación-acción misional ante la crisis colombiana del desplazamiento forzoso*, edited by Christopher M. Hays and Milton Acosta, 55–82. Eugene, OR: Wipf & Stock, 2022.

———. "Justicia económica y la crisis del desplazamiento interno en Colombia." In *Conversaciones teológicas del sur global americano: violencia, desplazamiento y fe*, edited by Milton Acosta and Oscar García-Johnson, 44–64. Eugene, OR: Wipf and Stock, 2016.

———. "La teología cristiana y el avance económico de las personas en situación de desplazamiento: aportes bíblico-teológicos a la superación financiera de las víctimas." In *Fe y Desplazamiento: la investigación-acción misional ante la crisis colombiana del desplazamiento forzoso*, edited by Christopher M. Hays and Milton Acosta, 247–68. Eugene, OR: Wipf & Stock, 2023.

———. *Luke's Wealth Ethics: A Study in Their Coherence and Character*. Wissenschaftliche Untersuchungen zum Neuen Testament II. Vol. 275. Tübingen: Mohr Siebeck, 2010.

———. *Renouncing Everything: Money and Discipleship in Luke*. Mahwah, NJ: Paulist, 2016.

———. "The State of Protestant Academic Theology in Colombia." In *Glaube und Theologie: Reformatorische Grundeinsichten in der ökumenischen Diskussion / Faith and Theology: Basic Insights of the Reformation in Ecumenical Debate*, edited by Wolfram Kinzig and Julia Winnebeck, 97–131. Veröffentlichungen der Wissenschaftlichen Gesellschaft für Theologie. Leipzig: Evangelische Verlagsanstalt, 2019.

———. "What Is the Place of My Rest? Being Migrant People(s) of the God of All the Earth." *Open Theology* 7, no. 2 (2021): 150–68.

Hays, Christopher M., and Milton Acosta. "A Colombian Theology and Theodicy of Forced Migration: Interpreting the Bible from and for the Colombian Displacement Crisis." In *Theologies of Migration*, edited by K. K. Yeo and Gene L. Green, forthcoming. Eugene, OR: Cascade, 2023.

———. "A Concubine's Rape, an Apostle's Flight, and a Nation's Reconciliation: Biblical Interpretation, Collective Trauma Narratives, and the Armed Conflict in Colombia." *Biblical Interpretation* 28 (2020): 56–83.

———. "Jesus as Missional Migrant: Latin American Christologies, the New Testament Witness, and Twenty-first Century Migration." In *Who Do You Say I Am? On the Humanity of Jesus*, edited by George Kalantzis, David B. Capes, and Ty Kieser, 158–77. Eugene, OR: Cascade, 2020.

Hays, Christopher M., Milton Acosta, and Saskia Donner, eds. *Research Reports of the Six Teams That Comprise the Project Integral Missiology and the Human Flourishing of Internally Displaced Persons in Colombia*, https://feydesplazamiento.org/investigacion.

Hays, Christopher M., Isaura Espitia Zúñiga, and Steban Andrés Villadiego Ramos. *La misión integral de la iglesia: cómo fortalecer o crear un ministerio a favor de personas en situación de desplazamiento: manual del facilitador*. Medellín: Publicaciones SBC, 2018.

Heimburger, Robert W., Christopher M. Hays, and Guillermo Mejía Castillo. "Forgiveness and Politics: Reading Matthew 18:21–35 with Survivors of the Armed Conflict in Colombia." *HTS Teologiese Studies / Theological Studies* 75, no. 4 (2019): 1–9.

Heimburger, Robert W., David López Amaya, Guillermo Mejía Castillo, Fernando Abilio Mosquera Brand, and Duberney Rojas Seguro. *Iglesia, política y desplazamiento: cartilla para profesionales.* 2nd ed. Medellín: Publicaciones SBC, 2020.

———. *Iglesia, política y desplazamiento: currículo para personas en situación de desplazamiento.* 2nd ed. Medellín: Publicaciones SBC, 2020.

Herr, Kathryn, and Gary L. Anderson. *The Action Research Dissertation: A Guide for Students and Faculty.* Thousand Oaks, CA: Sage, 2012.

Hofstede, Geerte. "What about Colombia?" https://geert-hofstede.com/colombia.html.

Holmes, Arthur F. *All Truth Is God's Truth.* Grand Rapids: Eerdmans, 1977.

Hwang Koo, Josephine, Lisseth Rojas-Flores, Larisa Grams-Benítez, Tommy Givens, and Francis Alexis Pineda González. *La iglesia y el trauma: una guía de recursos para profesionales de la salud mental cristianos que trabajan con personas en situación de desplazamiento en sus congregaciones.* 2nd ed. Medellín: Publicaciones SBC, 2020.

Ibáñez, Ana María, and Andrés Moya. "Do Conflicts Create Poverty Traps? Asset Losses and Recovery for Displaced Households in Colombia." In *The Economics of Crime: Lessons for and from Latin America*, edited by Rafael Di Tella, Sebastian Edwards, and Ernesto Schargrodsky, 137–72. Chicago: University of Chicago Press, 2010.

———. "Vulnerability of Victims of Civil Conflicts: Empirical Evidence for the Displaced Population of Colombia." *World Development* 38, no. 4 (2009): 647–63.

Ibáñez, Ana María, and Carlos Eduardo Vélez. "Civil Conflict and Forced Migration: The Micro Determinants and Welfare Losses of Displacement and Colombia." *World Development* 36, no. 4 (2008): 659–76.

Indepaz, Instituto de estudios para el desarrollo y la paz. "Informe de masacres en Colombia durantes el 2020 y 2021." Indepaz, http://www.indepaz.org.co/informe-de-masacres-en-colombia-durante-el-2020-2021/.

Jackson, Michael. *The Wherewithal of Life: Ethics, Migration, and the Question of Well-Being.* Berkley: University of California Press, 2013.

Jennings, Willie James. *Acts.* Belief: A Theological Commentary on the Bible. Louisville, KY: Westminster John Knox, 2017.

Jobs for Life, Alexander Fajardo Sánchez, and Christopher M. Hays. *Trabajos para la vida.* Medellín: Publicaciones SBC, 2018.

Jurisdicción especial para la paz. "Comunicado 019 de 2021." Bogotá, 2021.

Karlsen, Jan Irgens. "Action Research as Method: Reflections from a Program for Developing Methods and Competence." In *Participatory Action Research*, edited by William Foote Whyte, 143–57. London: Sage, 1991.

Keener, Craig S. *Acts: An Exegetical Commentary.* 4 vols. Grand Rapids: Baker Academic, 2012–2015.

Kindon, S., R. Pain, and M. Kesby. "Participatory Action Research." In *International Encyclopedia of Human Geography*, edited by Rob Kitchin and Nigel Thrift, 90–95. Amsterdam: Elsevier, 2009.

Kirkpatrick, David C. "C. René Padilla and the Origins of Integral Mission in Post-War Latin America." *Journal of Ecclesiastical History* 67, no. 2 (2016): 351–71.

Krause, Mariane. "Investigación-acción-participativa: una metodología para el desarrollo de la autoayuda, participación y empoderamiento." In *Experiencias y metodología de la investigación participativa*, edited by John Durston and Francisca Miranda, Políticas sociales, 41–56. Santiago, Chile: Naciones Unidas, 2002.

Kretzmann, John P., and John McKnight. *Building Communities from the Inside Out: A Path toward Finding and Mobilizing a Community's Assets*. Evanston, IL: Asset-Based Community Development Institute, 1993.

Leal, Eduardo. "La investigación acción participativa, un aporte al conocimiento y la transformación de Latinoamérica, en permanente movimiento." *Revista de investigación 67*, no. 33 (2009): 13–34.

Le Roux, Elisabet, and Laura Milena Cadavid Valencia. "'Las iglesias no pueden permanecer en silencio': debates y acciones frente a la violencia sexual en comunidades evangélicas en Colombia." *Revista colombiana de sociología* 45, no. 1 (2022): 243–65.

———. "Partnering with Local Faith Communities: Learning from the Response to Internal Displacement and Sexual Violence in Colombia." In *International Development and Local Faith Actors: Ideological and Cultural Encounters*, edited by Katherine Kraft and Olivia J. Wilkinson, Routledge Research in Religion and Development, 236–50. Oxon: Routledge, 2020.

———. "'There's No-One You Can Trust to Talk to Here': Churches and Internally Displaced Survivors of Sexual Violence." *HTS Teologiese Studies* 75, no. 4 (2019): 1–10.

Lewin, Kurt. "Action Research and Minority Problems." *Journal of Social Issues* 2, no. 4 (1946): 34–36.

Mackay, John A. *A Preface to Christian Theology*. New York: Macmillan, 1941.

Mackay, Juan A. *Prefacio a la teología cristiana*. Translated by Gonzalo Báez-Camargo. 3rd ed. México, D.F.: Casa Unida de Publicaciones, 1984.

Marshall, I. Howard. *Luke: Historian & Theologian*. 3rd ed. Guernsey, UK: Paternoster, 1988.

Martin, Ann W. "Action Research on a Large Scale: Issues and Practices." In *The SAGE Handbook of Action Research: Participative Inquiry and Practice*, edited by Peter Reason and Hilary Bradbury, 394–406. Los Angeles: SAGE, 2008.

Mathie, Alison, and Gord Cunningham. "From Clients to Citizens: Asset-Based Community Development as a Strategy for Community-Driven Development." *Development in Practice* 13, no. 5 (2003): 474–86.

McClintock Fulkerson, Mary. *Places of Redemption: Theology for a Worldly Church*. Oxford: Oxford University Press, 2007.

Mead, Geoff. "Muddling Through: Facing the Challenges of Managing a Large-Scale Action Research Project." In *The SAGE Handbook of Action Research: Participative Inquiry and Practice*, edited by Peter Reason and Hilary Bradbury, 629–42. Los Angeles: SAGE, 2008.

Mejía Castillo, Guillermo. "El equipo de Interacción con el sector público." In *Fe y Desplazamiento: la investigación-acción misional ante la crisis colombiana del desplazamiento forzoso*, edited by Christopher M. Hays and Milton Acosta, 185–202. Eugene, OR: Wipf & Stock, 2022.

———. "El lamento: terreno fértil de resiliencia política de las personas en situación de desplazamiento." In *Fe y Desplazamiento: la investigación-acción misional ante la crisis colombiana del desplazamiento forzoso*, edited by Christopher M. Hays and Milton Acosta, 310–27. Eugene, OR: Wipf & Stock, 2023.

Micah Network. "Vision and Mission." https://www.micahnetwork.org/visionmission/.

Míguez Bonino, José. *Christians and Marxists: The Mutual Challenge to Revolution*. Grand Rapids: Eerdmans, 1976.

———. *Doing Theology in a Revolutionary Situation*. Confrontation Books. Philadelphia: Fortress, 1975.

Moya, Andrés. "Violence, Emotional Distress and Induced Changes in Risk Aversion among the Displaced Population in Colombia." Working Paper No. 105, Programa dinámicas territoriales rurales: Rimisp - Centro Latinoamericano para el Desarrollo Rural, 2013.

Nel, Hanna. "A Comparison between the Asset-Oriented and Needs-Based Community Development Approaches in Terms of Systems Changes." *Practice* 30, no. 1 (2016): 33–52.

Opportunity International. *Holistic Community Assessment: An Immersive Story-Capture Approach: User's Guide*. Chicago: Opportunity International, 2018.

Orozco, Isabel, and H. Leonardo Ramírez. *Recorridos de Fe y Desplazamiento: memorias de una iniciativa de capacitación, movilización y reconstrucción*. Medellín: Publicaciones SBC, 2022.

Padilla, C. René, ed. *Bases bíblicas de la misión: perspectivas latinoamericanas*. Buenos Aires: Kairós, 1998.

———. "Ciencias sociales y compromiso cristiano." *Boletín teológico* 20, no. 31 (1988): 247–51.

———. *Economía humana y economía del Reino de Dios*. Buenos Aires: Kairós, 2002.

———. "Economía y plenitud de vida." In *Economía humana y economía del Reino de Dios*, 53–72. Buenos Aires: Kairós, 2002.

———. "Globalization, Ecology and Poverty." In *Creation in Crisis: Christian Perspectives on Sustainability*, edited by Robert S. White, 175–91. London: SPCK, 2009.

———. "Hacia una definición de la misión integral." In *El proyecto de Dios y las necesidades humanas*, edited by Tetsunao Yamamori and C. René Padilla, 19–33. Buenos Aires: Kairós, 2000.

———. "Introduction: An Ecclesiology for Integral Mission." In *The Local Church, Agent of Transformation*, edited by Tetsunao Yamamori and C. René Padilla, 19–49. Buenos Aires: Kairós, 2004.

———. "La trayectoria histórica de la misión integral." In *Justicia, misericordia y humildad: la misión integral y los pobres*, edited by Tim Chester, 55–80. Buenos Aires: Kairós, 2008.

———. *Misión integral: ensayos sobre el Reino y la iglesia*. Grand Rapids/Buenos Aires: Eerdmans/Nueva Creación, 1986.

———, ed. *The New Face of Evangelicalism: An International Symposium on the Lausanne Covenant*. Downer's Grove, IL: InterVarsity, 1976.

Padilla, Catalina F. de. "Los 'laicos' en la misión en el Nuevo Testamento." In *Bases bíblicas de la misión: perspectivas latinoamericanas*, edited by C. René Padilla, 405–35. Buenos Aires: Kairós, 1998.

Padilla DeBorst, Ruth Irene. "Integral Mission Formation in Abya Yala (Latin America): A Study of the *Centro de Estudios Teológicos Interdisciplinarios* (1982–2002) and Radical *Evangélicos*." PhD dissertation, Boston University, 2016.

Paredes, Rubén. "Fe cristiana, antropología y ciencias sociales." *Boletín teológico* 20, no. 31 (1988): 215–30.

Puyana García, German. *¿Cómo somos? Los colombianos: reflexiones sobre nuestra idiosincrasia y cultura.* 2nd ed. Bogotá: Bhandar, 2002.

Ramírez, H. Leonardo, and Isabel Orozco. *Asociados para el desarrollo: construcción de asociaciones de base eclesial para el desarrollo económico.* Medellín: Publicaciones SBC, 2019.

Red Nacional de Información. "Registro único de víctimas." https://www.unidadvictimas .gov.co/es/registro-unico-de-victimas-ruv/37394.

Restan Padilla, Ubaldo, and Miguel Bedoya Cárdenas. *70 años de historia y misión AIEC.* Sincelejo, Colombia: AIEC, 2015.

Restrepo, Gabriel. "Seguir los pasos de Orlando Fals Borda: religión, música, mundos de la vida y carnaval." *Investigación y desarrollo* 24, no. 2 (2016): 199–239.

Rojas-Flores, Lisseth. "Desplazamiento de centroamericanos y colombianos: violencia, trauma y el ministerio de la iglesia." In *Conversaciones teológicas del sur global americano: violencia, desplazamiento y fe,* edited by Oscar García-Johnson and Milton Acosta, 27–43. Eugene, OR: Wipf & Stock, 2016.

Rojas-Flores, Lisseth, Tommy Givens, Josephine Hwang Koo, Laura Milena Cadavid Valencia, Francis Alexis Pineda González, Elisabet le Roux, and Larisa Grams-Benítez. *Líderes de las iglesias como agentes de sanidad después del trauma.* 2nd ed. Medellín: Publicaciones SBC, 2020.

———. *Líderes de las iglesias como agentes de sanidad después del trauma.* Medellín: Publicaciones SBC, 2018.

Rojas-Flores, Lisseth, Josephine Hwang Koo, and Doribeth Tardillo. "El equipo de Psicología." In *Fe y Desplazamiento: la investigación-acción misional ante la crisis colombiana del desplazamiento forzoso,* edited by Christopher M. Hays and Milton Acosta, 167–84. Eugene, OR: Wipf & Stock, 2022.

Rojas Seguro, Duberney. *Torneo conciliadores de paz: una propuesta de desarrollo de capacidades en entornos de conflicto.* Medellín: Publicaciones SBC, 2018.

Romero Silva, Marco, Fabio Alberto Lozano, et al. "La crisis humanitaria en Colombia persiste: El pacífico en disputa: Informe de desplazamiento forzado en 2012". Interview with Consultoría para los Derechos Humanos y el Desplazamiento, Bogotá, 2013.

Rowe, C. Kavin. *World Upside Down: Reading Acts in the Graeco-Roman Age.* Oxford: Oxford University Press, 2009.

Salinas, J. Daniel. *Latin American Evangelical Theology in the 1970's: The Golden Decade.* Religion on the Americas. Leiden: Brill, 2009.

———. *Taking Up the Mantle: Latin American Evangelical Theology in the 20th Century.* Global Perspective. Carlisle, UK: Langham Global Library, 2017.

Sánchez G., Gonzalo, Andrés Fernando Suárez, and Tatiana Rincón. *La masacre de El Salado: esa guerra no era nuestra.* Bogotá: Ediciones Semana, 2009.

Spencer, F. Scott. "Neglected Widows in Acts 6:1–7." *Catholic Biblical Quarterly* 56 (1994): 715–33.

Stangeland Kaufman, Tone, and Jonas Ideström. "Why Matter Matters in Theological Action Research: Attending to the Voices of Tradition." *International Journal of Practical Theology* 22, no. 1 (2018): 84–102.

Stanley, Brian. *The Global Diffusion of Evangelicalism: The Age of Billy Graham and John Stott.* A History of Evangelicalism. Vol. 5. Downer's Grove, IL: IVP Academic, 2013.

———. *A World History of Christianity in the Twentieth Century.* Princeton History of Christianity. Princeton: Princeton University Press, 2018.

Stenschke, Christoph W. "Migration and Mission: According to the Book of Acts." *Missionalia* 44, no. 2 (2016): 129–51.

Stott, John. *The Lausanne Covenant: Complete Text with Study Guide.* Didasko files. Peabody, MA: Hendrickson, 2009.

Stringer, Ernest T. *Action Research.* 3rd ed. Los Angeles: Sage, 2007.

Swartz, David R. "Embodying the Global South: Internationalism and the American Evangelical Left." *Religions* 3 (2012): 887–901.

Unger, Hella von. "Partizipative Gesundheitsforschung: Wer partizipiert woran?" *Forum: Qualitative Sozialforschung* 13, no. 1 (2012): §§1–79.

Unidad de Restitución de Tierras. "Avances de restitución." https://www.restituciondetierras .gov.co/estadisticas-de-restitucion-de-tierras.

Vélez Caro, Olga Consuelo. "El quehacer teológico y el método de investigación acción participativa: una reflexión metodológica." *Theologica Xaveriana* 67, no. 183 (2017): 187–208.

Villadiego Ramos, Steban Andrés, and Andrés Steban Villadiego Ramos. "Una apropiación misio-teológica de una estrategia de desarrollo comunitario para la movilización de laicos y PSD (personas en situación de desplazamiento) en ministerios a favor de las PSD." Undergraduate thesis, Fundación Universitaria Seminario Bíblico de Colombia, 2018.

Walter, Maggie. "Participatory Action Research." In *Social Research Methods*, edited by Maggie Walter, 1–8. Oxford: Oxford University Press, 2010.

Watkins, Clare. "Reflections on Particularity and Unity." In *Ecclesiology in the Trenches: Theory and Method under Construction*, edited by Sune Fahlgren and Jonas Ideström, 139–53. Cambridge: James Clarke, 2015.

Whyte, William Foote. "Introduction." In *Participatory Action Research*, edited by William Foote Whyte, 1–14. London: Sage, 1991.

Wiens, Arnoldo. "La misión cristiana en un contexto de corrupción." In *Bases bíblicas de la misión: perspectivas latinoamericanas*, edited by C. René Padilla, 437–64. Buenos Aires: Kairós, 1998.

Witherington, Ben. *The Acts of the Apostles: A Socio-Rhetorical Commentary.* Grand Rapids: Eerdmans, 1998.

# Index

Acosta, Milton, 1, 12–13, 25–27, 30–31, 221–23

action research, 55–57. *See also* Missional Action Research (MAR); Participatory Action Research (PAR); Theological Action Research (TAR)

Acts of the Apostles: book of, 16–17, 111–16; Apostolic Council (Acts 15), 159, 212–21; Hellenistic widows (Acts 6), 76–79, 114, 161–62, 213; Jerusalem community (Acts 2, 4), 34–36, 76, 190; Paul's Areopagus speech (Acts 17), 132–39. *See also* Simon the Cyrenian (Luke 23; Acts 13)

Afro-Colombian: *mulato*, 73n48; people group, 4, 73, 109, 199; *zambo*, 73n48, 80

Antioquia, 8, 74, 140

armed conflict, 2–11, 49–51, 75, 81, 140–41, 147–48, 229–36

armed groups, 6–8, 51, 74, 80, 118, 141, 147, 164, 230. *See also* guerrilla; paramilitary groups

Asset-Based Community Development (ABCD), 128–31. *See also Skills Inventory*; *We Can* (game)

balcony, 21, 23–24, 33, 227

*barrio de invasión*, 75, 82, 108, 164

Bible, 58, 78; epistemic role, 15–18, 20, 201, 207, 209–12; interpretation of, 215, 219–26; role in Colombian Christianity, 15, 28, 164; role in curricula, 123, 128, 134, 136, 149–50, 158, 183; role in integral mission, 38, 42–43; role in Missional Action Research, 66–67, 69–71, 90, 99, 201. *See also lectura popular de la Biblia*

Bogotá: application of curricula in, 149–51, 155–56, 176, 179, 181; experiences of internally displaced persons in, 27–28, 230; role in research, 25, 75, 98, 125, 221

Cadavid Valencia, Laura Milena, 12, 14–15, 20, 45–46, 55, 65, 86, 107, 225

Cartagena, 57, 61, 75, 108, 151, 153, 176–78, 182, 184, 193–94, 199

Cauca: Piendamó, 75, 101, 108, 117–18; region of, 75, 222

Córdoba: Batata, 49–51, 75, 101, 125, 147, 152; Montería, 26, 30, 176, 184; Planeta Rica, 30, 80, 141; Puerto Libertador, 75, 80–83, 143, 148–49, 152, 155, 164; region of, 26, 30, 49, 75, 147, 157, 166, 234; Tierralta, 49–51, 75, 101, 125, 147, 149, 155–57

coresearcher: difficulties with, 89, 91, 131–32; in Missional Action Research, 72, 201–4; in Participatory Action Research, 61–65, 96; in the project, 30n54, 49, 74–76, 79, 98–99, 108, 116, 145–47, 157; research projects of, 123–25, 128. *See also* pilot communities

cyclicality, 58–61, 66–67, 70–72, 86, 90, 159, 186, 190–91, 201, 204–5

diploma course (*diplomado*), 169–86, 193, 195–96, 199–200, 205–6

discipleship, contemporary, 36, 40–41, 43–44, 104, 142, 191–92

102, 120, 126n4, 145–47, 158, 174. *See also* coresearcher
praxis, 58, 93, 209–12, 220–21, 227
prejudice, 11, 36, 73n47, 76–77, 195
professionals (nonacademic): curriculum for, 122–23, 127, 130, 139, 145–46, 151, 156, 170–72, 177, 180–81; participation in church ministry, 44, 102, 104, 110, 121; participation in Missional Action Research/Participatory Action Research, 55, 61, 69–70, 201, 226
psychology. *See* mental health
public sector interaction team, 25n47, 35n2, 46, 85, 90, 221, 223, 237–38

rape. *See* sexual violence
revenge. *See* vengeance
Rojas-Flores, Lisseth, 45, 107
Rojas Seguro, Duberney, 46, 127n6, 225

Scripture. *See* Bible
sexual violence, 8n16, 9, 27, 29, 46, 89, 99n25, 107, 225, 238–40
*Shalom Diagnostic*, 172–74, 179–80, 196. *See also* faith-based organization (FBO): Fundación AGAPE; faith-based organization (FBO): Opportunity International

Simon the Cyrenian (Luke 23; Acts 13), 158–63
*Skills Inventory*, 129–31, 145–47, 154–57, 173, 178–79, 185, 196. *See also* Asset-Based Community Development (ABCD)
social capital, 110, 234. *See also* sociology
social tissue, 85, 110, 186, 234. *See also* sociology
sociology, 55, 57–58, 68–69, 86, 88, 107, 209, 222–23; curriculum, 122, 127, 224; team, 35n2, 46, 85, 90, 99n25, 107, 110, 221, 224–25, 238–40. *See also* Cadavid Valencia, Laura Milena

Theological Action Research (TAR), 206–12
trauma: from displacement, 10–13, 22, 26, 50, 94, 101, 141, 165, 167, 232; recovery from, 104, 109, 127, 153, 224, 239; theory, 16, 107, 153, 222–25, 234

vengeance, 141, 225, 232–33, 238

Watkins, Clare, 18–20, 208, 212n21, 220
*We Can* (game), 129–30, 151, 166. *See also* Asset-Based Community Development (ABCD)